LEGAL

CRIMINAL LAW

Keyed To

Kadish, Schulhofer & Steiker

8th Edition

LEGAL PATH SERIES®

CRIMINAL LAW

Second Edition

Amy Cooper, Esq.

Seton Hall University School of Law

Mclaren Legal Publishers LLC

New York

ISBN 10: 0-9791306-7-0
ISBN 13: 978-0-9791306-7-0

Published by
Mclaren Legal Publishers LLC
136 West 21st Street, 8th Floor
New York, NY 10011

www.mclarenpublishing.com
Email: contact@mclarenpublishing.com

Printed in the United States of America

HOW TO USE THIS BOOK

This law school study aid is a "keyed" book. It summarizes all of the major cases in the text book to which it is linked and in the order those cases are printed. Our cases are presented in the IRAC format (Issue, Rule, Analysis and Conclusion). Each case uses a text symbol preceding the Issue, Rule, Analysis and Conclusion of the case referenced. The sentences that follow provide additional detail.

"Repetition is the Mother of Learning"

Throughout each case, many of the key Black Letter law and/or Issues are repeated. You may see the same legal conclusion repeated in the Issue, Rule, Analysis and/or Conclusion. This was done intentionally. All too often, the most important concepts in law school are mentioned only once by a law professor in a lecture hall. However, more often than not, what is mentioned the least is what is tested the most. We feel the more you see (and read) exactly what is important, the more likely you will remember it. Recalling key legal points quickly is the key to the successful application of those same rules on an exam. This *is* the difference between an "A" and a "C" for the course.

"All of what you need, none of what you don't"

Our law school study guides give you exactly what you need to understand the key principles of the case, including the sometimes elusive Black Letter law. We are not a replacement for an in depth legal analysis of the subject matter covered; however, we do present what is absolutely critical in a very concise format.

"Do it right in the beginning; it'll be easier in the end"

You may notice that the issues for each case are very specific. They are presented to you as accurately as we can print them. However, be mindful that there may be slight variations in their interpretation from lecture hall to lecture hall. With that in mind, our experience has taught us that if you do the labor-intensive, hard work in the beginning of the course and parse out the specific issue(s), rule(s) and conclusion, the analysis will be easier to formulate and write. It is the analysis of a case that separates the A, B and C grades on an exam (trust me).

"Who's the Plaintiff, who's the Defendant?"

You may notice that in some cases, a case title lists the Plaintiff v. Defendant in one order but the facts list the parties in the opposite order or may refer to the plaintiff/defendant as the petitioner/appellant/respondent etc. This is usually seen when the original party is appealing to a higher court (the defendant, for example, now appears as the petitioner in the facts section) or where various counterclaims and cross-claims are asserted by the parties. When you see the parties change in the facts, keep the procedural history (and the parties) of the case organized in your mind and don't get confused.

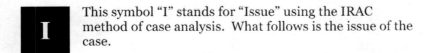

Abbreviations used in this book

I
This symbol "I" stands for "Issue" using the IRAC method of case analysis. What follows is the issue of the case.

R
This symbol "R" stands for "Rule" using the IRAC method of case analysis. What follows is the rule or black letter law of the case.

A
This symbol "A" stands for "Analysis" using the IRAC method of case analysis. What follows is the Analysis of the case.

C
This symbol "C" stands for "Conclusion" using the IRAC method of case analysis. What follows is the conclusion of the case.

* Use of the word "his" in this book is gender neutral and is meant to encompass both "his" and "her."

ALPHABETICAL TABLE OF CASES

People v. Zakowitz
New York Court of Appeals, 172 N.E. 466 (1930)

FACTS

On November 10, 1929, shortly after midnight, the Defendant Zackowitz shot Frank Coppola and killed him without justification or excuse. A crime is admitted. What is doubtful is the degree only. Coppola was one of four young men who were at work repairing an automobile on a Brooklyn street. A woman, the defendant's wife, walked by on the opposite side of the street and caught their attention. One of the men propositioned her (Zackowitz's wife). Her husband, the defendant, was not with her during this time as he had stopped to buy a newspaper. He returned to her only to find her in tears. He was told she had been insulted, though she did not then repeat the words. Enraged, he stepped across the street and yelled profanities at the offenders and informed them, so the survivors testify, that "if they did not get out of there in five minutes, he would come back and bump them all off." Rejoining his wife, he walked with her to their apartment house which was located close by. He was intoxicated with liquor which he had been drinking at a dance the two had attended that same evening. Within the apartment he induced her to tell him what the insulting words had been. A youth had asked her to lie with him, and had offered her two dollars. With rage aroused again, the defendant went back to the scene of the insult and found the four young men still working at the car. In a statement to the police, he said that he had armed himself at the apartment with a .25 caliber automatic pistol. In his testimony at the trial he said that this pistol had been in his pocket all evening. Words and blows followed, and then a shot. The defendant kicked Coppola in the stomach. There is evidence that Coppola went for him with a wrench. The pistol came from his pocket, and with a single shot killed Coppola. The defendant walked away and at the corner met his wife who had followed him from the home. The two took a taxicab to Manhattan where they spent the rest of the night at the dwelling of a friend. On the way the defendant threw his pistol into the river. He was arrested on January 7, 1930, about two months following the crime.

 As a part of its case-in-chief, can the prosecution submit into evidence, in a criminal case, evidence of a defendant's poor character?

 A prosecutor cannot present evidence of a defendant's bad character unless the defendant makes character an issue or submits evidence of his good character first.

 Here is a case where character evidence offered and received as probative of an essential element of the crime, used for that purpose, and for no other, repeatedly throughout the trial, is now about to be viewed as if accepted at a later stage and accepted for a purpose. This is not justice in accordance with the forms of law. "The practice of calling out evidence for one purpose, apparently innocent, and using it for another, which is illegal, is improper; and, if it is

People v. Zakowitz
New York Court of Appeals, 172 N.E. 466 (1930)

clear and manifest that the avowed object is colorable merely, its admission is error." Even more plainly is it a perversion to call out evidence for an avowed object manifestly illegal, and use it later on appeal as if admitted at another stage in aid of another purpose innocent and lawful. The endeavor was to generate an atmosphere of professional criminality. It was an endeavor the more unfair in that, apart from the suspicion attaching to the possession of these weapons, there is nothing to mark the defendant as a man of evil life. He was not in crime as a business. He did not shoot as a bandit shoots in the hope of wrongful gain. He was engaged in a decent calling, an optician regularly employed, without criminal record, or criminal associates. If his own testimony be true, he had gathered these weapons together as curios, a collection that interested and amused him. Perhaps his explanation of their ownership is false. There is nothing stronger than mere suspicion to guide us to an answer. Whether the explanation is true or false, he should not have been driven by the People to the necessity of offering it. Brought to answer a specific charge, and to defend himself against it, he was placed in a position where he had to defend himself against another, more general and sweeping. He was made to answer to the charge, pervasive and poisonous even if insidious. The purpose of this irrelevant evidence was to persuade the jury that Zackowitz was a man of vicious and dangerous propensities, who because of these propensities was more likely to kill with deliberate and premeditated design than a man of irreproachable life and amiable manners.

The judgment of conviction should be reversed and a new trial ordered.

Patterson v. New York
Supreme Court of the United States, 432 U.S. 197 (1977)

FACTS

After a brief and unstable marriage, Defendant-appellant Gordon Patterson, Jr., became estranged from his wife, Roberta. Roberta resumed an association with John Northrup, a neighbor to whom she had been engaged prior to her marriage to appellant. On December 27, 1970, Patterson borrowed a rifle and went to the residence of his father-in-law. There, he observed his wife through a window, semi-undressed, with John Northrup. He entered the house and killed Northrup by shooting him twice in the head. Patterson was charged with second-degree murder. In New York there are two elements of this crime: (1) "intent to cause the death of another person"; and (2) "caus[ing] the death of such person or of a third person." N. Y. Penal Law 125.25. Malice aforethought is not an element of the crime. In addition, the State permits a person accused of murder to raise an affirmative defense that he "acted under the influence of extreme emotional disturbance for which there was a reasonable explanation or excuse." New York also recognizes the crime of manslaughter. A person is guilty of manslaughter if he intentionally kills another person "under circumstances which do not constitute murder because he acts under the influence of extreme emotional disturbance." Appellant confessed before trial to killing Northrup, but at trial he raised the defense of extreme emotional disturbance. The jury was instructed as to the elements of the crime of murder. The trial court charged: "Before you, considering all of the evidence, can convict this defendant or anyone of murder, you must believe and decide that the People have established beyond a reasonable doubt that he intended, in firing the gun, to kill either the victim himself or some other human being . . ." and that the State holds the burden to prove that the defendant intended to kill in this instance beyond a reasonable doubt. The jury was further instructed, consistently with New York law, that the defendant had the burden of proving his affirmative defense by a preponderance of the evidence. The jury was told that if it found beyond a reasonable doubt that appellant had intentionally killed Northrup but that appellant had demonstrated by a preponderance of the evidence that he had acted under the influence of extreme emotional disturbance, it had to find appellant guilty of manslaughter instead of murder. The jury found appellant guilty of murder. Judgment was entered on the verdict, and the Appellate Division affirmed. While appeal to the New York Court of Appeals was pending, the U.S. Supreme Court decided *Mullaney v. Wilbur*, in which the Court declared Maine's murder statute unconstitutional. Under the Maine statute, a person accused of murder could rebut the statutory presumption that he committed the offense with "malice aforethought" by proving that he acted in the heat of passion on sudden provocation. In the Court of Appeals, appellant urged that New York's murder statute is functionally equivalent to the one struck down in Mullaney and that therefore his conviction should be reversed. The Court of Appeals rejected appellant's argument, holding that the New York murder statute is consistent with due process.

I If a state requires the accused to sustain the burden of proof regarding an affirmative defense, are the defendant's 14th amendment due process rights implicated?

Patterson v. New York

Supreme Court of the United States, 432 U.S. 197 (1977)

A state may require a defendant to sustain the burden of proving to a jury that he should not be found guilty of the crime charged because he has a valid affirmative defense without implicating his 14th Amendment Constitutional rights.

New York law requiring that the defendant in a prosecution for second-degree murder prove by a preponderance of the evidence the affirmative defense of extreme emotional disturbance in order to reduce the crime to manslaughter held not to violate the Due Process Clause of the Fourteenth Amendment. Such affirmative defense does not serve to negative any facts of the crime which the State must prove in order to convict, but constitutes a separate issue on which the defendant is required to carry the burden of persuasion. The Due Process Clause does not put New York to the choice of abandoning such an affirmative defense or undertaking to disprove its existence in order to convict for a crime which is otherwise within the State's constitutional powers to sanction by substantial punishment. If the State chooses to recognize a factor that mitigates the degree of criminality or punishment, it may assure itself that the fact has been established with reasonable certainty, and to recognize at all a mitigating circumstance does not require the State to prove beyond a reasonable doubt its nonexistence in each case in which the fact is put in issue, if in its judgment this would be too cumbersome, expensive, and inaccurate. Appellant argues that New York's statute is functionally equivalent to the statute we recently struck down in *Mullaney v. Wilbur* because it improperly places the burden of proof upon a defendant to disprove an element of the crime charged. We disagree. In *Mullaney*, defendant was charged with murder under a Maine statute which included a "malice aforethought" element. We struck down that statute because it unconstitutionally shifted the burden of proof from the prosecution to the defendant by requiring the defendant to prove that the killing occurred in the heat of passion. While the prosecution has the burden of proving each *element* of the crime charged beyond a reasonable doubt, the prosecution *does not* carry the burden of proving the nonexistence of all available affirmative defenses. In *Mullaney*, the statutory *presumption* was of malice aforethought because Maine's statute required the defendant to prove that he acted without malice, but New York's statute only requires that the prosecution show that Patterson intended to kill another person and did in fact kill such a person. The New York statute does not contain a malice aforethought element. As such, the affirmative defense of extreme emotional disturbance does not negate any of the elements of the crime charged, because such an element does not exist. It is a separate issue regarding mitigating circumstances and the defendant's burden to prove its existence. Just because New York recognizes mitigating circum-stances does not mean it is constitutionally required to prove their nonexistence in each case where it is at issue.

The New York Court of Appeals is affirmed.

Duncan v. Louisiana
Supreme Court of the United States, 391 U.S. 145 (1968)

FACTS

Defendant-appellant Gary Duncan, a black man, was driving on Highway 23 on October 18, 1966, he saw two younger cousins engaged in a conversation by the side of the road with four white boys. Duncan stopped the car, got out, and approached the six boys. At trial the white boys and a white onlooker testified, as did appellant and his cousins. The witnesses agreed that appellant and the white boys spoke to each other, that appellant encouraged his cousins to break off the encounter and enter his car. The whites testified that just before getting in the car appellant slapped Herman Landry, one of the white boys, on the elbow. The Negroes testified that appellant had not slapped Landry, but had merely touched him. The trial judge concluded that the State had proved beyond a reasonable doubt that Duncan had committed simple battery, and found him guilty. Duncan was convicted of simple battery in the Twenty-fifth Judicial District Court of Louisiana. Under Louisiana law simple battery is a misdemeanor, punishable by a maximum of two years' imprisonment and a $300 fine. Appellant sought trial by jury, but because the Louisiana Constitution grants jury trials only in cases in which capital punishment or imprisonment at hard labor may be imposed, the trial judge denied the request. Appellant was convicted and sentenced to serve 60 days in prison and pay a fine of $150. Appellant sought review in the Supreme Court of Louisiana, asserting that the denial of jury trial violated his constitutional rights. The Supreme Court denied appellant a writ of certiorari. Appellant then sought review in the U.S. Supreme Court, alleging that his Sixth and 14th Amendments were violated.

May a state deny a defendant the right to a trial by jury for a crime punishable by two years in prison when one would be guaranteed in federal court?

The Sixth Amendment's right to jury trial is a fundamental right, which must be afforded recognition by the states, and which is applicable to crimes punishable by two or more years in prison.

Since trial by jury in criminal cases is fundamental to the American scheme of justice, the Fourteenth Amendment guarantees a right of jury trial in all criminal cases which, were they tried in a federal court, would come within the Sixth Amendment's guarantee of trial by jury. The penalty authorized for a particular crime is of major relevance in determining whether it is a serious one subject to the mandates of the Sixth Amendment, and it is sufficient here, without defining the boundary between petty offenses and serious crimes, to hold that a crime punishable by two years in prison is a serious crime and that appellant was entitled to a jury trial.

Reversed and remanded.

United States v. Dougherty
U.S. Court of Appeals, 473 F.2d 1113 (D.C. Cir. 1972)

FACTS

Seven of the so-called "D.C. Nine," including Defendant-appellant Dougherty, bring this joint appeal from conviction arising from their arrest in relation to their entry into the Washington office of the Dow Chemical Company, and the destruction of certain property therein caused by them. After a jury trial, all seven appellants were each convicted of two counts of malicious destruction and all appeal their conviction on the grounds that 1) the trial judge erroneously refused to instruct the jury of its right to acquit the defendants without regard to the law and the evidence; and 2) the judge also refused to permit the appellants to argue that issue to the jury.

 Must a trial judge inform the jury that they may, at their own discretion, wholly disregard the law and the evidence and acquit a defendant in a criminal trial?

 While a jury has the power to acquit a defendant and discount the instructions on the law given by the trial judge, however, the judge need not expressly tell them so and may additionally instruct the jury that they are required to follow the instruction of the court on all matters of law.

 While juries have long enjoyed an unreviewable and unreversible power to acquit a defendant in disregard of the instructions on the law given by the trial judge, the judge may instruct the jury that they are required to follow the instructions of the court on all matters of law. Historically, as distrust for judges appointed and removed by the king receded, there came an increasing acceptance that under a republic the protection of citizens lay not in recognizing the right of each jury to make its own law, but in following democratic processes for changing the law. The right of jury nullification is put forward in the name of liberty and democracy, but its explicit avowal risks the ultimate logic of anarchy. The danger of the excess rigidity may now occasionally exist, but it is not as great as the danger of removing the boundaries of constraint provided by the announced rules. "To encourage individuals to make their determinations as to which laws they will obey and which they will permit themselves as a matter of conscience to disobey is to invite chaos." Moreover, to compel a juror to assume the burdens of the legislator or judge, as is implicit in the doctrine of nullification, is to put untoward strains on the jury system. To tell him [the juror] *expressly* of the nullification option is to inform him, in effect, that it is he who fashions the rule also condemns. That is an overwhelming responsibility, an extreme burden for the juror to take on.

 Affirmed.

Regina v. Dudley and Stevens
Queen's Bench Division, 14 Q.B.D. 273 (1884)

FACTS

Defendants Thomas Dudley (Dudley) and Edward Stephens (Stephens) were indicted for the murder of Richard Parker on the high seas on July 25, 1884. On July 5th, 1884, defendants, one Brooks, and Richard Parker (Parker) (a young seventeen or eighteen-year-old English boy) set out to sea on a yacht. Not long afterward, they were cast away in a storm at sea, 1,600 miles away from the Cape of Good Hope, and were compelled to put into an open boat belonging to the yacht. For three days, the four individuals only had two 1-lb. tins of turnips and no water to subsist upon. On the fourth day, they caught a small turtle, which was entirely consumed after twelve days. For eight days after, they had nothing to eat, and no fresh water, except for rain water they were able to catch in their oilskin capes. On July 24th, Dudley proposed to Stephen and Brooks, but not to Parker, that lots should be cast to see who should be put to death and be used for food to save the rest. Brooks refused and no lots were drawn. The next day, July 25th, when no vessel appeared to save them, Dudley and Stephens agreed to kill Parker, despite dissent by Brooks. Dudley offered a prayer asking for forgiveness. Dudley, with the assent of Stevens, approached the young boy, and cut his throat thus killing him. The men fed upon the boy, and were rescued by a passing vessel four days after the act. Dudley and Stephens were tried and convicted of murder.

Is a killing out of necessity grounds for punishment and subsequent conviction for murder?

A person may be punished and convicted of murder, even if the killing was done out of necessity.

We concede that there was no greater necessity than that which existed here. That under the circumstances, there appeared to the prisoners every probability that unless they fed, they would soon die of starvation. If the men had not fed upon the young boy, they probably would have not survived to be rescued. The young boy, being in a much weaker condition, was likely to have died before them anyway.

If upon the whole matter the Court finds that the killing of Richard Parker be felony and murder, then the jurors say that Dudley and Stephens were each guilty of felony and murder as alleged in the indictment.

United States v. Jackson
U.S. Court of Appeals, 835 F.2d 1195 (7th Cir. 1987)

FACTS

Defendant-appellant Dwight Jackson (Jackson), was released as part of a "work release program" on May 30, 1986, after being sent to prison on two bank robbery convictions. Thirty minutes after being let out, Jackson robbed another bank. He was back in prison before sunset that same day. 18 U.S.C. App. § 1202 provided that anyone who possesses any firearm and who has three previous felony convictions for robbery and/or burglary, shall be imprisoned not less than fifteen years, and shall not be eligible for parole. Jackson, who had been previously convicted of four armed bank robberies and one armed robbery, brandished his revolver, and robbed the Continental Bank of Oakbrook in Terrace, Illinois, while this statute was in force. Jackson was sentenced to life in prison under § 1202 which forbade release on parole and he appealed.

 Is the imposition of a life sentence a permissible punishment for a defendant?

 The imposition of life in prison is a permissible punishment for career criminals.

 Jackson concedes that the statute at issue permits the imposition of any term of years but insists that it allows only determinate numbers of years; therefore, it did not authorize a life sentence. However, when parole is forbidden, a judge may give either sentence to reach the same result. Jackson was 35 when he committed the crime. Unless there are startling advances in geriatric medicine, a long term of imprisonment (say, 60 years) and life sentence are the same sentence. Thus, it is ridiculous to read the statute as authorizing one but not the other. The imposition of a life sentence in prison on Jackson was permissible. The selection of a sentence within the statutory range is essentially free of appellate review. Armed robbery on the day of his release, coupled with various armed robbery convictions dating back to 1973 marked Jackson is a career criminal and specific deterrence had failed. The court was entitled to consider general deterrence and incapacitation. Although life without possibility of parole is the upper end of the scale of sanctions, the imposition of life in prison is a permissible punishment for career criminals who persist in possessing weapons.

C Affirmed.

United States v. Gementera
U.S. Court of Appeals, 379 F.3d 596 (9th Cir. 2004)

FACTS

Shawn Gementera, then 24, pilfered letters from several mailboxes along San Francisco's Fulton Street on May 21, 2001. After indictment, Gementera plead guilty to mail theft and the government dismissed a second count of receiving a stolen U.S. Treasury check. This was not his first encounter with the law; his criminal record was lengthy and was growing steadily more serious with each offense. On February 25, 2003, Judge Vaughn Walker of the U.S. District Court for the Northern District of California sentenced Gementera "perform 100 hours of community service" imposing several creative punishments along with a brief prison sentence. He was to watch postal patrons visit the lost and found window at a post office and deliver lectures about his crime to high school students. Walker also required Gementera to stand outside a post office wearing a placard reading: "I stole mail. This is my punishment." Gementera appealed, arguing that public humiliation as a form of punishment violated the Eight Amendment's ban on cruel and unusual punishment.

Is public humiliation as a form of punishment violative of the Eight Amendment's ban on cruel and unusual punishment?

The imposition of public humiliation as a form of punishment is not violative of the Eight Amendment's ban on cruel and unusual punishment under certain conditions.

Approving Judge Vaughn Walker's "Scarlet Letter" sentence, a divided court of appeals panel on Monday said it's OK to force a mail thief to wear a sandwich board announcing his crimes. Read in its entirety, the record unambiguously establishes that the district court imposed the condition for the stated and legitimate statutory purpose of rehabilitation and, to a lesser extent, for the general deterrence and for the protection of the public. Accordingly, we hold that the condition imposed upon Gementera reasonably related to the legitimate statutory objective of rehabilitation. We are careful not to articulate a principle broader than that presented by the facts of this case. With care and specificity, the district court outlined a sensible logic underlying its conclusion that a set of conditions, including the signboard provision, but also including reintergrative provisions, would better promote the defendant's rehabilitation than would a lengthier term of incarceration. By contrast, a *per se* rule that the mandatory public airing of one's offense can never assist the offender to reassure his duty of obedience to the law would impose a narrow penological orthodoxy not contemplated by the Guidelines [Sentencing Reform Act] express approval of "any other condition [the district court] considers appropriate."

Affirmed.

Lawrence v. Texas
Supreme Court of the United States, 539 U.S. 558 (2003)

FACTS

Responding to a reported weapons disturbance in a private residence, Houston police entered petitioner Lawrence's apartment and saw him and another adult man, petitioner Garner, engaging in a private, consensual sexual act. Petitioners were arrested and convicted of deviate sexual intercourse in violation of a Texas statute forbidding two persons of the same sex to engage in certain intimate sexual conduct. In affirming, the State Court of Appeals held, *inter alia*, that the statute was not unconstitutional under the Due Process Clause of the Fourteenth Amendment. The court considered *Bowers* v. *Hardwick,* 478 U.S. 186, controlling on that point.

 Does the Texas statute making it a crime for two persons of the same sex to engage in certain intimate sexual conduct violate the Due Process Clause?

 The Texas statute making it a crime for two persons of the same sex to engage in certain intimate sexual conduct violates the Due Process Clause.

 Resolution of this case depends on whether petitioners were free as adults to engage in private conduct in the exercise of their liberty under the Due Process Clause. For this inquiry the Court deems it necessary to reconsider its *Bowers* holding. The *Bowers* Court's initial substantive statement—"The issue presented is whether the Federal Constitution confers a fundamental right upon homosexuals to engage in sodomy ... ," 478 U.S., at 190–discloses the Court's failure to appreciate the extent of the liberty at stake. To say that the issue in *Bowers* was simply the right to engage in certain sexual conduct demeans the claim the individual put forward, just as it would demean a married couple were it said that marriage is just about the right to have sexual intercourse. Although the laws involved in *Bowers* and here purport to do not more than prohibit a particular sexual act, their penalties and purposes have more far-reaching consequences, touching upon the most private human conduct, sexual behavior, and in the most private of places, the home. They seek to control a personal relationship that, whether or not entitled to formal recognition in the law, is within the liberty of persons to choose without being punished as criminals. The liberty protected by the Constitution allows homosexual persons the right to choose to enter upon relationships in the confines of their homes and their own private lives and still retain their dignity as free persons.

 Reversed and remanded.

Commonwealth v. Mochan
Supreme Court of Pennsylvania, 110 A.2d 788 (1955)

FACTS

Mr. Mochan was indicted for intending to debauch, corrupt, embarrass and vilify Louise Zivkovich and the members of her family by telephoning her various times and referring to her as a lewd, immoral and lascivious woman of questionable character referencing intercourse and sodomy. Mrs. Zivkovich was a married woman with an outstanding character in the community and Mr. Mochan was a stranger to Mrs. Zivkovich. The Pennsylvania trial court convicted Mochan for his conduct, and he appealed alleging that his conduct was not punishable pursuant to either statutory or common law.

May conduct, which is not prohibited specifically by a criminal statute, nevertheless be found illegal if a criminal statutory provision permits punishment of common law offenses?

When the conduct alleged is not prohibited expressly by criminal statute, a violation of the legality principle does not exist if a statutory provision permits punishment of common law offenses.

When illicit conduct is not expressly prohibited by a criminal statute, such conduct may nevertheless be illegal if a criminal statute's provision permits the punishment of common law offenses. Section 1101 of the Pennsylvania Penal code of 1939 is one such statute; it permits punishment of common law offenses. Our state laws provide that the common law is sufficient to punish those acts that injure or intend to injure the public, affect public morality, and obstruct or pervert public justice. This includes conduct that openly outrages decency and is injurious to public morals; conduct that is scandalous and affects the morals or health of the community; and even that which maliciously vilifies the Christian religion. All are considered misdemeanors and are indictable at common law. To endeavor to persuade a married woman to commit adultery is not indictable under the common law of Pennsylvania. However, Mr. Mochan's conduct exceeds mere oral solicitation to commit adultery. His statements were accompanied by lewd, immoral, and filthy language and suggestions of sodomy. Moreover, defendant's statements were potentially injurious to public morality; including telephone operators, individuals who share Mr. Mochan's four party telephone line, and two persons in Mrs. Zivkovich's household who heard Mr. Mochan's statements. Mr. Mochan's conduct establishes a common law misdemeanor.

Judgment and sentences affirmed.

McBoyle v. United States

Supreme Court of the United States, 283 U.S. 25 (1931)

FACTS

The petitioner was convicted of transporting from Ottawa, Illinois, to Guymon, Oklahoma, an airplane that he knew to have been stolen, and was sentenced to serve three years' imprisonment and to pay a fine of $2,000. The judgment was affirmed by the Circuit Court of Appeals for the Tenth Circuit. A writ of certiorari was granted by the U.S. Supreme Court on the question whether the National Motor Vehicle Theft Act applies to aircraft. Act of October 29, 1919. That Act provides: 'Sec. 2. That when used in this Act: (a) The term 'motor vehicle' shall include an automobile, automobile truck, automobile wagon, motor cycle, or any other self-propelled vehicle not designed for running on rails. ... Sec. 3. That whoever shall transport or cause to be transported in interstate or foreign commerce a motor vehicle, knowing the same to have been stolen, shall be punished by a fine of not more than $5,000, or by imprisonment of not more than five years, or both.'

Does the National Motor Vehicle Theft Act apply to aircraft?

When a rule of conduct is laid down in words that evoke in the common mind only the pleura of vehicles moving on land, the statute should not be extended to aircraft simply because it may seem to us that a similar policy applies.

Section 2 defines the motor vehicles of which the transportation in interstate commerce is punished in Section 3. The question is the meaning of the word 'vehicle' in the phrase 'any other self-propelled vehicle not designed for running on rails.' No doubt etymologically it is possible to use the word to signify a conveyance working on land, water or air, and sometimes legislation extends the use in that direction, e. g., land and air, water being separately provided for, in the Tariff Act. But in everyday speech 'vehicle' calls up the picture of a thing moving on land. Thus in Rev. St. 4 (1 USCA 4) intended, the Government suggests, rather to enlarge than to restrict the definition, vehicle includes every contrivance capable of being used 'as a means of transportation on land.' And this is repeated, expressly excluding aircraft, in the Tariff Act, June 17, 1930, c. 497, 401(b), 46 Stat. 590, 708 (19 USCA 1401). So here, the phrase under discussion calls up the popular picture. For after including automobile truck, automobile wagon and motor cycle, the words 'any other self-propelled vehicle not designed for running on rails' still indicate that a vehicle in the popular sense, that is a vehicle running on land is the theme. It is a vehicle that runs, not something, not commonly called a vehicle, that flies. Airplanes were well known in 1919 when this statute was passed, but it is admitted that they were not mentioned in the reports or in the debates in Congress. It is impossible to read words that so carefully enumerate the different forms of motor vehicles and have no reference of any kind to aircraft, as including airplanes under a term that usage more and more precisely confines to a different class. The counsel for the petitioner have shown that the phraseology of the statute as to motor vehicles follows that of earlier statutes of Connecticut, Delaware, Ohio, Michigan and Missouri, not to mention the late Regulations of Traffic for the District of Columbia, title 6, c. 9, 242, none of which can be supposed to leave the earth.

Although it is not likely that a criminal will carefully consider the text of the law before he murders or steals, it is reasonable that a fair warning should be given to the world in language that the common world will understand, of what the law intends to do if a certain line is passed. To make the warning fair, so far as possible the line should be clear. When a rule of conduct is laid down in words that evoke in the common mind only the pleura of vehicles moving on land, the statute should not be extended to aircraft simply because it may seem to us that a similar policy applies, or upon the speculation that if the legislature had thought of it, very likely the picture of vehicles moving on land, the *United States v. Bhagat SinghThi nd*.

Judgment reversed

United States v. Dauray
United States Court of Appeals, 215 F.3d 257 (2nd Cir. 2000)

FACTS

Defendant-appellant Charles Dauray was arrested in possession of pictures cut from one or more magazines He was convicted following a jury trial of violating 18 U.S.C. sec. 2252(a)(40(B), which punishes the possession , inter alia, "matter," three or more in number, "which contain any visual description" of minors engaging in sexually explicit conduct ..." Dauray argued at trial that ach picture was in itself a "visual depiction" and therefore could not be "other matter which contain visual depiction." The district court concluded that the pictures Dauray possessed were "other matter" within the plain meaning of the statute and for the same reason denied Dauray's request to apply the rule of lenity. He was sentenced to 36 months imprisonment.

 How should a statute be interpreted when it can be read either to support or defeat an indictment; specifically, are individual pictures "other matter which contain any visual depiction" within the meaning of the statute?

 A statute should be interpreted in a way that avoids absurd results [the rule of lenity] to resolve ambiguity in the defendant's favor.

 A statute should be interpreted in a way that avoids absurd results [the rule of lenity: under the common law rule of lenity, courts must strictly construe penal statutes in order to avoid a violation of the due process rights of the accused. Thus, in criminal cases where two reasonable interpretations of a penal statute exist, one inculpating and the other exculpating a defendant, a court must employ the less harsh reading] to resolve ambiguity in the defendant's favor. If the plain language does not resolve the issue, courts should look to the canons of statutory interpretation. When the plain language and canons of statutory interpretation fail to resolve statutory ambiguity, we will resort to the legislative history. Unfortunately, here, "examination of [sec. 2252's] legislative history ... reveals no insight as to what Congress intended the precise scope of 'ordinary matter' to be."

 Reversed.

Keeler v. Superior Court

Supreme Court of California, 470 P.2d 617 (1970)

FACTS

Mrs. Teresa Keeler became pregnant by one Ernest Vogt, a man who was not her husband. This pregnancy occurred before she received a divorce from Defendant-petitioner Mr. Keeler. On February 23, 1969, after petitioner learned of the pregnancy, Mrs. Keeler was driving down a mountain road when she came upon the petitioner driving in the opposite direction. Upon seeing her, he blocked the road with his car and impeded Mrs. Keeler's passage. She pulled to the side of the road. He then walked over to Mrs. Keeler's car and confronted her about the pregnancy. When Mrs. Keeler did not respond, he assisted her out of her car. After Mr. Keeler looked at Mrs. Keeler's abdomen, he became extremely upset. He then pushed her against the car, shoved his knee into her abdomen, and struck her in the face with several blows. She fainted and regained consciousness after petitioner had departed. The blow to Mrs. Keeler's abdomen caused extensive bruising of the abdomen wall. A Caesarian section was performed on Mrs. Keeler and the fetus was examined *in utero* (in the uterus). Its head was severely fractured and it was delivered stillborn. The pathologist believed that the fetus's death was immediate; was caused by the skull fracture and that the injury could have been the result of Mr. Keeler shoving his knee into Mrs. Keeler's abdomen. Mrs. Keeler's obstetrician testified that the fetus had developed to a stage of viability prior to its death. The district attorney filed *an information* that charged Mr. Keeler with murder of the unborn fetus and infliction of traumatic injury and assault upon his wife. Petitioner then filed a *writ of prohibition* to halt the murder proceeding against him, and the Supreme Court of California granted review.

Is the Due Process Clause violated when (1) a court interprets a criminal statute contrary to the legislative intent and then (2) applies that interpretation retroactively to a defendant's conduct?

The Due Process Clause is violated when a court construes a criminal statue contrary to the legislative intent and then applies that interpretation retroactively to a defendant's conduct.

The Due Process Clause is violated when a court construes a criminal statue contrary to the legislative intent and then applies that interpretation retroactively to a defendant's conduct. California's Penal Code §187 defines murder as the unlawful killing of a human being with malice aforethought. Section 187 was enacted as part of the Penal Code of 1872; which took the language from an 1850 enactment. Thus the threshold question before us is whether the fetus at issue is a "human being" within the scope of the California law. To answer this question, we must begin our inquiry by examining the intent of the 1850 Legislature. Pursuant to the common law of 1850, a child must be born alive to support a charge of murder. The legislature of 1850 used common law language to define murder as the unlawful killing of a human being, and the common law at that time required a person to be born alive to support a charge of murder. Therefore, the legislature of 1850 intended that the

Keeler v. Superior Court

Supreme Court of California, 470 P.2d 617 (1970)

term *human being* refer to a person that is born alive and there is nothing in the legislative history that demonstrates the legislature of 1872 had a different intention when in enacted §187. We note that it is the policy of California to construe a penal statute in favor of the defendant with respect to its language and as the circumstances of its application permit. Thus, Mr. Keeler is entitled to the benefit of every reasonable doubt as to the true interpretation of section 187. Thus, in light of the above, we hold that the legislature intended to exclude the killing of an unborn fetus from the reach of §187. The People [of California] urge that the science of medicine allows for the survival of a viable fetus born prematurely in support of the argument that the killing of such a fetus is punishable under §187. We are unconvinced. The People's argument is challenged by two insuperable obstacles, one "jurisdictional" and one "constitutional." With respect to the former, the authority to define punishable crimes rests solely with the legislature. A court may construe a statute but it lacks authority to create offenses by enlarging a statute. The terms in §187 compels this court to reject enlarging the statute by construing its terms to cover an unborn but viable fetus. With respect to the latter, even if we could enlarge the statute to cover an unborn but viable fetus, such an enlargement would conflict with Mr. Keeler's Due Process Clause guarantees of fair notice of punishable acts. To apply a new definition of §187 to Mr. Keeler does not comport with constitutional notions of fair notice; it is an application wholly without any notice. The Ex Post Facto Clause's prohibition against retroactive penal legislation supports our reasoning.

See Rule above.

City of Chicago v. Morales
527 U.S. 41 (1999)

FACTS

In 1992, due to concerns over the increase in criminal street gang activity, the Chicago City Council enacted the Gang Congregation Ordinance, which prohibits "criminal street gang members" from "loitering" with one another or with other persons in any public place. Before the ordinance was adopted, the city council's Committee on Police and Fire conducted hearings to explore the problems created by the city's street gangs, and more particularly, the consequences of public loitering by gang members. Based on that evidence, it noted that in many neighborhoods throughout the city, "the burgeoning presence of street gang members in public places has intimidated many law abiding citizens;" that gang members "establish control over identifiable areas ... by loitering in those areas and intimidating others from entering those areas; and . . . [m]embers of criminal street gangs avoid arrest by committing no offense punishable under existing laws when they know the police are present . . . . [;]" and that "loitering in public places by criminal street gang members creates a justifiable fear for the safety of persons and property in the area . . . " The ordinance creates a criminal offense punishable by a fine of up to $500, imprisonment for not more than six months, and a requirement to perform up to 120 hours of community service. Commission of the offense involves four predicates. First, the police officer must reasonably believe that at least one of the two or more persons present in a "public place" is a "criminal street gang membe[r]." Second, the persons must be "loitering," which the ordinance defines as "remain[ing] in any one place with no apparent purpose." Third, the officer must then order "all" of the persons to disperse and remove themselves "from the area." Fourth, a person must disobey the officer's order. If any person, whether a gang member or not, disobeys the officer's order, that person is guilty of violating the ordinance. Two months after the ordinance was adopted, the Chicago Police Department promulgated General Order 92-4 to provide guidelines to govern its enforcement. That order purported to establish limitations on the enforcement discretion of police officers "to ensure that the anti-gang loitering ordinance is not enforced in an arbitrary or discriminatory way." The limitations confine the authority to arrest gang members who violate the ordinance to sworn "members of the Gang Crime Section" and certain other designated officers and established detailed criteria for defining street gangs and membership in such gangs. In addition, the order directs district commanders to "designate areas in which the presence of gang members has a demonstrable effect on the activities of law abiding persons in the surrounding community," and provides that the ordinance "will be enforced only within the designated areas." The City, however, does not release the locations of these "designated areas" to the public. Two trial judges upheld the ordinance's constitutionality, but eleven others ruled it invalid. The Illinois Appellate Court affirmed the latter cases and reversed the convictions in the former. The State Supreme Court affirmed, holding that the ordinance violates due process in that it is impermissibly vague on its face and an arbitrary restriction on personal liberties.

I Does the City of Chicago's criminal anti-loitering ordinance violate the Due Process Clause as being unconstitutionally vague?

City of Chicago v. Morales
527 U.S. 41 (1999)

A criminal law must provide specific limits on the discretion of law enforcement personnel <u>and</u> provide sufficient notice to the public of what conduct is prohibited in order to comply with the requirements of the Due process Clause and avoid a successful challenge based on vagueness.

The ordinance's broad sweep violates the requirement that a legislature establish minimal guidelines to govern law enforcement. The ordinance encompasses a great deal of harmless behavior: In any public place in Chicago, persons in the company of a gang member "shall" be ordered to disperse if their purpose is not apparent to an officer. Moreover, the Illinois Supreme Court interprets the ordinance's loitering definition - "to remain in any one place with no apparent purpose" - as giving officers absolute discretion to determine what activities constitute loitering. This Court has no authority to construe the language of a state statute more narrowly than the State's highest court. The three features of the ordinance that, the city argues, limit the officer's discretion - (1) it does not permit issuance of a dispersal order to anyone who is moving along or who has an apparent purpose; (2) it does not permit an arrest if individuals obey a dispersal order; and (3) no order can issue unless the officer reasonably believes that one of the loiterers is a gang member - are insufficient. Finally, the Illinois Supreme Court is correct that General Order 92-4 is not a sufficient limitation on police discretion. It was not improper for the state courts to conclude that the ordinance, which covers a significant amount of activity in addition to the intimidating conduct that is its factual predicate, is invalid on its face. An enactment may be attacked on its face as impermissibly vague if, *inter alia,* it fails to establish standards for the police and public that are sufficient to guard against the arbitrary deprivation of liberty. The freedom to loiter for innocent purposes is part of such "liberty." The ordinance's vagueness makes a facial challenge appropriate. This is not an enactment that simply regulates business behavior and contains a scienter requirement. It is a criminal law that contains no *mens rea* requirement, and infringes on constitutionally protected rights. Because the ordinance fails to give the ordinary citizen adequate notice of what is forbidden and what is permitted, it is impermissibly vague. The term "loiter" may have a common and accepted meaning, but the ordinance's definition of that term - "to remain in any one place with no apparent purpose" - does not. However, this vagueness about what loitering is covered and what is not dooms the ordinance. The city's principal response to the adequate notice concern--that loiterers are not subject to criminal sanction until after they have disobeyed a dispersal order--is unpersuasive for at least two reasons. First, the fair notice requirement's purpose is to enable the ordinary citizen to conform his or her conduct to the law. A dispersal order, which is issued only after prohibited conduct has occurred, cannot retroactively provide adequate notice of the boundary between the permissible and the impermissible applications of the ordinance. Second, the dispersal order's terms compound the inadequacy of the notice afforded by the ordinance, which vaguely requires that the officer "order all such persons to disperse and remove themselves from the area," and thereby raises a host of questions as to the duration and distinguishing features of the loiterers' separation.

This ordinance is unconstitutional, not because it provides insufficient notice, but because it does not provide sufficient minimal standards to guide the police. Affirmed.

Martin v. State

Alabama Court of Appeals, 17 So. 2d 427 (1944)

FACTS

Appellant appeals his conviction for being drunk on a public highway. Police officers arrested Mr. Martin at his home and took him onto a public highway. While on the highway, Martin manifested a drunken condition and used loud and profane language in a manner that suggested that he was intoxicated. Martin was convicted for violating a statute, which stated, in part, that "any person who, while intoxicated or drunk, appears in any public place where one or more persons are present ... and manifests a drunken condition by boisterous or indecent conduct, or loud or profane discourse, shall, on conviction, be fined." Martin appealed the conviction.

Must the accused perform the required physical act for each element of a crime that has an *actus reus* element?

The accused must perform the required physical act for each element of a crime that has an *actus reus* element.

The accused must perform the required physical act for each element of a crime that has an *actus reus* element. In the instant case, Martin was convicted for violating a statute that provides that an (1) individual in an intoxicated condition (2) who appears in a public place (3) where one or more persons are present and (4) manifest his intoxication by boisterous or indecent conduct, or loud and profane language shall be fined upon conviction. Under the plain terms of the statute, a voluntary appearance is presupposed: that is, a voluntary appearance in a public place is absolutely required. Thus, the State cannot prove public drunkenness by establishing that the arresting officer, while the defendant was intoxicated, involuntarily and forcibly carried the accused to the "public place."

Reversed and rendered.

People v. Newton
California District Court of Appeal, 87 Cal. Rptr. 394 (1970)

FACTS

At relevant times, John Frey and Herbert Heanes were officers of the Oakland Police Department. The criminal charges against defendant arose from a street altercation in which Frey was fatally wounded by gunfire, and Heanes and defendant were shot, on October 28, 1967. Through the testimony of Oakland police radio dispatcher Clarence Lord, who was on radio duty in the Oakland Police Administration Building, we learning the following: Officer Frey was also on duty, and alone in a police car, patrolling an assigned beat in Oakland. At about 4:51 a.m., he radioed Lord and requested a check on an automobile which was moving in his vicinity and which bore license number AZM 489. The next relevant radio call, received at 5:03 a.m., was "an officer needs assistance immediately" call from Officer Heanes at Seventh and Willow Streets. Officer Heanes testified for the People as follows: He arrived at Seventh and Willow Streets "three to four minutes" after responding by radio to Officer Frey's "cover call." Officer Frey's police car was parked at the south curb of Seventh Street, east of Willow Street. A beige Volkswagen was parked directly in front of it. Heanes parked his car behind Frey's, and walked to the right rear of the Volkswagen. At this time, two men were seated in the Volkswagen, both in the front seat; Officer Frey was standing near the driver's door of the vehicle, writing a citation. At some point, Officer John Frey ordered Newton to get out of his car. An altercation ensued and the State's witnesses testified that Newton drew a gun and, during the struggle for possession of the gun, it went off and wounded Police Officer Heanes. As the thrashing about continued, Officer Heanes fired a shot into Newton's stomach. At some point, Newton wrested the gun from Officer Frey and fire it at him (Frey). Officers Frey and Heanes were taken to Merritt Hospital, where Frey was dead on arrival. He had been shot five times, at approximately the same time but in an unknown order. Newton somehow appeared at a local hospital where he requested treatment for a gunshot wound to his stomach. Newton testified that he was unarmed at the time of the altercation and that a struggle with Frey ensued when Frey struck Newton for resisting arrest. According to Newton, as Frey stumbled backwards he drew his revolver and shot Newton in his stomach. Newton then claims to remember nothing else until he found himself at the entrance of Kaiser Hospital with no knowledge of how he got there testifying that he was "unconscious or semiconscious" during this time [of the fatal shooting] and only "semiconscious" when he appeared at the hospital's entrance seeking medical attention. The defense called Bernard Diamond, M.D., who testified that defendant's recollections were "compatible" with the gunshot wound he had received; and that "[a] gunshot wound which penetrates in a body cavity, the abdominal cavity or the thoracic cavity is very likely to produce a profound reflex shock reaction, that is quite different than a gunshot wound which penetrates only skin and muscle and it is not at all uncommon for a person shot in the abdomen to lose consciousness and go into this reflex shock condition for short periods of time up to half an hour or so." The trial judge failed to give Newton's requested instruction to the jury on the defense of unconsciousness. Newton appealed to the Court of Appeal arguing that the failed instruction by the trial judge on the defense of unconsciousness was reversible error.

People v. Newton
California District Court of Appeal, 87 Cal. Rptr. 394 (1970)

Must the trial judge instruct the jury on the defense of unconsciousness?

When a person commits a criminal act that requires the element of "voluntariness," proof of a lack of consciousness provides a complete defense to that crime.

Although the evidence of the fatal affray is both conflicting and confused as to who shot whom and when, some of it supported the inference that defendant had been shot in the abdomen before he fired any shots himself. Given this sequence, defendant's testimony of his sensations when shot - supplemented to a degree, as it was, by Dr. Diamond's opinion based upon the nature of the abdominal wound - supported the further inference that defendant was in a state of unconsciousness when Officer Frey was shot. Defendant's testimony suggested that Officer Frey wounded him with the first shot fired. However, the absence of powder deposits on his (defendant's) clothing would indicate that Officer Heanes, not Frey, shot him. Grier's testimony was explicit as to this sequence: i.e., that Heanes, struck by the first bullet fired, shot at defendant before the latter commenced firing at Frey. Heanes' account, while less precise on this subject also supports the inference that he shot defendant (in the "midsection") before Officer Frey was shot by anyone. Where not self-induced, as by voluntary intoxication or the equivalent (of which there is no evidence here, unconsciousness is a complete defense to a charge of criminal homicide. "Unconsciousness," as the term is used in the rule just cited, need not reach the physical dimensions commonly associated with the term (coma, inertia, incapability of locomotion or manual action, and so on); it can exist - and the above-stated rule can apply - where the subject physically acts in fact but is not, at the time, conscious of acting. The statute underlying the rule makes this clear, as does one of the unconsciousness instructions originally requested by defendant. Thus, the rule has been invoked in many cases where the actor fired multiple gunshots while inferably in a state of such "unconsciousness" Because defendant presented some evidence of unconsciousness, the trial judge's refusal to give the requested instruction on the subject is prejudicial error.

Reversed.

FACTS

Defendant-appellant Jones was found guilty of involuntary manslaughter because of her failure to provide proper care for Anthony Lee Green, an infant child. The infant Green was placed with Jones, who was a family friend. Shirley Green, the infant's single mother, had lived with Jones for some time, but there is a conflict as to how long. It is also *unclear* from the evidence whether Jones was paid to take care of the infant. Uncontested medical evidence showed that Jones had ample means to provide food and medical care. Jones takes exception to the failure of the trial court to instruct that the jury that it must find, beyond a reasonable doubt that he was under a legal duty to provide food and other necessities to the infant. Jones appealed.

Must a court instruct a jury that it must find, beyond a reasonable doubt that a defendant was under a legal duty to provide food and other necessities to the infant before they find the defendant guilty or not guilty of a crime of omission such that a failure to give such an instruction constitutes reversible error?

A legal duty of care owed the victim by the defendant must have existed [and is an element of the offense charged] before a jury can find a defendant guilty of a crime of omission; the failure to give such an instruction by the court constitutes reversible error.

There are at least four situations in which a failure to act may constitute breach of a legal duty: 1) where a statute imposes a duty to care for another; 2) where one stands in a certain status relationship to another, such as a parent to a child; 3) where one has assumed a contractual duty to care for another; and 4) where one has voluntarily assumed the care of another and so secluded the helpless person so as to prevent others from rendering aid. The prosecution contends that either the third or fourth ground is applicable here. However, in any of the four there are critical issues of fact that the jury must pass on – specifically in this case is whether Jones had entered into a contract with the child's mother for the care of the infant or, alternatively, whether Jones assumed the care of the child and secluded him from the care of his mother. With respect to both of these issues, the evidence is in direct conflict. That is, Jones insisting that the mother was actually living with her and the infant, while the mother testified that she was living with her parents and was paying Jones to care for the child. Notwithstanding this conflict, the court failed to even suggest the necessity for finding a legal duty of care. The only reference to a duty of care was in the reading of the indictment. A finding of legal duty is the critical element of the crime and failure to instruct the jury on this requirement is plain error.

Reversed and remanded.

Pope v. State

Maryland Court of Appeals, 396 A.2d 1054 (1979)

FACTS

Defendant Joyce Lillian Pope allowed a Melissa Norris, the mother of a three month old infant who suffered from a serious mental illness and experienced episodes of violent religious frenzy, to stay in her home on Friday night after church services because the two did not have any other place to go. During the weekend in question, Pope fed the two and looked after the infant in a variety of ways. On Sunday, Norris experienced one of her attacks and claimed she was God and that Satan had hidden himself in the body of her child. With Pope present, Norris beat, ripped, and tore at the infant, causing the child serious injury. During the prolonged period of this episode, Pope took no action to protect the child, summon the authorities or seek medical assistance. That evening, the infant died from the beatings received from Norris. Pope was convicted of felony child abuse under §35A, a statute that imposed criminal liability for abuse occurring to a child when the defendant was " . . . responsible for the supervision of a minor child . . . AND caused, by being in some manner accountable for, by act of commission or omission, abuse to the child in the form of (a) physical injury or injuries sustained by the child as the result of (i) cruel or inhumane treatment, or (ii) malicious act or acts by such person . . . " when the defendant had "permanent or temporary care or custody or responsibility for the supervision of [the] minor child." Pope was also convicted under the common law crime of "misprision of felony," for "hiding one's felonies from law enforcement officers."

1) May criminal liability be imposed on another for a failure to take action when a parent is abusing his or her child? 2) May criminal liability be imposed under the common law rule of "misprision of felony" for a failure to report it?

Notwithstanding an exception [statutory or otherwise] to the contrary, the laws does not impose a duty to take affirmative action upon bystanders in emergency situations if they are not responsible for the situation.

Pope's failure to prevent the mother's child abuse and her failure to seek medical attention for the child constitute cruel and inhumane treatment within the meaning of the statute. However, Pope was not within class of persons specified by the statute: she was neither the child's parent, nor adoptive parent, and that there is no evidence sufficient to show Pope had the "permanent or temporary care or custody." Hence, we are left with the only remaining relevant question to be answered with respect to Pope's liability under the statute, or lack thereof: Was Pope "responsible for the supervision of" the child." The record shows that at all times the child's mother was present. Since Pope had no right to take over the role of parent and as long as the mother was present, Pope cannot be held responsible for the definitive well-being of the child. Any reading to the contrary would be simply illogical. While Pope may have had a moral obligation to intervene, she had no legal obligation to do so; and we do not punish those who fail to live up to society's image of what a moral obligation should be. In sum, we hold that the evidence was insufficient to demonstrate that Pope fell within the class of persons to whom the child abuse statute applies. We turn now to issues of liability under the common law crime of misprision of felony. We assume, *arguendo* ["for the sake of argument"], that misprision was a crime under the English common law. The question is whether it is a crime in modern times and within our jurisdiction. We hold that it is not. We are satisfied, considering its origin, the impractical and discriminate width of its scope, and its long non-use, that it is now incompatible with our general code of laws and jurisprudence. If the legislature feels otherwise, it may enact a statute making it a crime. We therefore hold that misprision of felony is no longer a chargeable offense in this state.

Reversed.

Barber v. Superior Court

California District Court of Appeal, 195 Cal. Rptr. 484 (1983)

FACTS

Petitioner Robert Nejdl, M.D., performed surgery on Clarence Herbert; Petitioner Neil Barber, M.D., was Herbert's attending internist. Shortly after the successful surgery, Herbert suffered cardiac arrest and was revived and immediately placed on life support. Within three days, Barber and other physicians determined that Herbert had severe brain damage, leaving him in a vegetative state from which he would probably not recover although there remained some brain activity. Petitioners informed Herbert's family of his slim chances for recovery. At that point, the family drafted a written request to the hospital, stating that they wished to take Herbert off life support. When they took him off, Herbert continued to breathe without the equipment, but showed no signs of improvement. After two more days, petitioners, after consulting with the family, order the removal of the intravenous tubes which provided hydration and nourishment. Herbert died some time later.

 When a person removes the life support from a patient who is comatose, but not brain dead, has murder been committed?

 Removal of artificial life support equipment from a patient who is in a vegetative state and not expected to recover is the conduct of an omission (to carry on treatment via the life support measures) rather than an affirmative action, such that if it is in harmony with the patient's or his surrogate's wishes, does not give rise to criminal liability.

 Murder is the *unlawful* killing of a human being with *malice* aforethought. Recent advances in medicine have resulted in the instant prosecution and its attendant legal dispute. As such, in order to resolve the dispute with the existing legal framework, we must determine if petitioners' conduct was, in fact, *unlawful*. All parties agree that Herbert was not dead by either statutory or historical standards, since there was still minimal brain activity. If he were "brain dead," this prosecution could not have been instituted because one cannot be charged with killing a dead person. As a predicate to our analysis of whether petitioner' conduct rose to the level of an "unlawful killing," we conclude that cessation of "heroic" life support measures is not an affirmative act, but rather the withdrawal or omission of treatment. And while the treatments are self-propelled to a degree, in reality each pulsation of the respirator or each drop of fluid introduced into a patient's blood stream by an intravenous method is comparable to a manually administered injection or medication. The People (plaintiff) argue that a murder charge may be supported by the failure to feed a child. We agree, but this case is easily distinguishable. A parent clearly has duty to feed an otherwise healthy child, while the duty of a physician is clearly different. A physician has no duty to continue treatment, once it has proved to be ineffective. The patient's desires are the key ingredients of the decision making process; and where it is not possible to ascertain the choice the patient himself, the surrogate [usually the family] ought to be guided by their knowledge of the patient's feelings and desires. If the patient's desires are unknown, the surrogate should be guided by the patient's best interests. Here, there is evidence that Mr. Herbert did not want to be kept alive by machines and his wife and children decided that his treatment should be discontinued. Thus, we find no legal requirement that prior judicial approval was necessary in the absence of legislative guidance.

Writ prohibiting prosecution issued.

Regina v. Cunningham
Court of Criminal Appeal, 2 Q.B 396 (1957)

FACTS

Defendant-appellant Cunningham appeals his conviction claiming that the judge erroneously instructed the jury as to the meaning of the word "malicious." Cunningham was engaged to Sarah Wade's daughter. Mrs. Wade owned two houses that had once existed as a single home. After the single building had been converted into two separate homes, a wall had been erected to divide the cellars of the two homes; a wall which was loosely cemented. Mrs. Wade lived on one side with her husband and Appellant Cunningham was to live on the other side after his marriage to the Wades' daughter. The other side was, at the time, unoccupied. On evening, in need of money, appellant went into the basement of the unoccupied house and stole a gas meter. He admitted that he "wrenched the gas meter from the gas pipes and stole it, together with its contents. He got 8 shillings from the meter and then discarded the meter. Although there was a shut off valve within 2 feet of the meter, Cunningham did not turn off the gas. Consequently, gas leaked through the basement wall and into Mrs. Wade's house, where it partially asphyxiated her while she was sleeping in her bedroom. Cunningham was indicted for violating Section 23 of the Offenses against the Person Act, 1861. The Act made it a felony to unlawfully and maliciously administer poison to a person, or cause poison to be administered to a person, so as to endanger the person's life. The trial judge instructed the jury that the term "malicious" was defined in the statute to mean "wicked." The jury convicted Cunningham and he appealed.

Is the *mens rea* requirement of "maliciousness" satisfied when the accused has acted "wickedly" with respect to the crime charged?

The *mens rea* requirement for maliciousness is satisfied by a showing of either an actual intention to do particular kind of harm or by reckless conduct; but not by a showing of malice or wickedness.

The *mens rea* requirement for maliciousness is satisfied by a showing of either an actual intention to do particular kind of harm or by reckless conduct. Criminal liability may still be found where the accused did not intend to bring about the harm, but was able to foresee that the harm could occur and persisted in his actions anyway. In such a case, the accused would be acting recklessly because he chose to disregard a foreseeable risk of harm and acted anyway. In the instant case, it does not appear that Cunningham intentionally released the gas to poison Mrs. Wade. Rather, he admitted that he was in need and money and stole the meter to that effect. The trial judge instructed the jury that the statutory concept of "malicious" was synonymous with the word "wicked;" such that the jury could convict Cunningham if they found that he was doing something he knew was wrong (the poisoning of Mrs. Wade, not the stealing of the meter). However, we think that such a definition was too broad because in the context of the statute at issue, an act is "malicious" if it is done intentionally or recklessly, but not wickedly. Hence, in our view, it should have been left to the jury to decide whether, even if the appellant did not intend to injure Mrs. Wade, he foresaw that the removal of the gas mater might cause injury to someone but removed it anyway. In such a case, the jury may have found that he had been acting recklessly. Because the jury was erroneously instructed as to the meaning of "malicious," we cannot be sure beyond a reasonable doubt that they found that Cunningham acted with the requisite state of mind.

Appeal allowed and conviction quashed.

Regina v. Faulkner

13 Cox Crim. Cas. 550, 555, 557 (1877)

FACTS

On June 26, 1876, Defendant Robert Faulkner was on board the ship *The Zemindar*, which was the property of Sandback, Tenne, and Co., on a voyage on the high seas, feloniously, unlawfully, and maliciously, did set fire to the said ship, with intent thereby to prejudice the said Sandback, Parker, and other, the owners of certain goods and chattels then laden, and being on board said ship." *The Zemindar* was on her voyage home with a cargo of rum, sugar, and cotton, worth £50,000. The defendant, who was a seaman on board, went into the bulk head and entered the area where the rum was stored. He had no business being there and no authority to go there but went for the purpose of stealing some rum. To do so, he bored hole in the cask with a gimlet, whereupon the rum ran out, and when he tried to plug the hole while holding a lighted match in his hand to see, the rum caught fire. Faulkner himself was burned on the arms and neck and that the ship caught fire and was completely destroyed. At the close of the case for the Crown [the trial], counsel for the defendant asked for a direction of an acquittal on the ground that on the facts proved the indictment was not sustained, nor the allegation that he had unlawfully and maliciously set fire to the ship proved. The Crown contended that the prisoner [defendant] was at the time engaged in the commission of a felony, the indictment was sustained, and the allegation of the intent was held immaterial.

Is one who commits a felony criminally liable for every consequence resulting from it?

One who commits a felony criminally liable for every consequence resulting from it, unless such a collateral crime is the probable and natural consequence of the initial felonious act or is the type that could have been reasonably foreseen as the result of the former act.

One who commits a felony is not criminally responsible for every result which occurs during the initial crime committed unless such a collateral crime is the probable and natural consequence of the initial felonious act or is the type that could have been reasonably foreseen as the result of the former act. A very broad argument has been put forth by the Crown, namely, that if a person is engaged in a felony, or, having committed it, is endeavoring to conceal his act, and accidentally does some collateral act which if done willfully would be another felony, he is nonetheless guilty of the latter felony. No express authority either by way of decision or dictum from a judge or legal scholar has been cited in support of this preposition. Thus, I shall consider myself bound for the purpose of this case by the authority of *Reg. v. Pembliton*. That case must be taken as deciding that to constitute an offence under the Malicious Injuries to Property Act, sect. 51, the act done *must* be in fact intentional and willful, although the intention and will may (perhaps) be held to exist in, or be proved by, the fact that the accused knew that the injury would be the probable result of his unlawful act, and yet did the act reckless of such consequences. The present indictment charges the offence to be under the same Act, and it is not disputed that the same construction must be applied to both cases. The jury was instructed to give a verdict of guilty upon the simple ground that the fire which destroyed the ship, though accidental, was caused by an act done in the course of, or immediately consequent upon, a felony, and no question of the prisoner's malice or intent, constructive or otherwise, was left to the jury. I am of opinion that, according to *Reg. v. Pembliton*, that direction was erroneous, and that the conviction should be quashed.

The conviction should be quashed.

Santillanes v. New Mexico
849 P.2d 358 (1993)

FACTS

Defendant Santillanes cut his 7-year-old nephew's neck with a knife during an altercation and was convicted under a statute defining child abuse as "negligently" causing a child to be placed in a situation that may endanger the child's life or health. At the close of all the evidence, Santillanes's counsel submitted jury instructions that included a criminal negligence standard patterned on the definition provided in the Model Penal Code Section 2.02(2)(d). The trial court refused to give this instruction, opting instead to instruct the jury on a civil negligence standard which provided that "An act, to be 'negligence,' must be one which a reasonably prudent person would foresee as involving an unreasonable risk of injury to himself or to another and which such a person, in the exercise of ordinary care, would not do." Santillanes maintains that felony punishment should attach only to criminal acts or acts involving criminal negligence, but not to ordinary civil negligence.

When the legislature is silent as to the level of negligence required, should civil negligence be applied?

Unless specifically stated in the statute, "negligence" shall be defined as calling for criminal negligence.

When the legislature has not defined the level of intent required in a criminal statute, we do not automatically default to either a no-fault or strict liability crime and we must additionally presume criminal intent is required unless the legislature clearly intended to omit the *mens rea* element. The issue before us is when the *mens rea* has been included in a criminal statute [here the term "negligently"] but not defined the term, what degree of negligence is required. The intended scope of proscribed conduct under the child abuse statute is, at best, open to debate. As such, we must strictly construe the statutory language as requiring the criminal negligence standard, in the absence of clear legislative intent to the contrary. This is because we construe the intended scope of the statute as aiming to punish conduct that is morally culpable. We therefore interpret this statute to require criminal negligence instead of ordinary civil negligence.

See Rule above.

United States v. Jewell
U.S. Court of Appeals, 532 F.2d 697 (9th Cir. 1976)

FACTS

Defendant-appellant Jewell was driving a car from Mexico to the U.S. containing 110 pounds of marijuana concealed in a secret compartment under the rear seat and in the trunk. He was caught, charged and put on trial. Jewell testified that while he knew the compartment existed, he did not know that it contained marijuana. Jewell requested a jury instruction that in order to find him guilty of possession of marijuana, the jury must also find that he actually knew he was carrying the drug. The requested instruction was rejected. In its place, the court instructed the jury that it must find "beyond a reasonable doubt" that Jewell "knowingly" possessed the marijuana and that if he "was not actually aware that there was marijuana in the vehicle he was driving when he entered the United States his ignorance in that regard was solely and entirely a result of his having made a conscious purpose to disregard the nature of that which was in the vehicle, with a conscious purpose to avoid learning the truth." The jury found Jewell guilty of the charge.

When an offence requires "knowledge" as an essential element of the crime, does such a requirement imply actual positive knowledge only?

To act with "knowledge" is not necessarily to act only with actual positive knowledge, but also to act with an awareness of a high probability of the existence of the fact in question.

Appellant's narrow interpretation of the word "knowingly" is inconsistent with the Drug Control Act' general purpose to deal with the nation's dug problems. Deliberate "willful" ignorance and positive knowledge are the same in the following respect – both impugn guilt. Thus, when one acts with an "awareness of the high probability that some fact exists," he is also acting "knowingly" with respect to that fact. We distinguish the foregoing from the situation in which one has an actual belief the fact does not exist. This rule is meant to keep actors from escaping liability through "willful blindness" when the accused is aware of the probable existence of a material fact but does not certify that it does not actually exist. Hence, a court can find willfulness only where it can be proven that the defendant actually knew of the material fact(s). However, when the state proves that the defendant would have known of the material fact(s) but for his conscious intention to evade learning the truth, the government has proven "knowledge" as set forth by the statute. No legitimate interest is prejudiced by such a standard, and society's has an interest in a system of criminal law that is enforceable and that imposes sanctions upon all who are equally culpable.

Affirmed.

Regina v. Prince

Court of Crown Cases Reserved, L.R. 2 Cr. Res. 154 (1875)

FACTS

Defendant Prince was convicted under a criminal statute for what is commonly known today as statutory rape. Specifically, Price was convicted of "unlawfully taking or causing to be taken any unmarried girl under the age of sixteen years, out of the possession and against the will of her father or mother, or of any person having the lawful care or charge of her." A person so charged shall be guilty of a misdemeanor. The jury found that the girl, only fourteen years old, had told Prince that she was eighteen before he took her away. Moreover, testimony was proffered to the effect that Prince honestly and reasonably believed the girl was eighteen. After his conviction, Prince appealed on the ground that the statute at issued requires that the person accused not believe that the girl taken is under sixteen.

 When a statute is silent as to any requirement that the illicit act be done with knowledge of its illegality, does a reasonable mistake of fact form a valid defense?

 A mistake of fact defense *does not* apply to criminal statutes which clearly do not require the proscribed conduct to be done "knowingly" [these are strict liability crimes].

 I find it necessary to read into the statute language requiring that a person not believe the girl is over the age of 16 and thus uphold the conviction. This Court is not bound to read such a *mens rea* requirement into the statute: The act forbidden is wrong in itself - I do not say illegal. It is what the statute contemplates. The legislature has decided that anyone who does this act does so at the risk of being wrong – that she is in fact under sixteen. This opinion gives full scope and accord to the doctrine of *mens rea*. If the taker believes he has the father's permission, though wrongly, he would have no *mens rea*. In such a case he would not know he was doing the act forbidden by statute; an act which, if he knew she was in the possession of another's charge, he would know was a crime. The same principle holds true in other situations. For example, a man will be held liable for striking a police officer in the execution of his duty, though he did not know the man was a police officer. Why? Because the act is wrong in and of itself. It seems to me impossible to say that where a person takes girl out of her father's possession, not knowing whether she is or is not under sixteen, that he is not guilty; and equally impossible when he believes, erroneously, that she is old enough for him to do a wrong act with safety. I think the conviction should be affirmed.

 Judgment of conviction affirmed.

People v. Olsen
Supreme Court of California, 685 P.2d 52 (1984)

FACTS

Defendant-appellant Olsen was convicted of committing a lewd or lascivious act with Shawn M., a child of 13 years and 10 months at the time. At trial, the victim testified that she was staying in her family's trailer in their driveway because a number of houseguests were staying at her house and in her room. That during the third night she'd locked the trailer as directed by her parents and was sleeping when she was awakened by Olsen knocking on the window and asking to be let in. A half hour later, another person named Garcia came and also knocked on the window asking to enter. Once again she did not answer and Garcia left. That she was once again awoken by barking dogs and by Garcia who had a knife by her side and his hand over her mouth. Although Shawn testified that she locked the trailer, she failed to explain how Garcia gained entry. Garcia is then said to have called out to Olsen to enter the trailer. Garcia allegedly told Shawn to let appellant "make love" to her or he [Garcia] would stab her. That upon entering the trailer, Olsen proceeded to do just that. That while Olsen was having intercourse with Shawn, her father entered the trailer and was stabbed by Garcia in order to free Olsen from his [the father's] grasp. Shawn also testified that she knew Garcia "pretty well" and that she was very good friends "off and on" with Olsen and that for one three month period she'd spent almost every day at Olsen's house. Also, that at the time of the incident she considered Garcia her boyfriend. Shawn also admitted telling both Garcia and Olsen that she was over sixteen and Patricia Alvarez, a police officer, testified that appellant told her that he thought she was 17. Garcia, not unexpectedly, testified to a different set of events. He stated that the day before the incident, Shawn had invited him to spend the night in the trailer so they could have sex. He and Shawn had engaged in intercourse about four times that evening and that she'd invited him to come back the next evening at midnight. After Garcia unsuccessfully tried to enter the trailer on two prior occasions, he and Olsen were told by Shawn to come back at midnight. When they did, they were greeted at the door by Shawn wearing only panties. She allegedly told them that she wanted "to make love" with Olsen first. When Shawn's father, Mr. M., entered the trailer, Olsen was on top of Shawn. Garcia denied threatening Shawn with a knife, taking her nightgown off, breaking into her trailer or forcing her to have sex. The court found both Garcia and Olsen guilty of violating Penal Code §288, which makes it a crime to "willfully and lewdly commit any lewd or lascivious act . . . with a child under the age of 14 years . . ." Subdivision (a) contains no knowledge requirement concerning the child's age. Appellant was convicted to a term of three years in state prison. This appeal followed.

Does a good faith, reasonable mistake as to the victim's age form a valid defense to a charge of a lewd or lascivious act with a child under fourteen years of age?

A reasonable mistake of age is not a valid affirmative defense when the accused is charged with a lewd or lascivious act with a child under fourteen years of age.

People v. Olsen

Supreme Court of California, 685 P.2d 52 (1984)

The language of §288 is silent as to whether a good faith, reasonable mistake as to the victim's age constitutes a defense to a charge under that statute. We have previously held, against precedent, in *People v. Hernandez* that an accused's good faith and reasonable belief that a victim was 18 years or more of age <u>was</u> a defense to a charge of statutory rape. One Court of Appeal has declined to apply this holding to a case where a marijuana dealer made out a reasonable mistake of age defense to a charge of offering or furnishing marijuana to a minor [*People v. Lopez*]. The *Lopez* Court distinguished that case from *Hernandez* by noting that the act of furnishing marijuana is illegal regardless of the age of the recipient and that when the recipient is a minor the crime is viewed as being more serious. Thus, "A mistake of fact relating only to the gravity of the offense will not shield a deliberate offender from the full consequences of the wrong actually committed." Section 288 was enacted with the specific purpose to protect children of tender years. Even the *Hernandez* court recognized this consideration when it made clear that it did not contemplate applying the mistake of age defense when the victim was of "tender years." This conclusion is also supported by the legislature's enactment of § 1203.066, subd. (a)(3) which makes people convicted of the instant crime eligible for probation if they "honestly and reasonably believed the victim was 14 years old older." If these persons, including convicted Olsen, are eligible for parole under the foregoing circumstances, there is a strong suggestion that the legislature did not intend for a mistake of age to be a *defense* against such a charge; else why include a "parole" provision. To hold otherwise [that a valid defense does exist for honestly and reasonably believing the victim was 14 years old older] would be to nullify § 1203.066, subd. (a)(3) altogether. We also find support in other legislative provisions: the legislature has determined that persons who commit sexual offenses on children under 14 should receive a more severe punishment than those who've committed such offenses against children under 18. Thus, the legislative purpose of §288 wouldn't be served by recognizing the defense of reasonable mistake of age.

Affirmed.

Morissette v. United States

Supreme Court of the United States, 342 U.S. 246 (1952)

FACTS

On a large tract of uninhabited and untilled land in a wooded and sparsely populated area of Michigan, the Government established a practice bombing range over which the Air Force dropped simulated bombs at ground targets. These bombs consisted of a metal cylinder about forty inches long and eight inches across, filled with sand and enough black powder to cause a smoke puff by which the strike could be located. At various places about the range signs read "Danger - Keep Out - Bombing Range." Nevertheless, the range was known as good deer country and was extensively hunted. Spent bomb casings were cleared from the targets and thrown into piles "so that they will be out of the way." They were not stacked or piled in any order but were dumped in heaps, some of which had been accumulating for four years or upwards, were exposed to the weather and rusting away. Defendant Morissette, in December of 1948, went hunting in this area but did not get a deer. He thought to meet expenses of the trip by salvaging some of these casings. He loaded three tons of them on his truck and took them to a nearby farm, where they were flattened by driving a tractor over them. After expending this labor and trucking them to market in Flint, he realized $84. Morissette, by occupation, is a fruit stand operator in summer and a trucker and scrap iron collector in winter. The loading, crushing and transporting of these casings were all in broad daylight, in full view of passers-by, without the slightest effort at concealment. When an investigation was started, Morissette voluntarily, promptly and candidly told the whole story to the authorities, saying that he had no intention of stealing but thought the property was abandoned, unwanted and considered of no value to the Government. He was indicted, however, on the charge that he "did unlawfully, willfully and knowingly steal and convert" property of the United States of the value of $84, in violation of 18 U.S.C. 641, which provides that "whoever embezzles, steals, purloins, or knowingly converts" government property is punishable by fine and imprisonment. Morissette was convicted and sentenced to imprisonment for two months or to pay a fine of $200. The Court of Appeals affirmed. The U.S. Supreme Court granted certiorari.

If the Legislature is silent as to any requirement of intent in the codification of a common law crime which does require intent, can a criminal defendant be found guilty without a showing of intent?

The legislature's omission of a *mens rea* element in a criminal statute which can be found in its common law counterpart does not turn the codified crime into a strict offense; in such a case, the statute will be interpreted to require the *mens rea* element of its common law counterpart.

A criminal intent is an essential element of an offense under 18 U.S.C. §641, which provides that "whoever embezzles, steals, purloins, or knowingly converts" property of the United States is punishable by fine and imprisonment. Mere omission from §641 of any mention of intent is not to be construed as eliminating that element from the crimes defined. The history and

Morissette v. United States

Supreme Court of the United States, 342 U.S. 246 (1952)

---

purposes of §641 afford no ground for inferring any affirmative instruction from Congress to eliminate intent from the offense of "knowingly converting" or stealing government property. Where intent of the accused is an ingredient of the crime charged, its existence is a question of fact which must be submitted to the jury for determination in the light of all relevant evidence; and the trial court may not withdraw or prejudge the issue by instructing the jury that the law raises a presumption of intent from a single act.

 Reversed.

Staples v. United States

Supreme Court of the United States, 511 U.S. 60 (1994)

FACTS

The National Firearms Act criminalizes possession of an unregistered "firearm," 26 U.S.C. 5861(d), including a "machinegun," 5845(a)(6), which is defined as a weapon that automatically fires more than one shot with a single pull of the trigger, 5845(b). Petitioner Staples was charged with possessing an unregistered machinegun in violation of 5861(d) after officers searching his home seized a semiautomatic rifle - i.e., a weapon that normally fires only one shot with each trigger pull - that had apparently been modified fire continuously and automatically [like a machinegun]. At trial, Defendant Staples testified that the rifle had never fired automatically while he possessed it, and that he had been ignorant of any automatic firing capability. He was convicted after the District Court rejected his proposed jury instruction under which, to establish a 5861(d) violation, the Government would have been required to prove beyond a reasonable doubt that Staples knew that the gun would fire fully automatically. The Court of Appeals affirmed, concluding that the Government need not prove a defendant's knowledge of a weapon's physical properties to obtain a conviction under 5861(d). The U.S. Supreme Court granted certiorari.

 Should a statute be interpreted with respect to the background rules of the common law pertaining to that crime in which the requirement of a *mens rea* element is present, even when no such requirement exits in the statute as written?

 A criminal Act that omits a *mens rea* element will be construed in light of the background rules of the common law pertaining to that crime in which the requirement of a *mens rea* element is present, even when no such requirement exits in the statute as written, unless there is an explicit indication that the legislature intended there to be no such requirement.

 To obtain a 5861(d) conviction, the Government should have been required to prove beyond a reasonable doubt that Staples knew that his rifle had the characteristics that brought it within the statutory definition of a machinegun. The common law rule requiring *mens rea* as an element of a crime informs interpretation of 5861(d) in this case. Because some indication of congressional intent, express or implied, is required to dispense with *mens rea*, 5861(d)'s silence on the element of knowledge required for a conviction does not suggest that Congress intended to dispense with a conventional *mens rea* requirement, which would require that the defendant know the facts making his conduct illegal. The Court rejects the Government's argument that the Act fits within the Court's line of precedent concerning "public welfare" or "regulatory" offenses, and thus that the presumption favoring *mens rea* does not apply in this case. In cases concerning public welfare offenses, the Court has inferred from silence a congressional intent to dispense with conventional *mens rea* requirements in statutes that regulate potentially harmful or injurious items. In such cases, the Court has reasoned that, as long as a defendant knows that he is dealing with a dangerous device of a character that places him in

Staples v. United States
Supreme Court of the United States, 511 U.S. 60 (1994)

responsible relation to a public danger, he should be alerted to the probability of strict regulation, and is placed on notice that he must determine at his peril whether his conduct comes within the statute's inhibition. Guns, however, do not fall within the category of dangerous devices as it has been developed in public welfare offense cases. In contrast to the selling of dangerous drugs at issue in *United States v. Balint* or the possession of hand grenades considered in *Freed*, private ownership of guns in this country has enjoyed a long tradition of being entirely lawful conduct. Thus, the destructive potential of guns in general cannot be said to put gun owners sufficiently on notice of the likelihood of regulation to justify interpreting 5861(d) as dispensing with proof of knowledge of the characteristics that make a weapon a "firearm" under the statute. The Government's interpretation potentially would impose criminal sanctions on a class of persons whose mental state - ignorance of the characteristics of weapons in their possession - makes their actions entirely innocent. Had Congress intended to make outlaws of such citizens, it would have spoken more clearly to that effect. The potentially harsh penalty attached to violation of 5861(d) - up to 10 years' imprisonment - confirms the foregoing reading of the Act. Where, as here, dispensing with *mens rea* would require the defendant to have knowledge only of traditionally lawful conduct, a severe penalty is a further factor tending to suggest that Congress did not intend to eliminate a *mens rea* requirement. The holding here is a narrow one that depends on a common sense evaluation of the nature of the particular device Congress has subjected to regulation, the expectations that individuals may legitimately have in dealing with that device, and the penalty Page III attached to a violation. It does not set forth comprehensive criteria for distinguishing between crimes that require a mental element and crimes that do not.

Reversed and remanded.

State v. Guminga

Supreme Court of Minnesota, 395 N.W.2d 344 (1986)

FACTS

Defendant George Joseph Guminga, restaurant owner, was charged with violating Minn. Stat. §340.941, which imposes vicarious criminal liability on an employer whose employee serves intoxicating liquor to a minor. As part of an undercover operation, two undercover investigators entered the restaurant with a 17-year-old woman on March 29, 1985. All three ordered alcoholic beverages. The minor had never been in the restaurant before and the waitress did not ask the minor her age or request any identification. When the waitress returned with the drinks the minor paid for all three. Once the officers confirmed the drinks contained alcohol they arrested the waitress for serving intoxicating liquor to a minor in violation of Minn. Stat. §340.73 (1984). At defendant's trial, the State did not contend that Guminga was aware of or sanctioned the waitress's actions. Subsequently, Guminga moved to dismiss the charges on the ground that §340.941 violates the Due Process Clauses of the federal and state constitutions. The trial court denied his motion to dismiss. The court of appeals asked the State Supreme Court to take jurisdiction over the question.

 Are a defendant's Due Process rights violated under either federal or state constitutions when he is held vicariously and criminally liable for his employee's sale of alcohol to a minor?

 Vicarious criminal liability will not violate the accused's due process rights if the state's [public] interest outweighs the interest of the offender to be free from intrusion into his personal liberty, while at the same time taking into account any possible alternative means of achieving the state interest.

 We find that the statute in question does violate the due process clauses of the Minnesota and the United States Constitutions and thus answer the certified question in the affirmative. Under Minnesota law, a defendant who commits a gross misdemeanor may be sentenced to "imprisonment for not more than one year or to payment of a fine of not more than $3,000 or both." In addition, a defendant convicted under §340.941 may, at the discretion of the licensing authority, have his license suspended, revoked or be unable to obtain a new license. A due process analysis of a statute involves the balancing of the public interest against the intrusion on personal liberty while taking into account any alternative means by which to achieve the same end. Section 340.941 serves the public interest by providing additional deterrence to violation of the liquor laws. The private interests affected, however, include liberty, damage to reputation and other future disabilities arising from Criminal prosecution. Such an intrusion upon personal liberty is not justified by the public interest protected, especially when there are alternative means by which to achieve the same end, such as civil fines or license suspension, which do not entail the legal and social ramifications of a criminal conviction. The dissent argues that vicarious liability is a necessary deterrent and that limiting punishment to a fine allows bar owners to view their liability as nothing more than the cost of doing business. But we

State v. Guminga

Supreme Court of Minnesota, 395 N.W.2d 344 (1986)

---

believe it is deterrent enough that the employee who does sell to a minor can be charged under the statute and that the business is subject to fines or suspension or revocation of license. The certified question is thus answered in the affirmative.

 The certified question is thus answered in the affirmative..

State v. Baker
Kansas Court of Appeal, 571 P.2d 65 (1977)

FACTS

Defendant Baker was convicted of driving at a speed of 70 m.p.h. in a 55 m.p.h. zone in violation of K.S.A. 1976 Supp. 8-1336(a)(3), a strict liability statute. Before trial the state moved to suppress evidence offered by Baker that: 1) Defendant's cruise control stuck in the "accelerate" position causing the car to accelerate beyond the posted speed limit; 2) The defendant attempted to deactivate the cruise control by hitting the off button, and the coast button and tapping the breaks; 3) These actions were not immediately successful in deactivating the cruise control; 4) Subsequent to the date of the incident, Baker had the defective cruise control repaired. The trial court sustained the motion, thus preventing Baker from introducing the proffered evidence. Subsequently, Baker was fined $10 plus costs, but both were suspended pending this appeal. Baker readily concedes a violation of the applicable strict liability statute; however, he argues that the offense requires a voluntary act which was not proven by the government in his case.

Do strict liability crimes also necessitate a voluntary act by the defendant?

Strict liability crimes still require a voluntary act by the accused.

Baker readily admits a violation of the applicable speeding statute as a strict liability offense and agrees that any evidence of the defective cruise control would be inadmissible if introduced merely to negate an intent or culpable state of mind on the part of the motorist. Nevertheless, Baker argues that the evidence was offered to show that his speeding was not a voluntary act, therefore negating liability. We do not doubt that if Baker were able to establish that his speeding was the result of an unforeseen occurrence, which was not caused by him and which he could not prevent, that such would constitute a valid defense to the charge. But the evidence that was proffered suggests a malfunction of a device attached to the vehicle, over which he had or should have had absolute control. Baker has not suggested that the operation of the vehicle on the day of the offense was anything but a voluntary act on his part nor that anyone else activated the cruise control, which may have caused his excessive speed. In the New York case *People v. Shaughnessy*, a passenger in a vehicle that drove onto a person's private property was found not guilty of trespassing because he was just a passenger and the state failed to show an overt voluntary act or omission by the defendant. In *State v. Kremer,* the Court held that a defendant could not be guilty of running a red stop light when the evidence showed that the defendant's breaks had failed with no prior warning because, again, there was no voluntary act. In *State v. Weller,* a Connecticut court found no voluntary act when a man's throttle malfunctioned with no prior warning. In our view though,

State v. Baker
Kansas Court of Appeal, 571 P.2d 65 (1977)

---

unexpected break failure and unexpected malfunction of a vehicle's throttle mechanism, both being essential components to the operation of the vehicle, differ significantly from the malfunction of a cruise control device to which the driver has voluntarily handed over at least partial control of the automobile to the mechanism. It must be said that the defendant assumed the full operation of his motor vehicle and when he did so and activated the cruise control attached to that automobile; he clearly was the agent in causing the act of speeding.

Judgment Affirmed.

Regina v. City of Sault Ste. Marie
Supreme Court of Canada, 85 D.L.R.3d 161 (1978)

FACTS

None stated.

Is there a level of criminal wrongdoing which fulfills the goals of the public welfare offenses while still not punishing the entirely blameless; or, stated another way, is there a type of offense that does not require full *mens rea* and where the defendant may still offer evidence he was not negligent?

There is a "middle level" of offenses; those where the state is not required to show any required *mens rea*, but where the defendant may present an affirmative defense that he took all reasonable care.

Various arguments are advanced to justify absolute liability in public welfare offenses. Two predominate. First, it is argued that the protection of social interests requires a high standard of care and that absolute liability will cause people to pay more attention to such standards if they know ignorance or mistake will not excuse a failure to adhere to them. The second argument is based on administrative efficiency. Because of the difficulty of proving mental culpability and the high number of cases that come before the courts and taken time to unravel, proof of fault is just too great a burden in time and money to place upon the prosecution. It is therefore argued that absolute liability is the most efficient and effective way of ensuring compliance with minor regulatory legislation and the social ends to be achieved are of such importance as to override the unfortunate by-product of punishing those who may be free of moral turpitude. Arguments of greater force are advanced against absolute liability though. Strongest is that it violates fundamental principles of penal liability. In serious crimes, the public interest is even more involved and *mens rea* must still be proven. We therefore declare that there are compelling grounds to add another category of offenses to the two that already exist and that have heretofore been recognized. This third category encompasses those offenses in which there is no necessity for the state to prove the existence of *mens rea*; the doing of the prohibited act is prima facie proof of the offense, leaving it open to the defendant to avoid liability by proving that he took all reasonable care. The wording of a particular statute would dictate its category: Offenses which are criminal in the truest sense or that which requires proof of *mens rea* would fall in the first category. Public welfare offenses would fall into the middle category, unless the statute includes such words as "willfully," "with intent," "knowingly," or "intentionally," in which case the offense would fall into the first category. Offenses of absolute liability would be those which the Legislature made clear that guilt would follow proof merely of the proscribed act. The over-all regulatory pattern of the Legislature, its subject-matter, the importance of the penalty, and the precision of the language used will be primary considerations in determining whether the offense falls into the third category.

See Rule above.

People v. Marrero
New York Court of Appeals, 507 N.E.2d 1068 (1987)

FACTS

Defendant Marrero, a *federal* corrections officer, was convicted of unlawful possession of a loaded .38 caliber pistol in violation of New York Penal Law §265.02. However, §265.02(a)(1) provided an exemption from prosecution for "peace officers." The statutory definition of "peace officers" included "correction officers of any state correction facility or of any penal correctional institution." The trial court dismissed the charge, but the Appellate Division reinstated the indictment and ruled that only state and not federal officers were covered by the provision. At trial, the court refused the defendant's request for a jury instruction which stated that it [the jury] should acquit Marrero if he reasonably believed himself to be a peace officer under the statutory definition.

 Does the misunderstanding and misinterpretation of a statute excuse criminal conduct in violation of a statute when the statute omits a *mens rea* requirement?

 An erroneous interpretation of the law, even if based on a reasonable mistake, does not excuse a violation of the law.

 A mistake of law is generally no excuse to a violation of the law. However, the mistake of law defense is available to defendants who have relied on an "official statement" of the law, either expressed in a statute or by a public servant/agency charged with administering, enforcing, or interpreting the law. Here, Marrero claims that his conduct was based on an official statement of the law contained in the statute itself. Marrero argues that his mistaken interpretation was a "reasonable" interpretation falls in light of the above. We disagree. Allowing this exception would make mistake of law a generally applied or available defense, rather than an unusual exception. The Government counters and argues that misconstruing the statute is allowed only when the statute relied upon actually permitted the conduct in question and was only later found to be in error. The bolster its argument, the Government analogizes New York's *official statement* defense to the approach taken by Model Penal Code. The Model Penal Code provides that the *official statement* defense only applies when the accused acts in reliance on a statute that actually authorizes his conduct. If the *official statement* of the law is afterward determined to be invalid or erroneous, the *official statement* defense protects those who mistakenly acted in reliance. Reviewing the legislative history, it is evident that the legislature intended the New York official statement defense statute to be similarly construed. Defendant's conduct was never approved by statute, he simply believed it was. To allow otherwise would be to permit the exception to swallow the rule.

 The conviction is affirmed.

Cheek v. United States
Supreme Court of the United States, 498 U.S. 192 (1991)

FACTS

Petitioner Cheek, a pilot for American Airlines, was charged with six counts of willfully failing to file a federal income tax return in violation of 7203 of the Internal Revenue Code (Code) and three counts of willfully attempting to evade his income taxes in violation of 7201. Cheek represented himself at trial and testified in his defense. He admitted that he had not filed personal income tax returns during the years in question. He testified that, as early as 1978, he had begun attending seminars sponsored by, and following the advice of, a group that believes, among other things, that the federal tax system is unconstitutional. Some of the speakers at these meetings were lawyers who purported to give professional opinions about the invalidity of the federal income tax laws. Cheek produced a letter from an attorney stating that the Sixteenth Amendment did not authorize a tax on wages and salaries, but only on gain or profit. Petitioner's defense was that, based on the indoctrination he received from this group and from his own study, he sincerely believed that the tax laws were being unconstitutionally enforced and that his actions during the 1980-1986 period were lawful. He therefore argued that he had acted without the willfulness required for conviction of the various offenses with which he was charged. In instructing the jury, the court stated that an honest but unreasonable belief is not a defense, and does not negate willfulness, and that Cheek's beliefs that wages are not income and that he was not a taxpayer within the meaning of the Code were not objectively reasonable. It also instructed the jury that a person's opinion that the tax laws violate his constitutional rights does not constitute a good-faith misunderstanding of the law. Cheek was convicted, and the Court of Appeals affirmed. The U.S. Supreme Court granted certiorari.

Is mistake of law a valid, enforceable defense to a crime if it negates the willfulness element (specific intent) required for conviction?

A good-faith mistake of law, reasonable or not, is a valid defense to a crime if it negates the specific intent required for conviction.

A good-faith misunderstanding of the law or a good-faith belief that one is not violating the law negates willfulness, whether or not the claimed belief or misunderstanding is objectively reasonable. Statutory willfulness, which protects the average citizen from prosecution for innocent mistakes made due to the complexity of the tax laws, *United States v. Murdock*, is the voluntary, intentional violation of a known legal duty, *United States v. Pomponio*. Thus, if the jury credited Cheek's assertion that he truly believed that the Code did not treat wages as income, the Government would not have carried its burden to prove willfulness, however unreasonable a court might deem such a belief. Characterizing a belief as objectively unreasonable transforms what is normally a factual inquiry into a legal one,

Cheek v. United States

Supreme Court of the United States, 498 U.S. 192 (1991)

---

thus preventing a jury from considering it. And forbidding a jury to consider evidence that might negate willfulness would raise a serious question under the Sixth Amendment's jury trial provision, which this interpretation of the statute avoids. Of course, in deciding whether to credit Cheek's claim, the jury is free to consider any admissible evidence showing that he had knowledge of his legal duties. It was proper for the trial court to instruct the jury not to consider Cheek's claim that the tax laws are unconstitutional, since a defendant's views about the tax statutes' validity are irrelevant to the issue of willfulness, and should not be heard by a jury. Unlike the claims in the *Murdock-Pomponio* line of cases, claims that Code provisions are unconstitutional do not arise from innocent mistakes caused by the Code's complexity. Rather, they reveal full knowledge of the provisions at issue and a studied conclusion that those provisions are invalid and unenforceable. Congress could not have contemplated that a taxpayer, without risking criminal prosecution, could ignore his duties under the Code and refuse to utilize the mechanisms Congress provided to present his invalidity claims to the courts and to abide by their decisions. Cheek was free to pay the tax, file for a refund, and, if denied, present his claims to the courts. Also, without paying the tax, he could have challenged claims of tax deficiencies in the Tax Court.

Vacated and remanded.

Lambert v. California

Supreme Court of the United States, 355 U.S. 225 (1957)

FACTS

Section 52.39 of the Los Angeles Municipal Code prohibits any person ever convicted of a felony to be or remain in Los Angeles for more than five days without registering with the Chief of Police. Section 52.43(b) makes the failure to register a continuing offense, with each day's failure constituting a separate offense. Defendant-appellant Lambert, arrested on suspicion of another offense, was charged with a violation of this registration law. The evidence showed that she had been at the time of her arrest a resident of Los Angeles for over seven years. Within that period she had been convicted in Los Angeles of the crime of forgery, an offense which California punishes as a felony. Though convicted of a crime punishable as a felony, she had not at the time of her arrest registered under the Municipal Code. At the trial, appellant asserted that 52.39 of the Code denies her due process of law and other rights under the Federal Constitution, unnecessary to enumerate. The trial court denied this objection. The case was tried to a jury which found appellant guilty. The court fined her $250 and placed her on probation for three years. Appellant, renewing her constitutional objection, moved for arrest of judgment and a new trial. This motion was denied. On appeal the constitutionality of the Code was again challenged. The Appellate Department of the Superior Court affirmed the judgment, holding there was no merit to the claim that the ordinance was unconstitutional. The case is here on appeal. The U.S. Supreme Court noted probable jurisdiction, and designated amicus curiae to appear in support of appellant. The case having been argued and reargued, we now hold that the registration provisions of the Code as sought to be applied here violate the Due Process requirement of the Fourteenth Amendment.

May a person be convicted of violating a mandatory registration law without proof that they actually knew of the obligation or had probable knowledge of such a necessity?

A conviction for the violation of a registration law mandating that specific groups of people register with authorities is not valid unless the person 1) has actual knowledge of the requirement or 2) has probable reason to know of his duty to register.

The registration provision, carrying criminal penalties, applies if a person has been convicted "of an offense punishable as a felony in the State of California" or, in case he has been convicted in another State, if the offense "would have been punishable as a felony" had it been committed in California. No element of willfulness is by terms included in the ordinance or read into it by the California court as a condition necessary for a conviction. We must assume that appellant had no actual knowledge of the requirement that she register under this ordinance, as she offered proof of this defense which was refused. The question is whether a registration act of this character violates due process where it is applied to a person who has no actual knowledge of his duty to register, and where no showing is

Lambert v. California

Supreme Court of the United States, 355 U.S. 225 (1957)

---

made of the probability of such knowledge. We do not agree with Blackstone in saying that "a vicious will" is necessary to constitute a crime, for conduct alone without regard to the intent of the doer is often sufficient. There is wide latitude in the lawmakers to declare an offense and to exclude elements of knowledge and diligence from its definition. But we deal here with conduct that is wholly passive - mere failure to register. It is unlike the commission of acts, or the failure to act under circumstances that should alert the doer to the consequences of his deed. The rule that "ignorance of the law will not excuse" is deep in our law, as is the principle that all the powers of local government, the police power is "one of the least limitable." On the other hand, due process places some limits on its exercise. Engrained in our concept of due process is the requirement of notice. Notice is sometimes essential so that the citizen has the chance to defend charges. Notice is required before property interests are disturbed, before assessments are made, before penalties are assessed. Notice is required in a myriad of situations where a penalty or forfeiture might be suffered for mere failure to act. Recent cases illustrating the point are *Mullane v. Central Hanover Trust Co.; Covey v. Town of Somers; and Walker v. Hutchinson City*. These cases involved only property interests in civil litigation. But the principle is equally appropriate where a person, wholly passive and unaware of any wrongdoing, is brought to the bar of justice for condemnation in a criminal case. Registration laws are common and their range is wide. Many such laws are akin to licensing statutes in that they pertain to the regulation of business activities. But the present ordinance is entirely different. Violation of its provisions is unaccompanied by any activity whatever, mere presence in the city being the test. Moreover, circumstances which might move one to inquire as to the necessity of registration are completely lacking. At most the ordinance is but a law enforcement technique designed for the convenience of law enforcement agencies through which a list of the names and addresses of felons then residing in a given community is compiled. The disclosure is merely a compilation of former convictions already publicly recorded in the jurisdiction where obtained. Nevertheless, this appellant on first becoming aware of her duty to register was given no opportunity to comply with the law and avoid its penalty, even though her default was entirely innocent. She could but suffer the consequences of the ordinance, namely, conviction with the imposition of heavy criminal penalties thereunder. We believe that actual knowledge of the duty to register or proof of the probability of such knowledge and subsequent failure to comply are necessary before a conviction under the ordinance can stand. As Holmes wrote in The Common Law, "A law which punished conduct which would not be blameworthy in the average member of the community would be too severe for that community to bear." Its severity lies in the absence of an opportunity either to avoid the consequences of the law or to defend any prosecution brought under it. Where a person did not know of the duty to register and where there was no proof of the probability of such knowledge, he may not be convicted consistently with due process. Were it otherwise, the evil would be as great as it is when the law is written in print too fine to read or in a language foreign to the community.

Reversed.

State v. Rusk
Court of Appeals of Maryland, 424 A.2d 720 (1981)

FACTS

The prosecutrix (victim) was a twenty-one-year-old mother of a two-year-old son, separated but not divorced from her husband. After leaving her son with her mother, the victim attended a high school reunion, after which she and a female friend went bar hopping in the Fells Point area of Baltimore, driving in separate cars. At the third bar, the victim met Defendant-appellant Edward Salvatore Rusk (Rusk), and after talking with him for 10 minutes, he requested and was subsequently driven to his home by the victim. When they arrived at Rusk's home, the victim parked at the curb on the side of the street opposite from Rusk's rooming house, but did not turn off the ignition. Rusk asked the victim numerous times to come up to his apartment, which, as the victim testified, made her afraid. While the victim tried to convince Rusk that she didn't want to go up to his apartment, stating that she was separated and that it might cause her marital problems especially if she was followed by a detective, Rusk took the keys out of the car and walked over to her side of the car. Rusk then opened the door and said, "Now will you come up?" She agreed, testifying that at that point she was scared because she did not have her car keys, know where she was, whether to run, and could not think of anything else to do. After following Rusk to the room, the victim was left alone while Rusk went to the bathroom. She made no attempt to leave. When Rusk came back, he sat on the bed and pulled the victim onto the bed. The victim stated that she then removed her slacks and removed his clothes because Rusk asked her to. After undressing, the victim testified that she was still begging Rusk to let her leave, but that Rusk continued to say "no." At which point the victim stated that she was really scared, more from the look in his eyes. Not knowing what to say, the victim asked Rusk, "If I do what you want, will you let me go without killing me?" The victim then began to cry, and Rusk putting his hands on the victim's throat, began to lightly choke her. At this point the victim asked, "If I do what you want, will you let me go?" After Rusk said yes, the victim proceeded in doing what Rusk desired. After the victim performed oral sex on Rusk, they had sexual intercourse. After the incident and upon arriving at home, the victim sat in her car and wondered about what Rusk would have done if she did not assent to his wishes. Believing that the right thing to do was to report the incident, she immediately proceeded to Hillendale to find a police car. Rusk was convicted of rape in the second degree and of assault. Rusk appeals only the conviction for rape.

Can the element of force for rape be satisfied by an implied threat?

An implied threat is sufficient to satisfy the element of force for rape.

State v. Rusk
Court of Appeals of Maryland, 424 A.2d 720 (1981)

An implied threat is sufficient to satisfy the element of force for rape. The reversal by the Court of Special Appeals was in error for the fundamental reason so well expressed in the dissenting opinion. The reasonableness of the victim's apprehension of fear was plainly a question of fact for the jury to determine. Reversed and remanded to the Court of Special Appeals with direction that it affirm the judgment of the Criminal Court of Baltimore.

See Rule above.

State [of New Jersey] in the Interest of M.T.S.

New Jersey Supreme Court, 609 A.2d 1266 (1992)

FACTS

On May 21, 1990 fifteen-year-old C.G. was living in a town home with her mother, her three siblings, and several others including Defendant M.T.S. and his girlfriend. 17 year old M.T.S. was temporarily living at the home with the permission of C.G.'s mother and slept downstairs on the couch, while C.G. had her own room on the second floor. At approximately 11:30 p.m., C.G. went upstairs after watching television with her mother, M.T.S. and M.T.S.'s girlfriend. According to C.G., earlier that day M.T.S. had told her three or four times that he "was going to make a surprise visit up in [her] bedroom," but she did not take him seriously. She also testified that M.T.S. had attempted to kiss her on numerous other occasions and at least once had attempted to put his hands inside of her pants, but that she had rejected all of his previous advances. On May 22, at approximately 1:30 am, C.G. awoke to use the bathroom. As she got out of bed, she found M.T.S. standing in the doorway fully clothed. C.G. testified that M.T.S. stated that, "he was going to tease [her] a little bit," but that she thought nothing of it. She then walked past him, used the bathroom, and then returned to bed, falling into a "heavy" sleep. The next event C.G. alleged to have recalled was waking up with M.T.S. on top of her, her underpants and shorts removed, with his penis in her vagina. She immediately slapped M.T.S. in the face and "told him to get off [her] and get out." She did not scream or cry out, and M.T.S. complied in less than one minute after being struck. C.G. said that after M.T.S. left the room, she fell asleep crying because she couldn't believe that he did what he did to her. She did not immediately tell anyone of the events that morning because she was "scared and in shock." According to M.T.S., he and C.G. had been good friends for a long time, and their relationship "kept leading on to more and more." He testified that three days preceding the incident they had been "kissing and necking," and had discussed sexual intercourse. M.T.S. also stated that C.G. encouraged him to "make a surprise visit up in her room." At exactly 1:15 am on May 22, he entered C.G.'s bedroom as she was walking to the bathroom. When she returned the two began kissing and eventually moved to the bed. After continuing to kiss and touch for about five minutes, the two proceeded to engage in sexual intercourse. According to M.T.S., he "stuck it in" and "did it [thrust] three times, and then the fourth time," C.G. pushed him off and told him to stop and get off and M.T.S. "hopped off right away." After about one minute, M.T.S. asked C.G. what was wrong and she replied with a slap to his face. He recalled asking her what was wrong a second time, and her replying, "How can you take advantage of me something like that." The trial court found M.T.S, guilty of 2nd degree sexual assault. The Appellate Division reversed determining that the absence of force beyond that involved in the act of sexual penetration precluded a finding of second-degree sexual assault. The State petitioned the Supreme Court of New Jersey for certification.

 Is the element of "physical force" met simply by an act of non-consensual penetration involving no more force than is necessary to accomplish the result?

State [of New Jersey] in the Interest of M.T.S.

New Jersey Supreme Court, 609 A.2d 1266 (1992)

Resistance is not a required element of rape.

Resistance is not a required element of rape. Under New Jersey law "sexual assault" is defined as the commission "of sexual penetration . . . with another person" with the use of "physical force or coercion." An unconstrained reading of the statutory language indicates that both the act of "sexual penetration" and the use of "physical force or coercion" are separate and distinct elements of the offense. However, the Code does not provide assistance in interpreting the words, "physical force" and the statutory words are ambiguous on their face and can not be understood and applied in accordance with their plain meaning. Thus, because of the conflicting interpretations of "physical force," we must turn to the legislative intent, relying on legislative history and the contemporary context of the statute. Under the common law, rape was defined as "carnal knowledge of a woman against her will." Although American jurisdiction generally adopted the English view, over time they added the requirement that the knowledge have been forcible. As of 1796, New Jersey statutory law defined rape as "carnal knowledge of a woman, forcibly, and against her will." Under traditional rape law, in order to prove that a rape had occurred, the state had to show both that force had been used and that the penetration had been against the woman's will. The presence or absence of consent often turned on credibility. To demonstrate that the victim had not consented to the intercourse, and also that sufficient force had been used to accomplish the rape, the state had to prove that the victim had resisted. In urging that the "resistance" requirement be abandoned, reformers sought to break the connection between force and resistance. The circumstances surrounding the actual passage of the current law reveal that it was conceived as a reform measure to address an evil and to effectuate an important public policy. We are thus satisfied that an interpretation of the statutory crime of sexual assault to require physical force in addition to that entailed in the act of involuntary or unwanted sexual penetration would be fundamentally inconsistent with the legislative purpose to eliminate any consideration of whether the victim resisted or expressed non-consent. Because the statute avoids any reference to the victim's will or resistance, the standard defining the role of force in sexual penetration must prevent the possibility that the formation of the crime will turn on the alleged victim's state of mind or responsive behavior. We conclude, therefore, that any act of sexual penetration engaged in by the defendant without the affirmative and freely-given permission of the victim to the specific act of penetration constitutes the offense of sexual assault. Therefore, physical force in excess of that inherent in the act of sexual penetration is not required for such penetration to be unlawful. Persons need not expressly announce their consent to engage in intercourse for there to be affirmative permission. Permission to engage in an act of sexual penetration can be and indeed often is indicated through physical action rather than words. It is enough that a reasonable person would have believed that the alleged victim had affirmatively and freely given

State [of New Jersey] in the Interest of M.T.S.

New Jersey Supreme Court, 609 A.2d 1266 (1992)

authorization to the act. Therefore, in a case such as this one, in which the State does not allege violence or force extrinsic to the act of penetration, the factfinder must decide whether the defendant's act of penetration was undertaken in circumstances that led the defendant to reasonably believe that the alleged victim had freely given affirmative permission to the specific act of sexual penetration. Such permission can be indicated through words or actions that, when viewed in the light of all the surrounding circumstances, would demonstrate to a reasonable person affirmative authorization for the specific act of sexual penetration. The focus must be on the nature of the defendant's actions. The role of the factfinder is to decide whether the defendant's belief that the alleged victim had freely given affirmative permission was reasonable. Neither the alleged victim's subjective state of mind nor the reasonableness of the alleged victim's actions can be deemed relevant to the offense. In sum, in order to convict under the sexual assault statute in cases such as these, the State must prove beyond a reasonable doubt that there was sexual penetration and that it was accomplished without the affirmative and freely-given permission of the alleged victim. If there is evidence that the defendant reasonably believed that such permission had been given, the State must demonstrate either that defendant did not actually believe that affirmative permission had been freely-given or that such a belief was unreasonable under the circumstances. The trial court concluded that the victim had not expressed consent to the act of intercourse, either through her words or actions. We conclude that the record provides reasonable support for the trial court's disposition.

Reversed.

M.C. v. Bulgaria

European Court of Human Rights [2003] ECHR 39272/98

FACTS

Applicant, a Bulgarian national, alleges that she was raped twice in two consecutive days by two perpetrators who were friends with each other, and acquaintances of the applicant. At the time of the alleged rape the applicant was 14 years and 10 months of age, and thus was of the age of consent (14 years) according to Bulgarian legislation. Immediately after the first rape, the applicant was accompanied by the perpetrator and his friends, amongst which was the second perpetrator, to a restaurant and was witnessed there to have acted "normally." The applicant returned home that evening, and the following night, was raped for the second time at the residence of a friend of the second perpetrator. After she failed to return home that night, the Applicant´s mother sought her whereabouts and located her, immediately accompanying the applicant to the hospital, where a medical examination was conducted. The Applicant´s hymen was found to have been freshly torn, and minor abrasions were found on her body. At that time, the applicant reported only the first incident, citing feelings of shame in light of the conservative nature of her upbringing and environment. That evening, the perpetrator of the first assault visited the applicant at her familial residence where he sought forgiveness and assured the Applicant´s mother of his desire to marry the applicant. The mother, while initially accepting the idea, approached the parents of the first perpetrator, where she was informed of the second rape. Upon the return home of the Applicant´s father, the family promptly decided to file a complaint with authorities and on the same day, both perpetrators were arrested. An investigation was conducted by the police, which included a psychological assessment of the Applicant indicating the typicality of the Applicant´s reaction to the two assaults in light of her age. However, the district attorney decided to close the case as he believed that there was a lack of evidence of resistance, and use of force or threats could not be established beyond a reasonable doubt.

Does the failure of the State to fully investigate the allegations of rape by the Applicant in a contextually-sensitive manner amount to a failure to establish and effectively apply a criminal law regime to punish rape and sexual abuse?

The European Court of Human Rights determined that the failure of the State to fully investigate the allegations of rape by the Applicant in a contextually-sensitive manner amounted to a failure to establish and effectively apply a criminal law regime to punish rape and sexual abuse, which constituted a violation of Articles 3 and 8 of the European Convention on Human Rights. The Court held that there was no further issue under either Articles 13 or 14 of the Convention.

Articles 3 and 8

The Court dealt with Articles 3 and 8 jointly, first describing the evolution of the definition of rape in international law away from an approach requiring the use of force and towards a more progressive one that is centered on individual autonomy and non-consent. The Court further read Articles 3 and 8 as requiring the effective penalization of any non-consensual sexual act, including in the absence of physical resistance, and found that a requirement by investigators of proof of resistance effectively eviscerated the validity of any attempt to penalize. Both the legal regime of the State and its application were subjected to the scrutiny of the Court, which acknowledged that even in the absence of a legal apparatus that fully embraced the progressive approach described above, a State may fulfill its obligations through the application of a contextually-sensitive interpretation of the law. However, in the instant case, the Court found that the government had failed to disprove that it had pursued a restrictive rather than progressive application of its legislative framework, evidenced by firstly, the inadequacy of the investigation undertaken by authorities, and secondly, the absence of case law put forth by the government demonstrating an application of the law not requiring the use of force. The investigation was described as contextually insensitive, due to the authorities' failure to take into consideration the age of the Applicant and the likely effect it would have on her reaction to the rape, as well as the failure of the authorities to challenge the credibility of the testimony of several witnesses.

Article 13
The Court held that no separate issue arose under Article 13.

Article 14
The Court held that in light of its findings with respect to Articles 3 and 8, it was not necessary to examine the complaint under Article 14 of the Convention.

Article 41
Due to the "distress and psychological trauma" suffered by the Applicant as a result of the shortcomings of the authorities' investigatory approach, the Court awarded the Applicant EUR 8,000 on an equitable basis. It awarded costs to the Applicant at the hourly rate of EUR 40 for a total of EUR 4,110, subtracting the amount the Applicant had received in legal aid from the Council of Europe.

The Court found violations of Articles 3 and 8, and awarded the Applicant EUR 12,110 in non-pecuniary damages and costs.

People v. Evans

Supreme Court, New York County, Trial Term, 379 N.Y.S. 2d 912 (1975)

FACTS

Defendant Evans was charged with committing first degree rape. The relevant statute defined first degree rape as engaging in sexual intercourse by forcible compulsion, where "forcible compulsion" was defined as "physical force that overcomes earnest resistance; or a threat, express or implied, that places a person in fear of immediate death or serious physical injury." Evans was a thirty-seven-year-old bachelor; the person he alleged to have raped, Miss P., was a twenty-year-old student college student, who was, according to proffered testimony, gullible, trusting and naïve. Sometime after meeting Miss P., she was invited to come up to Evans' apartment. Two hours after they entered the apartment, Evans began making advances. Miss P. rejected him. He made statements such as "How do you know that I am who I say I am," and "I could kill you or rape you or hurt you physically." Evans "thereafter changed his tactics" and told Miss P. a story about his lost love who died when she drove her car off of a cliff. Evans said that Miss P. reminded him of his lost love. Miss P. became sympathetic and went to Evans to put her arms around him. He grabbed her at that time, saying "you're mine, you are mine." The two had sexual intercourse; oral-genital contact and then a second act of sexual intercourse approximately one-half hour later. Before Miss P. left Evans' apartment about seven o'clock the next morning, there was an additional sexual act. There were no items of torn clothing and Miss P. had no scratches or bruises.

Does sexual intercourse obtained by deception constitute a valid consent so as to negate a rape conviction?

A woman's consent to sexual intercourse, obtained by deception or misrepresentation, constitutes valid consent which will preclude a conviction for rape.

The question in this case is whether the act that occurred between Evans and Miss P. was rape according to our Penal Code. Rape requires forcible compulsion. The lesser crime of seduction, recognized in some states, consists of engaging in sexual intercourse after obtaining consent by artifice, deception, flattery, fraud or promise. Our state does not recognize either a criminal or civil action for seduction. The evidence makes clear that Miss P. was intimidated or at least confused; however it is equally clear that Evans did not exert to actual physical force. And while threats can be considered physical compulsion, it is not so clear-cut that Evans' statements of "I could kill you," "I could rape you," and "I could hurt you physically" were sufficient to show threats of a type espoused by the statute. This is the question we are called upon to decide. Evans' words are subject to two different interpretations: 1) an actual treat of hard or death - that she better do what he said or he would hurt her; or 2) an exposure of her foolishness - in effect, showing her how unwise she had been to go up to the apartment with a strange man. Evans could have been trying to show her the folly of making herself so vulnerable and defenseless. Our analysis involves an examination of Evan's intent in speaking them, not by the effect they had on Miss P. Without a doubt, the intent behind these words is ambiguous. In such circumstances, it is impossible to declare with any degree of certainty that Evans had the requisite intent beyond a reasonable doubt. While his trickery and deceit were morally reprehensible, they were not criminal.

See Rule above.

Commonwealth v. Sherry

Supreme Judicial Court of Massachusetts, 437 N.E.2d 224 (1982)

FACTS

The victim, a registered nurse, and defendants Sherry, Hussain and Lefkowitz, all doctors, were employed at the same hospital in Boston. On September 5, 1980, Sherry, along with another doctor, was a host at a party for some hospital staff. According to her testimony, the victim had a conversation with Hussain, during which he made sexual advances toward her. Some time later, Hussain and Sherry grabbed the victim by her arms and pulled her out of the apartment, as Lefkowitz said, "We're going up to Rockport." The victim verbally protested but did not physically resist the men because she thought that they were just "horsing around." Nor was she physically restrained as they rode down an elevator with an unknown fifth person, or as they walked through the lobby of the apartment building. The victim testified that once outside, Hussain carried her over his shoulder to Sherry's car and held her in the front seat as the four drove to Rockport. En route she engaged in superficial conversation with the three defendants. She testified that she was not in fear at this time. When they arrived at Lefkowitz's home in Rockport, she asked to be taken home. Instead Hussain carried her into the house. Once in the house, the victim and two of the men smoked marijuana, and all of them toured the house. After being invited by Lefkowitz to view an antique bureau in a bedroom, all of them entered and the men began to disrobe. Although the victim was frightened and began to verbally protest, the three men proceeded to undress her and maneuver her onto the bed. One of the defendants attempted to have the victim perform oral sex on him while another attempted intercourse. After the victim told them to stop, two of the defendants left the room temporarily. Each defendant separately had intercourse with the victim in the bedroom. The victim testified that she felt physically numbed, humiliated, and disgusted and could not fight. After this sequence of events, the victim claimed that she was further sexually harassed and forced to take a bath. According to defendants' version of the events, Lefkowitz invited Sherry to accompany him from the party to a home that his parents owned in Rockport. The victim, upon hearing this, inquired as to whether she could go along. As the three were leaving, Sherry extended the invitation to Hussain. At no time did the victim indicate her unwillingness to accompany the defendants. Upon arrival in Rockport, the victim wandered into the bedroom where she inquired about the antique bureau. She sat down on the bed and kicked off her shoes, whereupon Sherry entered the room, dressed only in his underwear. Sherry helped the victim get undressed, and she proceeded to have intercourse with all three men separately in turn. Each defendant testified that the victim consented to the acts of intercourse. Sherry, Hussain and Lefkowitz were convicted of rape without aggravation. All three appeal.

On the issue of consent [to intercourse], must the defense of mistake-of-fact be based on a reasonable, good faith standard?

The defense of mistake-of-fact must be based on a reasonable good faith standard.

Commonwealth v. Sherry
Supreme Judicial Court of Massachusetts, 437 N.E. 2d 224 (1982)

All three defendants contend that the judge's jury charge was inadequate and the cause of prejudicial error. However the instructions given by the trial judge placed before the jury the essential elements of the crime required to be proved. The judge instructed the jury that intercourse must be accomplished with force sufficient to overcome the woman's will or by threats of bodily harm, inferred or expressed, which engendered sufficient fear so that it was reasonable for her not to resist. These instructions correctly stated the elements of proof required for a rape conviction. To the extent that defendants appear to have been seeking to raise a defense of good faith mistake on the issue of consent, they would require the jury to find beyond a reasonable doubt that the accused had *actual knowledge* of the victim's lack of consent. They argue that mistake-of-fact negating criminal intent is a defense to the crime of rape. However, a defense of mistake-of-fact must be based on a reasonable good faith standard. Whether a reasonable good faith mistake-of-fact as to consent is a defense to the crime of rape has never, to our knowledge, been decided in this Commonwealth. Nevertheless, we do not reach the issue whether a reasonable and honest mistake to the fact of consent could be a valid defense, for even if we assume it to be, the defendants did not request a jury instruction based on a reasonable good faith mistake of fact. We are aware of no Court of last resort that recognizes mistake-of-fact, without consideration of its reasonableness as a defense; nor do the defendants cite such authority.

Affirmed.

Commonwealth v. Fischer

Superior Court of Pennsylvania, 721 A.2d 1111 (1998)

FACTS

Defendant-appellant Fischer, an eighteen year-old college freshman, was charged with involuntary deviate sexual intercourse (IDSI), aggravated indecent assault and related offenses in connection with an incident that occurred in a Lafayette College campus dormitory. The victim was another freshman student appellant met at school. At trial, both the victim and appellant testified that a couple of hours prior to the incident at issue, the two went to appellant's dorm room and engaged in intimate contact. The victim testified that the couple's conduct was limited to kissing and fondling. Appellant, on the other hand, testified that during this initial encounter, he and the victim engaged in "rough sex" which culminated in the victim performing oral sex on him. After the encounter, both students separated and went to the dining hall with their respective friends. They met up again later in appellant's dorm room. According to the victim, appellant forcibly penetrated her with his fingers; ejaculated on her face, hair and sweater and attempted to penetrate her anally. Throughout the incident, appellant said "I know you want it," "I know you want my dick in your mouth" and "Nobody will know where you are." When the victim attempted to leave, appellant blocked her path. Only after striking him in the groin with her knee was the victim able to escape. Not surprisingly, appellant characterized the second meeting in a far different light. He stated that as he led the victim into his room, she told him it would have to be "a quick one." Thereafter, according to appellant, he began to engage in the same type of behavior the victim had exhibited in their previous encounter. Appellant admitted that he held the young woman's arms above her head, straddled her and placed his penis at her mouth. He testified that at that point he told her "I know you want my dick in your mouth." When she replied "no," appellant answered "No means yes." After another verbal exchange that included the victim's statement that she had to leave, appellant again insisted that "she wanted it." This time she answered "No, I honestly don't." Upon hearing this, appellant no longer sought to engage in oral sex and removed himself from her body. However, as the two lay side by side on the bed, they continued to kiss and fondle one another. The jury returned a guilty verdict on virtually all counts and Fischer was sentenced to two to five years in prison. After his conviction and sentence, appellant filed a direct appeal and argued, among other things, that the trial court erred in refusing to instruct the jury "that if the defendant reasonably believed that the [victim] had consented to his sexual advances that this would constitute a defense to the rape and involuntary deviate sexual intercourse charge."

Is a mistake of fact regarding the victim's consent a valid defense to rape?

A mistake of fact regarding the victim's consent is not a valid defense to rape.

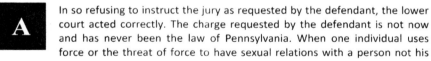

Commonwealth v. Fischer

Superior Court of Pennsylvania, 721 A.2d 1111 (1998)

A In so refusing to instruct the jury as requested by the defendant, the lower court acted correctly. The charge requested by the defendant is not now and has never been the law of Pennsylvania. When one individual uses force or the threat of force to have sexual relations with a person not his spouse and without the person's consent he has committed the crime of rape. If the element of the defendant's belief as to the victim's state of mind is to be established as a defense to the crime of rape then it should be done by our legislature which has the power to define crimes and offenses. We refuse to create such a defense. In *Commonwealth v. Williams,* the defendant drove victim to dark place and threatened to kill her if she did not have sex, and victim said "go ahead." Under those facts, we held that a mistake of fact instruction was not available and that it is up to the legislature, not the courts, to decide whether a defendant's mistaken belief about the victim's state of mind should be a defense to rape. Fischer makes a number of arguments to the contrary, none of which we find convincing. He first distinguishes *Williams* from the facts at bar by arguing that *Williams* involved a rape by a stranger rather than an acquaintance and that the laws with respect to rape have changed significantly in the last ten or so year since *Williams* was decided. Specifically, the legislature has broadened the definition of the "forcible compulsion." This new, broad definition prompts the need for a mistake of fact instruction because the new definition inextricably links the consent issue with *mens rea*. Thus, to ask a jury to consider whether "intellectual or moral force" was used [a *mens rea* consideration] while denying an instruction as to how to consider the defendant's mental state at the time of the alleged encounter is patently unfair to the accused. Although the logic of this argument is persuasive, and we agree that the rule in *Williams* is inappropriate in a date rape case, we must abide by *Williams'* holding that the law does not require a mistake of fact instruction and that the judiciary has no authority to change the law. Moreover, because this appeal is based on ineffective assistance of counsel, we must determine whether Fischer's prior counsel made a mistake by not asking for an instruction that would have changed the law. We cannot change the law and find counsel ineffective for refusing to predict the same.

Affirmed.

People v. Liberta

New York Court of Appeals, 474 N.E.2d 567 (1984)

FACTS

Defendant-appellant Mario Liberta and Denise Liberta were married in 1978. After the birth of their son, Mario began to beat Denise. Denise sought a protective order against him in early 1980. The Family Court issued a temporary protective order in April, 1980, which required Mario to move out and remain away from the family home. He was, however, allowed to see his son once every weekend. In March of 1981, Mario convinced Denise and their 2 ½ old son to join him in a hotel room, where forced her to perform fellatio on him and raped her, all while making his wife tell their son to watch what his father was making his mother do. He was indicted on charged of rape in the first degree and sodomy; the trial court dismissed the indictment on the "marital exception" to rape; the appellate division reinstated the indictment and the defendant was convicted of rape in the first degree and sodomy in the first degree; the conviction was affirmed by the appellate division; defendant appealed to the Court of Appeals, New Yolk's highest court.

Does the marital exemption for rape violate equal protection in that it exempting females from criminal liability for forcible rape while holding men liable?

The common-law marital exception for rape is unconstitutional as against due process.

Appellate Division did not err in considering defendant husband "not married" for the purposes of the New York Penal Law rape statute where the man raped his wife while they were living apart pursuant to a Family Court order. The marital exception under which men cannot be convicted of raping their wives is a violation of the equal protection clause because there is no rational basis for distinguishing between marital rape and nonmarital rape. Thus, the statute exempting females from criminal liability for forcible rape while holding men responsible violates the equal protection clause of the Fourteenth Amendment. Section 130.35 of the Penal Law, the relevant statute at issue, provides that a man is guilty of rape in the first degree when he engages in sexual intercourse by forcible compulsion with a woman to whom he is not married. "Not married" is defined as including cases where the husband and wife are no longer living together pursuant to a court order or decree or a written separation agreement. Accordingly, the statute contains a marital exemption for rape. We first turn to the applicability of the marital exemption. Under the statute, Mario and Denise were "not married" at the time of the attack, by statutory definition [they were not living together at the time] so the marital exemption as written did not apply to Mario. Mario argues, however, that the marital exemption as written is unconstitutional because it violates equal protection by treating him differently than another man similarly situated. The Equal Protection Clause does not prohibit a State from creating classifications of persons, so long as it does not arbitrary burden a particular class of persons and as long as there is a rational basis for doing so. In our state, to find such a distinction constitutional, there must be some rational basis for treating marital rape differently from non-marital rape. We cannot find any rational basis for doing so. Those rationales that have been advanced in support of such an exemption are out-dated and indefensible: 1) that there is implied consent because the woman and man are married. This preposition is absurd we need not expound on it any further. 2) A married woman is the property of her husband. We no longer consider women chattel or property and therefore, these archaic notions cannot provide a rational basis for retaining the marital exemption. 3) That it protects marital privacy and encourages reconciliation. We similarly reject this argument because we feel that, in a marriage that has degraded to where a husband must resort to forcible rape, there is little left to reconcile. Thus, we hold that the marital exemption for rape violates the equal protection clauses of both our state and federal constitutions. Consequently, we opt to invalidate only the marital exemption portion of the statute rather than the whole statute itself. We feel that by doing so, any disparate treatment of married and non-married individuals will be removed. The effect of our decision is to leave that part of the statute intact under which Mario was convicted. Hence, his conviction is affirmed.

Conviction affirmed.

United States v. Wiley

U.S. Court of Appeals, 492 F.2d 547 (D.C. Cir. 1974)

FACTS

The court held that the victim's testimony had not been adequately corroborated by independent evidence as was then required under D.C. Law in a rape prosecution before the court. Judge Bazelon wrote a concurring opinion which highlighted some of the issues surrounding the corroboration requirement and the arguments for its preservation with respect to the state's rape laws.

 Is independent corroboration to support a rape conviction based upon the victim's allegations?

 Independent corroboration of at least some of the victim's story is required to support a rape conviction.

 Historically, the common law has rejected the corroboration requirement for all crimes except perjury; thus no such requirement existed for sex crimes. Today, about 35 states have similarly rejected the corroboration requirement, and of those jurisdictions that do retain it, including the District of Columbia, do so in the absence of legislation. I feel there must be independent corroboration sufficient such that a jury could find beyond a reasonable doubt that the victim's rendition of the facts, was in, fact genuine. I shall now recite the justifications advanced for the corroboration requirement. 1) A charge of rape is unusually difficult to defend against. Juries are said to be unusually sympathetic to a woman who alleges rape, which in turn weakens the presumption of innocence in criminal cases. 2) False charges of rape are more prevalent than false charges of other crimes. It is contended that women sometimes fabricate allegations of rape to give explanation for a pregnancy, because they are ashamed and bitter toward the man for having consented to the intercourse or because they wish to blackmail. But there are countervailing reasons for a woman not to report a rape. A victim may be stigmatized by society and/or there may be humiliating publicity or harsh treatment by the police or hospital personnel. 3) The requirement evolved as a method of protecting men. It has been said that to a "good" woman, being raped is a "fate worse than death" and she will therefore fight to the death to resist it. Absent evidence of this struggle, though, the theory says that it is more likely than not that the woman enticed the man and the man is therefore blameless in the situation. Such a rationale stems from discrimination against women. Still, I feel that the requirement is a necessity, at least to a somewhat limited extent. Corroborating evidence was absent in the instant case, thus I concur with the court's judgment in reversing the conviction.

 Conviction reversed.

State ex rel. Pope v. Superior Court
Supreme Court of Arizona, 545 P.2d 946 (1976)

FACTS

The County Attorney of Mojave County, acting on behalf of the state of Arizona, brought a special action requesting the Arizona Supreme Court to reconsider the existing evidentiary law, which allowed an accused rapist to introduce evidence of the alleged victim's unchaste character in a prosecution for first degree rape.

Is a defendant charged with rape allowed to introduce evidence of the victim's unchaste character?

Evidence of the victim's unchaste character is generally inadmissible in rape cases.

Generally, evidence of the victim's unchaste character is inadmissible in rape cases. The leading case on point in our jurisdiction is the Arizona case of *State v. Wood,* which held that when consent is at issue, evidence of the victim's unchastity is relevant and material. Our rational in *Wood* stemmed from the reasoning that a woman who has once strayed from virtue is more likely to have done so again. Today, we expressly overrule *Wood,* as such a justification no longer is supported by our modem society and because we no longer think it appropriate to imply that a woman who has once consented to sexual intercourse is more likely to have done so at future dates. The reasoning advanced by this court has consistently barred evidence of prior bad acts of a witness in a criminal case, and in a rape prosecution, it applies with even greater force because "it interjects collateral issues into the case which tend to divert the jury's attention [away] from the real issue." We recognize that there will be some limited instances where the evidence of the victim's past sexual history's probative value outweighs its prejudicial effect. These include evidence of prior sexual intercourse with the defendant or testimony which directly refutes physical or scientific evidence, such as the victim's alleged loss of virginity. However, taken as a whole, we believe that the inflammatory nature of such evidence generally outweighs any probative value. In cases where this is not the case, i.e., the probative value of the evidence outweighs its prejudicial effect, a court should hold a hearing outside of the presence of the jury to determine the admissibility of the evidence. If the defendant can show that the proffered evidence falls into one of these limited exceptions, the court should admit the evidence after a hearing and a determination that the evidence is credible.

See Rule above.

State v. DeLawder

Maryland Court of Special Appeals, 344 A.2d 446 (1975)

FACTS

Defendant Lee Franklin DeLawder was found guilty after a jury trial of carnal knowledge of a female under the age of 14 and was sentenced to 15 years in prison. At his rape trial, his counsel was not permitted to ask the victim about her past sexual history. His conviction was affirmed by the Maryland Court of Special Appeals on direct appeal. He later sought post-conviction relief, arguing that the U.S. States Supreme Court decision in *Davis v. Alaska* affected the validity of his conviction. The *Davis* Court held that the right of confrontation guaranteed by the Sixth Amendment applies to state as well as federal criminal defendants.

In light of *Davis*, do the rules of evidence, which bar a defendant from cross-examining an alleged rape victim, violate the Sixth Amendment [Confrontation Clause]?

A criminal defendant must be allowed an opportunity to confront the witnesses against him.

An accused must be permitted to effectively cross-examine the witnesses against him. *Davis* was decided after we affirmed DeLawder's conviction. At that time, we held that the trial court properly excluded the defense's attempts to cross-examine the victim regarding her prior sexual relations with other men. The trial judge correctly applied the general rule that because consent is not an issue in carnal knowledge prosecution, evidence of the victim's sexual relations with others is irrelevant. When the Supreme Court decided in *Davis,* it held that the right of an accused to confront the witnesses against him is secured in both state and federal criminal proceedings. Not to be allowed to do so was a violation of the defendant's Sixth Amendment rights. We now examine *Davis* to see whether it affects DeLawder's conviction in the instant case. DeLawder's counsel was prohibited from examining the victim regarding her past sexual history. The defense made it clear from the onset that its theory was to discredit the prosecution's witness and prove that the victim fabricated the rape charges because she was actually pregnant and did not want to tell her mother that she had consensual sexual intercourse with others. In light of *Davis*, defense counsel should have been permitted to pursue this line of questioning. While we can not say with any degree of certainty that the jury would have been swayed one way or the other, they nonetheless should have been able to hear the defense's arguments, as they would then have been able to more accurately determine the reliability and credibility of the witness. The jury was deprived of this opportunity; and by denying defense counsel the opportunity to effectively cross-examine the alleged victim, the trial court violated DeLawder's right to confrontation.

Reversed.

Government of the Virgin Islands v. Scuito
United States Court of Appeals, 623 F.2d 869 (3rd Cir. 1980)

FACTS

The victim worked at the Drunken Shrimp restaurant as a waitress. Defendant Scuito, a frequent patron of the restaurant, was asked by the owner on July 9, 1978 to take the complainant [the alleged victim] to her apartment after she'd worked her shift. It was undisputed that Scuito took a detour down a beach road on the way to the complainant's apartment and the two had sexual intercourse. The crucial issue at trial, therefore, was whether the victim consented. According to the complainant, Scuito turned down a beach road to relieve himself, then stopped in a turnaround and began kissing her. She said she expressed no interest, but that Scuito told her he had a knife and would throw her into the ocean if she did not cooperate. She testified that she did not see a knife but felt something metal cut into her neck in the dark and then she stopped resisting. There was evidence presented at trial that the victim did have a cut on the side of her neck after the alleged incident. She testified that Scuito took off her clothes then raped and sodomized her. During the course of the attack, the victim allegedly recited her mantra [a sound aid used while meditating] and prayed. After Scuito dropped her off, she said she kissed him on the forehead because she was praying for him. Scuito, on the other hand, testified that he casually knew the woman and her sister and had driven them both home from the restaurant on a number of occasions. He said that on the night in question, the alleged victim seemed "a little space, not all there" and that she offered him marijuana. He testified that they stopped on the beach road to smoke it and that they later engaged in consensual sexual intercourse. Prior to the first trial the prosecution and defense agreed not to mention that Scuito had previously raped a woman by threatening her with a flare gun. The first trial ended in a mistrial when the prosecutor indirectly referred to the previous rape. Scuito moved, prior to the second trial, for a court order compelling the victim to undergo a psychiatric evaluation. In a supporting affidavit, defense counsel represented that he had been informed by others and personally observed the woman "spaced out" or in a trance-like state and that he had been told by others that she frequently used mind-altering substances. Defense counsel also noted in the affidavit that the victim's frequent use of LSD and other mind altering drugs were highly indicative of a personality that fantasizes to extremes and one that might therefore be inclined to fabricate a story of rape. The trial court denied the motion and Scuito was convicted of forcible rape. Scuito appealed, contending that the trial court abused its discretion by refusing to order the psychiatric evaluation.

May a trial judge to refuse a defendant's request to compel an alleged rape victim to undergo a psychiatric evaluation?

A judge may order a psychological examination of a rape victim if the judge, in his discretion, believes that one is necessary.

Government of the Virgin Islands v. Scuito

United States Court of Appeals, 623 F.2d 869 (3rd Cir. 1980)

The decision to order a psychiatric evaluation of an alleged rape victim is up to the sole discretion of the trial judge. Scuito does not press the extreme theory endorsed by Wigmore that a psychiatric evaluation of the complainant should be ordered in *all* sexual offenses. Rather, defense counsel argues that while such discretion to do so exists, the trial judge in the instant case abused that discretion. Notwithstanding this discretion, there are countervailing considerations which weigh against ordering such an examination. So called "rape shield laws" protect the victim's privacy. A psychological examination may seriously encroach upon the victim's privacy. It may also increase the trauma she experienced or be used as a tool of harassment. Federal Rule of Evidence 412 specifically addresses these concerns by restricting the use of prior sexual history in sexual offenses. The Rule is intended to "protect rape victims from the degrading and embarrassing disclosure of intimate details about their private lives." We hold today that this line of reasoning applies to a judge's decision not to order a psychiatric evaluation of a rape victim as well. We find no evidence of an abuse of discretion by the trial judge in this case. Evidence of the victim's reputation for drug use and tendency to engage in conduct related thereto could have been introduced by other means, such as direct testimony.

Judgment of the trial court is affirmed.

Commonwealth v. Carroll
Supreme Court of Pennsylvania, 194 A.2d 911 (1963)

FACTS

Defendant Mr. Carroll was married to his wife, Mrs. Carroll in 1955. Three years later, Mrs. Carroll fractured her skull while trying to get out of her car during an argument with her husband. She was later diagnosed as a "schizoid personality type." In January, 1962, the defendant was selected to attend an electronics school in North Carolina for nine days. Mrs. Carroll responded to the news by striking up a violent argument. So that she would feel safe during this time, defendant left a loaded .22 caliber pistol on the windowsill above their bed. When he returned from North Carolina, defendant informed his wife that he would be taking a teaching job in Chambersburg, requiring him to be out of town for four nights out of seven during a ten week period. Another violent and protracted argument ensued. Sometime between 3 and 4 a.m., Mr. Carroll remembered the gun on the windowsill, picked it up, and shot Mrs. Carroll twice in the head. Hen then wrapped his wife's body in the bedding and carried her to the cellar, cleaned up the bloody mess, and later transported the body to a desolate spot near a trash dump. He took his children to his parents' home in New Jersey and was arrested the following Monday at his new job. He pled guilty to an indictment charging him with murder and was tried without a jury. A psychiatrist testified that Mr. Carroll did not premeditate the killing. Nevertheless, the court found him guilty of first degree murder and sentenced him to life imprisonment. Mr. Carroll appealed.

Under Pennsylvania law, is a court required to mitigate a first degree murder charge to second degree murder when evidence of the defendant's good character is submitted together with expert psychological testimony that the homicide was not premeditated?

A court is not required to reduce a first degree murder charge to second degree murder, under Pennsylvania law, when evidence of the defendant's good character is submitted together with expert psychological testimony that the homicide was not premeditated and [the court] will disregard the length of time it took for the defendant to form the intention to kill.

Under Pennsylvania's murder statute, first degree murder includes killings by poison, lying in wait "or any other kind of willful, deliberate and premeditated killing." A specific intent to kill is necessary to constitute first-degree murder. Factors including the defendant's words and conduct and the circumstances surrounding the homicide help courts make such a determination; and a specific intent to kill may be inferred when the defendant has used a deadly weapon on a vital body part of another human being. Thus, even if everything defendant alleged was true, his act still constituted murder in the first degree. Defendant first argues that there was insufficient time for premeditation in light of his good reputation and bases this first argument on the axiom that "no time is too short for a wicked man to frame in his mind the scheme of murder." He reasons, conversely, that a long time is necessary for a good man to form the intent to kill. However, under Pennsylvania case law whether the premeditation occurred in a short period of time

Commonwealth v. Carroll
Supreme Court of Pennsylvania, 194 A.2d 911 (1963)

before the killing or an extended period of time before the act is immaterial to an analysis of whether a killing was willful, deliberate, and premeditated. Mr. Carroll's second argument is that the time place and manner of the crime; the difficulty he experienced in moving and hiding the body and his lack of an organized escape plan cut against a showing of any premeditation. This is a "jury argument" clearly devoid of merit on appeal. Lastly, Mr. Carroll's argues that his mental state in the moments leading up to the crime preclude a finding of premeditation, based upon the expert's testimony. The psychiatrist gave *his* opinion that "rage," "desperation," and "panic" produced "an uncontrollable impulse rather than out of intentional premeditation" in the defendant. However, this court is not required to believe the testimony offered by any witness as the psychiatrist's opinion was based on statements made to him by Mr. Carroll. Moreover, defendant's own testimony helped to convict him: Mr. Carroll made it clear that during his argument with his wife, he remembered the gun, took it from the windowsill, and deliberately fired two shots into her head; and defendant makes no argument that he was insane at the time of the killing.

Judgment and sentence affirmed.

State v. Guthrie

Supreme Court of Appeals of West Virginia, 461 S.E.2d 163 (1995)

FACTS

Defendant Dale Edward Guthrie and Steven Todd Farley worked together as dishwashers in the Danny's Rib House restaurant in Nitro, West Virginia. On the evening of February 12, 1993, Farley began to make fun of Guthrie, who appeared to be in a bad mood, telling him to "lighten up" and snapping Guthrie several times with a dish towel. When Farley snapped Guthrie's nose, Guthrie became enraged and started towards Farley, who responded "Ooo, he's taking his gloves off." Guthrie then took out a pocket knife and stabbed Farley in the neck and arm. Wounded, Farley cried, "Man, I was just kidding around," to which Guthrie responded, "Well, man, you should have never hit me in my face." Farley died as a result. Evidence at trial showed that Guthrie suffered from a host of psychiatric problems. The trial court instructed the jury that, to establish that a killing was deliberate and premeditated, it was *not* necessary to prove that the intent to kill existed for any *particular* time prior to the killing; it was only necessary to prove that the intent to kill have existed at the time of the killing, or prior thereto. Guthrie appealed his conviction.

Was the jury instruction in error? Specifically, in order to convict on a charge of murder in the first-degree based on premeditation and deliberation, must proof that defendant contemplated his decision to kill be proffered?

Some proof that the defendant considered and weighed his decision to kill must be offered in order to establish that a killing was done with premeditation and deliberation.

Some proof that the defendant considered and weighed his decision to kill must be offered in order to establish that a killing was done with premeditation and deliberation. The jury instruction given by the trial court fails to make clear to the jury the differences between first and second-degree murder. It erroneously equates "premeditation and deliberation" with "an intent to kill." Premeditation and deliberation are not measured by any specific period of time, but there must be some period between the formation of the intent to kill and the actual killing which indicates that the killing is by prior calculation and design. This means that there is an opportunity for some reflection on the intention to kill after it is formed – but a showing of an elaborate plan or scheme is not necessary. Any other spontaneous and non-reflexive intentional killing is second degree murder.

Reversed and remanded for a new trial.

Girouard v. State

Court of Appeals of Maryland, 583 A.2d 718 (1991)

FACTS

Defendant-petitioner Steven S. Girouard (Steven) and Joyce M. Girouard (Joyce) were married for about two months before Joyce's death. Both served in the army. The marriage was often tense and strained, and there was some evidence that Joyce had been unfaithful with an old boyfriend. On the night of Joyce's death Steven overheard Joyce talking on the phone with a friend about a discharge because her husband did not love her anymore. He asked her what the conversation was about and she refused to answer him. He then kicked over the food she was eating and left the room and went to lie down in the bedroom. She followed him into the bedroom, got up onto the bed, onto his back and pulled his hair and said, "What are you going to do, hit me?" She continued to taunt him saying, "I never did want to marry you and you are a lousy fuck and you remind me of my dad." The barrage of insults and taunts continued. She then told him she had reported him to the Judge Advocate General (JAG) for spousal abuse and that he would probably be court-marshaled. Through all of this she continually asked, "What are you going to do about it?" Steven then got out of bed, went into the kitchen with his pillow and got a knife. He returned to the bedroom with the knife behind the pillow. Joyce continued to harangue him. Steven testified that he kept waiting for her to say that she was kidding. When Joyce paused for a moment and asked Steven what he was going to do about it, he stabbed her 19 times. After the killing, Steven dropped the knife and took a shower. He attempted to slit his wrists but was unsuccessful. He then called the police and told them he had murdered his wife. He was found wandering outside the apartment, distraught, talking about how much he loved his wife and that could not believe what he had done. At his trial, psychiatrist William Stejskal testified that Steven "reached the limit of his ability to swallow his anger." He was convicted of 2nd murder and sentenced to 22 years in prison. Petitioner relies primarily on out of state cases to support his argument that manslaughter should include all criminal homicides that lack the malice element and that court should thus extend the definition of what constitutes adequate provocation to his case. The State, on the other hand, argues that the court should not extend the definition of adequate provocation to include provocation *by words alone* because by doing so, any domestic argument leading to murder could be reduced to a conviction of manslaughter.

Do words alone constitute the adequate provocation necessary to mitigate a charge of murder to manslaughter?

Words alone do not constitute the adequate provocation necessary to reduce a charge of murder to manslaughter.

As a preliminary matter, we note the difference between murder and manslaughter: manslaughter lacks the malice element that is present in a murder. Thus, voluntary manslaughter has been defined as an *"intentional* killing done in a sudden heat of passion caused by adequate provocation before there has been a reasonable opportunity for the passion to cool." There are certain facts which may mitigate what would normally be murder to manslaughter. They are, but are not limited to: 1) discovering one's spouse having sex with someone else; 2) being engaged in mutual combat; 3) assault and battery by the victim; 4) discovering injury to a family relative or third party; 5) death resulting from an illegal arrest. In order to determine whether murder should be mitigated to manslaughter, we look to the circumstances surrounding the homicide. Within the framework of these facts and circumstances, we superimpose the Rule of Provocation. The Rule of Provocation requires: 1) adequate provocation; 2) that the killing be the result of a sudden heat of passion; 3) there has been no opportunity to cool off; and 4) there must be a causal connection between the provocation and the fatal act. We will assume all of these criteria have been met except for 1) adequate provocation, which is the ultimate issue at bar. In order for provocation to be "adequate" it must be capable of causing a *reasonable man* to loose reason and act/react out of passion. Thus, the issue we must resolve then is whether Joyce's words were enough to inflame the passion of a reasonable man such that he would be sufficiently infuriated to strike out in a passionate rage and kill her. However, Maryland case law indicates that words alone are not adequate provocation, without more. And while we recognize that Joyce's words were a "significant provocation," they do not rise to the level of an "adequate provocation." Moreover, we are not convinced that it was reasonable to assume she was threatening Steven with physical harm such that he was forced to protect himself; she was considerably smaller than Steven and was not armed with a weapon of any kind. Thus, without reservation, we hold that words alone are not enough to cause a reasonable man to stab his provoker and kill her in the heat of passion; there was no adequate provocation necessary to mitigate murder down to manslaughter.

 We affirm.

Maher v. People

Supreme Court of Michigan, 81 Am. Dec. 781 (1862)

FACTS

Defendant Maher was charged with assault with intent to kill and murder Patrick Hunt. Defendant suspected that his wife had had sexual intercourse with another man, Patrick Hunt. One day, he followed his wife and Hunt as they entered the woods together and then followed them to a saloon when they left the woods a ½ hour later. Just before he entered the saloon, a fried told him that Hunt and Maher's wife had intercourse in the woods a day before. When Maher arrived at the saloon, he was sweaty, agitated and excited. Maher approached Hunt, who was standing with a group of people at the bar. Maher shot Hunt in the head, causing Hunt to lose partial hearing in his left ear and to be confined to bed for a week. Maher was charged with assault with intent to commit murder. At trial, Maher tried to introduce evidence that he had learned of his wife's affair less than an hour before the assault. The trial court suppressed the evidence and Maher appealed.

 Under Michigan law, can evidence of the defendant's belief that the victim was engaged in a sexual relationship with his wife constitute provocation evidence necessitating a reduction of a charge of an assault with intent to murder to a lesser charge?

 A jury may consider the words and conduct of the victim, as well as the defendant's perceptions and motivations in a determination as to whether an assault was committed with intent to murder.

 In order to decide whether Maher is guilty of assault and battery or assault with intent to murder, the court must examine his motivation for his actions. To do so, the court must look at the ask, hypothetically, if Hunt had died as a result of the injuries Maher inflicted, would Maher have been guilty of murder or manslaughter? If he would have been guilty of manslaughter, he cannot be found guilty of assault with intent to murder. As part of its analysis, the court must look at the events leading up to the assault to decide whether sufficient provocation was present. Its presence would reduce Maher's act from assault with intent to murder to assault and battery. What the law considers *reasonable* provocation is a determination left to the judge; however, whether adequate provocation existed is a matter of fact, not a question of law, and is a matter left to the jury to decide. It is the judge's role to allow the jury access to any evidence that could reasonably affect its decision in the case. Here, that evidence is whether Maher's provocation was sufficient to reduce a crime of premeditation to one of passion. On a related issue, the jury should likewise be allowed to weigh evidence of a cooling off period. Maher's suppressed evidence might have shown that when Hunt and Maher's wife disappeared into the woods, she was committing adultery. Under these circumstances, evidence of adultery can constitute provocation and a jury should have been permitted to weigh that proof.

 Judgment reversed and case remanded for new trial.

People v. Casassa
New York Court of Appeals, 404 N.E.2d 1310 (1980)

FACTS

Defendant-appellant Victor Casassa (Casassa) and Victoria Lo Consolo (Lo Consolo) lived in the same apartment complex, dated a few times casually, until eventually Lo Consolo informed him that she was not "falling in love" with him. Casassa says that this rejection devastated him and that his behavior turned bizarre. He broke into the apartment below her so on several occasions so that he could eavesdrop on her. He claims the things he heard further devastated him. He broke into her apartment and lay naked in her bed with a knife. He later told police that he had a knife with him at that time of the break-in because he was going to either kill her or commit suicide. On his final trip to her apartment, on February 28, 1977, he brought several bottles of wine and liquor to her as a gift. When she did not accept this gift he pulled out a steak knife and stabbed her in the throat, after which he pulled her to the bathroom and submerged her body in the tub to make sure she was dead. These facts are undisputed. He waived a jury trial and proceeded with a bench trial before a judge with only one witness, a psychiatrist, who testified, in essence, that Casassa had become obsessed with Lo Consolo and that her rejection combined with his peculiar personality attributes had placed him under the influence of an extreme emotional disturbance at the time of the killing. In rebuttal, the State produced several witnesses. Among them was another psychiatrist, who testified, in effect, that while Casassa was emotionally disturbed, he was not under the influence of "extreme emotional disturbance" because his disturbed state was not the product of external factors but rather the result of internal stresses created within himself in dealing mostly with fantasy and a refusal to accept the reality of the situation. The trial court found Casassa guilty of murder in the 2nd degree. Defendant appeals arguing that the trial court erred in failing to afford him the benefit of the affirmative defense of "extreme emotional disturbance" and that by refusing to apply a wholly subjective standard the trial court misconstrued New York's applicable penal law, §125.25.

Is the test of whether the accused can show that he acted under the influence of an "extreme emotional disturbance" for which there was a reasonable explanation or excuse determined from the subjective point of view of the killer or by objective evidence?

The test of whether the killer can show that he acted under the influence of an "extreme emotional disturbance" for which there was a reasonable explanation or excuse depends on a reasonable evaluation of the external circumstances that the killer believed he was facing and not on the killer's personal point of view.

We decide this case applying §125.25 of the New York Penal Code, which provides that if the killer can show that he acted under the influence of an extreme emotional disturbance for which there was a reasonable explanation or excuse, he qualifies for an affirmative defense reducing murder in the second degree to manslaughter. In enacting §125.5, the legislature

People v. Casassa
New York Court of Appeals, 404 N.E.2d 1310 (1980)

adopted the language of the manslaughter provisions of the Model Penal Code. The "extreme emotional disturbance" defense in the Model Penal Code is an outgrowth of the "heat of passion" doctrine, but it is considerably broader: 1) it eliminates entirely the provision which required that there be *no* cooling off period; and 2) it eliminates the rigid rules concerning the sufficiency of adequate provocation. Thus, we consider the Comments to the Model Penal Code, from which §125.25 was drawn. The defense of "extreme Emotional Disturbance" has two principal but separate components. The first component requires that the act must have actually been done in a state of "extreme emotional disturbance," and is considered *subjectively* from the killer's point of view. The second component requires that there be a reasonable explanation or excuse for that emotional disturbance, measured objectively. Applying both components above to the facts of the instant case, we find that Casassa has no problem meeting the first component. He was acting out of extreme emotional disturbance and the judge, as fact finder, reached the conclusion that this emotional disturbance was based on factors specific to Casassa. Because these factors were peculiar to him, the judge held that there was no reasonable explanation or excuse. This conclusion is consistent with statue at issue. In the end, we believe that what the Legislature intended in enacting the statute was to allow the finder of fact, in this case the judge, the discretionary power to mitigate the penalty and the definition of manslaughter from the Model Penal Code intentionally leaves the finder of fact with such discretion. The judge made his decision. Overturning his finding here would be inconsistent with the intention of the Act.

 We affirm.

Commonwealth v. Welansky
Massachusetts Supreme Judicial Court, 55 N.E.2d 902 (1944)

FACTS

The New Cocoanut Grove, Inc. was a nightclub in Boston. The club had one entrance, a single revolving door, and a small number of emergency exits. Three of the emergency exits were poorly marked and located in obscure areas, and while two others were marked with "Exit" lights and equipped with panic bars, one door was blocked and the other was kept locked. On November 28, 1942, one of the busiest nights of the year, the club was crowded with patrons. At around 10 p.m., a waiter accidentally ignited a nearby palm tree, which in turn ignited the club's cloth ceiling. The fire spread and the customers panicked. The door at the head of the stairway had been locked so that the panic bar could not operate and it was not opened until firefighters broke it down with an ax, as were two other emergency doors. A great number of patrons and many employees died inside the building. Defendant Barnett Welansky completely dominated the enterprise. He had been in the hospital at the time of the fire, but he had closely supervised and inspected the club's business before falling ill. Welansky was charged with numerous count of involuntary manslaughter based on the club's overcrowding, flammable decorations, absence of fire doors, and failure to maintain proper emergency exits. Welansky was found guilty and sentenced to between 12 and 15 years hard labor for each count, sentences to be served concurrently.

Under Massachusetts law, can a defendant be found guilty of involuntary manslaughter based on his wanton or reckless conduct when in breach of a duty of care owed to his customers?

An individual is guilty of involuntary manslaughter when his wanton or reckless breach of duty of care causes the death of another.

Under Massachusetts law, a defendant who owes a duty for the safety of business visitors and breached a duty resulting in their deaths through his wanton or reckless conduct can be found guilty of involuntary manslaughter. Liability in this case is impugned to Welansky, as the dominant and controlling party in the New Cocoanut Grove Corporation. Despite his absence from the nightclub on that deadly night, Welansky stilled owed a duty of care for the safety of the patrons of his club. He was, at the very least, responsible for not impeding their safety, and his disregard of the probable consequences of his failure constitute wanton or reckless conduct. As a preliminary matter, we distinguish wanton or reckless conduct from the negligence or gross negligence. With respect to wanton or reckless conduct, it is the conduct that is intentional, not the harm caused by the conduct; and the standard applied is *both* subjective and objective. The defendant must have chosen to take the risk that harm would not occur rather than change his conduct in order to prevent the harm from certainly occurring. Thus, if the evidence shows that the defendant knew [subjective standard] there was a danger, his decision to run the

Commonwealth v. Welansky

Massachusetts Supreme Judicial Court, 55 N.E.2d 902 (1944)

---

risk will constitute wanton or reckless conduct even if the hypothetical "reasonable man" [objective standard] did not perceive it. Hence, "wanton" and "reckless" express a difference in the degree of risk taken; they are terms that denote a higher degree of risk of liability than "negligence" or "gross negligence." Here, in order to convict Welansky of involuntary manslaughter, the prosecution did not need to show that he caused the fire through a wanton or reckless *act*. It was enough for the prosecution to show his wanton or reckless *disregard* for the safety of the club's patrons as evidenced by knowingly disregarding the consequences of keeping the emergency exists locked and obstructed in the event of a fire.

Judgment affirmed.

People v. Hall
Supreme Court of Colorado, 999 P.2d 207 (2000)

FACTS

On April 20, 1997, the last day of the ski season, Hall worked as a ski lift operator on Vail Mountain. When he finished his shift and after the lifts closed, Hall skied down toward the base of the mountain. The slopes were not crowded. On the lower part of a run called "Riva Ridge," just below where the trail intersects with another called "North Face Catwalk," Hall was skiing very fast, ski tips in the air, his weight back on his skis, with his arms out to his sides to maintain balance. He flew off of a knoll and saw people below him, but he was unable to stop or gain control because of the moguls. Hall then collided with Cobb, who had been traversing the slope below Hall. The collision caused major head and brain injuries to Cobb, killing him. Cobb was taken to Vail Valley Medical Center, where efforts to resuscitate him failed. Hall's blood alcohol level was .009, which is less than the limit for driving while ability impaired. A test of Hall's blood for illegal drugs was negative.

The People charged Hall with manslaughter (a class 4 felony) and misdemeanor charges that are not relevant to this appeal. At the close of the prosecution's case at the preliminary hearing, the People requested that, with respect to the manslaughter count, the court consider the lesser-included charge of criminally negligent homicide (a class 5 felony). The county court held a preliminary hearing to determine whether there was probable cause to support the felony charges against Hall. Ultimately, the county court dismissed the manslaughter count. The prosecution appealed the county court's decision to the district court pursuant to Crim. P. 5(a)(4)(IV). The district court agreed with the county court that the prosecution failed to establish probable cause. The court held that Hall's conduct did not involve a substantial risk of death because any risk created by Hall had a less than fifty percent chance of causing another's death. The district court relied on language from our decisions in *People v. Thomas* and *People v. DelGuidice* to determine that for a risk of death to be substantial, "it should be at least more likely than not that *death* would result." The court ruled that when viewed in the light most favorable to the People, the facts showed that Hall was "skiing too fast for the snow conditions." The district court held that while such conduct may involve a substantial risk of injury, a person of ordinary prudence and caution would not infer that skiing too fast for the conditions creates at least a fifty percent chance of death. Thus, the court held that the prosecution failed to meet its burden and affirmed the county court's finding of no probable cause.

The People petitioned this court pursuant to C.A.R. 49, and we granted certiorari to consider the following: (1) Whether the district court erred by establishing "*more likely than not*" as the level of substantial risk of death that a defendant must disregard for a finding of probable cause that he caused the death of another recklessly; and (2) Whether the district court reviewed the wrong criteria and neglected the evidence relating specifically to this case in affirming the county court's dismissal of a manslaughter charge at preliminary hearing.

People v. Hall
Supreme Court of Colorado, 999 P.2d 207 (2000)

I (1) Did the district court err by establishing "*more likely than not*" as the level of substantial risk of death that a defendant must disregard for a finding of probable cause that he caused the death of another recklessly; and (2) Did the district court review the wrong criteria and neglect the evidence relating specifically to this case in affirming the county court's dismissal of a manslaughter charge at preliminary hearing?

R Although this statute may not form the basis of criminal liability, it establishes the minimum standard of care for uphill skiers and, for the purposes of civil negligence suits, creates a rebuttable presumption that the skier is at fault whenever he collides with skiers on the slope below him. A violation of a skier's duty in an extreme fashion, such as here, may be evidence of conduct that constitutes a "gross deviation" from the standard of care imposed by statute for civil negligence.

A We hold that Nathan Hall must stand trial for the crime of reckless manslaughter. While skiing on Vail Mountain, Hall flew off of a knoll and collided with Allen Cobb, who was traversing the slope below Hall. Cobb sustained traumatic brain injuries and died as a result of the collision. The People charged Hall with felony reckless manslaughter. At a preliminary hearing to determine whether there was probable cause for the felony count, the county court found that Hall's conduct "did not rise to the level of dangerousness" required under Colorado law to uphold a conviction for manslaughter, and the court dismissed the charges. On appeal, the district court affirmed the county court's decision. The district court determined that in order for Hall's conduct to have been reckless, it must have been "at least more likely than not" that death would result. Because the court found that "skiing too fast for the conditions" is not "likely" to cause another person's death, the court concluded that Hall's conduct did not constitute a "substantial and unjustifiable" risk of death. Thus, the district court affirmed the finding of no probable cause.

The charge of reckless manslaughter requires that a person "recklessly cause[d] the death of another person." § 18-3-104(1)(a), 6 C.R.S. (1999). For his conduct to be reckless, the actor must have consciously disregarded a substantial and unjustifiable risk that death could result from his actions. *See* §18-1-501(8). We hold that, for the purpose of determining whether a person acted recklessly, a particular result does not have to be more likely than not to occur for the risk to be substantial and unjustifiable. A risk must be assessed by reviewing the particular facts of the individual case and weighing the likelihood of harm and the degree of harm that would result if it occurs. Whether an actor consciously disregarded such a risk may be inferred from circumstances such as the actor's knowledge and experience, or from what a similarly situated reasonable person would have understood about the risk under the particular circumstances.

People v. Hall
Supreme Court of Colorado, 999 P.2d 207 (2000)

We hold that under the particular circumstances of this case, whether Hall committed the crime of reckless manslaughter must be determined by the trier of fact. Viewed in the light most favorable to the prosecution, Hall's conduct - skiing straight down a steep and bumpy slope, back on his skis, arms out to his sides, off-balance, being thrown from mogul to mogul, out of control for a considerable distance and period of time, and at such a high speed that the force of the impact between his ski and the victim's head fractured the thickest part of the victim's skull - created a substantial and unjustifiable risk of death to another person. A reasonable person could infer that the defendant, a former ski racer trained in skier safety, consciously disregarded that risk. For the limited purposes of a preliminary hearing, the prosecution provided sufficient evidence to show probable cause that the defendant recklessly caused the victim's death. Thus, we reverse the district court's finding of no probable cause and we remand the case to that court for trial.

Dismissal reversed; case remanded for trial.

State v. Williams

Court of Appeals of Washington, 484 P.2d 1167 (1971)

FACTS

Defendant-appellants Walter and Bernice Williams, husband and wife, were charged with manslaughter for negligently failing to supply their 17 month old child with necessary medical education, resulting in his death. Walter Williams was a 24-year-old Sheshont Indian with a 6th grade education. His wife, Bernice Williams, was a 20-year-old part-Indian with an 11th grade education. At the time of the marriage, Bernice had two children, the younger of whom was a 14-month-old son, whom they both loved very much. The child became ill on September 1, of which they were aware, but "were ignorant" in that they did not realize how sick he actually was. Thinking he had only a toothache, which they did not believe to be life-threatening, they gave him aspirin in hopes of improving his condition. He was not taken to a doctor out of fear that the Welfare Department would take him from them. The abscessed tooth developed into an infection of the mouth and cheeks, eventually becoming gangrenous. This condition, accompanied by the child's inability to eat, brought on malnutrition, which lowered the child's resistance and eventually produced pneumonia, causing death on September 12. The infection lasted about two weeks. Dr. Gale Wilson, the autopsy surgeon and chief pathologist testified that the infection would have to have been treated within the first 5 days in order to save the child. The Williams were convicted of manslaughter for not seeking medical treatment for the child.

 Can negligence support a conviction for manslaughter?

 Proof of ordinary negligence can be sufficient to support a conviction for manslaughter.

 A parent has an affirmative duty to provide food and medical care to a dependent, minor child. Under the common law, involuntary manslaughter could be proven by a breach of duty which exceeding mere ordinary or simple negligence—a showing of gross negligence was required. In our state, however, a showing of simple or ordinary negligence is all that is required to prove manslaughter. The concept of ordinary negligence requires a failure to exercise the "ordinary caution" necessary to make out the defense of excusable homicide. Ordinary caution is the kind of caution that a man of reasonable prudence would exercise under the same or similar conditions. If the conduct of a defendant, regardless of his ignorance, good faith, or good intentions, fails to measure up to this standard, he is guilty of ordinary negligence. If such negligence proximately causes the death of the victim, the defendant is guilty of manslaughter. While the law does not require that a parent call a doctor at the first sign of illness, timeliness in the furnishing of medical care must be considered in terms of "ordinary caution." The testimony from the defendants indicates that they noticed the child was ill 2 weeks before he died. In the critical days in which it would have been possible to save the child's life, the parents noticed that the child was fussy, could not keep food down, and that his cheek turned a "bluish color like." The defendants thought that dentists would not pull a tooth "when it's all swollen up like that." Also, both parents feared that the child would be taken away from them if they took him to a doctor. Thus, there is sufficient evidence that the defendants were put on notice of the symptoms of the baby's illness and lack of his improvement of condition to have required them to have obtained medical care. They did not and so such negligence and failure to exercise "ordinary caution" is sufficient to support a conviction for manslaughter.

Judgment affirmed.

Commonwealth v. Malone

Supreme Court of Pennsylvania, 47 A.2d 445 (1946)

FACTS

Defendant Malone, a 17-year-old boy, went to the movies one evening and brought with him a .32 caliber revolver that he had taken from his uncle's house the day before. That afternoon, William H. Long, a 13-year-old boy and friend of Malone, procured a cartridge for the gun from his father's room. After leaving the theater, Malone met Long at a dairy store, took the gun out of his pocket in the rear of the store and loaded the chamber to the right of the firing pin. The two then sat at the lunch counter and ate. Malone then suggested that they play "Russian Poker" a/k/a "Russian Roulette." Long replied, "I don't care; go ahead." Malone held the gun against Long's right side and pulled the trigger three times. The third pull resulted in the fatal shot to Long. He died two days later. At trial, Malone testified that he did not "expect to have the gun go off" and that he did not intend to hurt his friend. Nevertheless, Malone was found guilty of second degree murder and sentenced to 5 to 10 years in prison. His motion for a new trial was denied and he appealed post-sentencing.

Under Pennsylvania law, can a defendant be convicted of murder in the second degree when has killed without hostility toward the victim when a second degree murder conviction requires a showing of malice in that jurisdiction?

Under Pennsylvania law, a defendant can be convicted of murder in the second degree if his actions show a callous disregard for human life and the consequences of his actions - under such circumstances, he will have exhibited the type of malice, the so-called "wickedness of disposition," that sets second-degree murder apart from involuntary manslaughter.

In our jurisdiction, a conviction of second-degree murder requires a showing of malice on the part of the killer. However, "malice" does not necessarily mean hostility toward the victim, but can include a "wicked disposition" among other things. When an individual acts in a grossly reckless way and must have reasonably anticipated that another person's death would likely result therefrom, he is demonstrating the kind of "wickedness of disposition, hardness of heart, cruelty, recklessness of consequences" that can form non-hostile "malice." In this case, Long died as a result of Malone's intentional reckless and wanton act committed in clear disregard of the consequences. There was at least a 60% chance that a shot would kill Long [statistically speaking, one bullet loaded into a gun and fired it three times = 60% probability that a live round would fire into Long's side]. The fact that Malone had no specific motive for killing Long is irrelevant.

Judgment affirmed.

United States v. Fleming
United States Court of Appeals, 739 F.2d 945 (1984)

FACTS

Defendant David Earl Fleming was driving southbound on the George Washington Memorial Parkway in Virginia 70 to 100 m.p.h in a 45 m.p.h. zone on the afternoon of June 15, 1983. The Parkway is within the federal jurisdiction. On more than one occasion, Fleming drove his car into oncoming traffic in order to avoid the heavy congestion. At some point on the parkway, Fleming lost control of his vehicle, slid across the oncoming lanes of traffic, and hit a curb on the northbound side of the Parkway before finally colliding with a car driven by Mrs. Haley who was traveling in the opposite direction. At the moment of impact, Fleming's car was traveling at between 70 and 80 miles per hour. The impact killed Mrs. Haley, but Fleming survived. His blood alcohol level was .315%. Fleming was convicted of second-degree murder.

Under federal law, can a defendant be convicted of second degree murder, requiring malice aforethought, for an unintentional killing resulting from a motor vehicle accident while he was intoxicated?

Under federal law, drunk and reckless driving can constitute malice aforethought [second degree] murder when 1) proof of a risk of serious harm can be ascribed to the defendant's actions and 2) where the defendant *knew* the risk but nevertheless disregarded it; that is, he *intended* to operate his car in the manner in which he did with a heart that was without regard for the life and safety of others.

"Malice aforethought" is that part of 2nd degree murder that separates murder from manslaughter. Proof of malice need not include evidence that the defendant harbored any hostility toward his victim, or intended to kill his victim, and may be established by showing that the defendant acted recklessly, wantonly, or violated a gross breach of the standard of care such that his actions created a risk of death or serious bodily harm. Here, the government had only to show that Fleming intended to drive without regard for the lives and safety of others, but not that he intended to kill his victim - this is acting with malice aforethought. Fleming argues that his conviction should be reduced to involuntary manslaughter because he did not intend to kill anyone. As we have already said, intent to kill is not the correct prerequisite for malice aforethought. The difference between malice and gross negligence, a required showing for a conviction of involuntary manslaughter, is one of degree. Here again, Fleming's actions show a recklessness or wantonness that is different in degree from that found in most vehicular homicide cases. It is this reckless conduct, made more dangerous by his drunkenness, which constitutes malice aforethought.

Judgment affirmed.

Regina v. Serne

Central Criminal Court, 16 Cox Crim. Cas. 311 (1887)

FACTS

Defendant Leon Serne, in 1887, lived with his wife, two daughters and two sons in a house above a store at No. 274 Strand, London. The Sernes were in severe debt. By September of that same year, Serne had taken out a life insurance policy on his 14-year-old son, Sjaak, who was mentally retarded, had insured the inventory of his store below, all of his furniture, and his rent. Shortly thereafter, the store and house burned down, resulting in the deaths of both of his sons. At trial, the prosecution submitted evidence that he and Codefendant John Henry Goldfinch had been seen together in the shop shortly before the fire started. Two fires broke out on the lower floor of the building, and two on the second floor such that, it was posited, escape could still be made to the roof. Serne, Goldfinch, and Serne's wife and daughters escaped to the roof of their house and then to the roof of the house next door. Serne's sons burnt to death. The body of one of the sons was found on the floor near the window through which the Sernes had escaped. The body of the other son was found in the basement. Serne and Goldfinch were indicted for the willful murder of Sjaak Serne.

Under English law, does any act done with intent to commit a felony and which causes death constitutes murder?

An act known to be dangerous to life and likely in and of itself to cause the death of another, done for the purpose of committing a felony which causes death, should be considered felony murder.

Murder is the unjustified killing of a human being committed with malice aforethought. "Malice aforethought" is 1) the killing of another person by an act done with an intention to commit a felony or 2) an act done with the knowledge that that action will probably cause the death of another person. If Serne and/or Goldfinch killed Sjaak Serne either with intent to commit insurance fraud [a felony] or through an action done with the knowledge that that action will probably cause the death of another person, then the party or parties responsible will be guilty of murder. Historically, the definition of "felony murder" was quite broad, but its current definition includes any act *known* to be dangerous to human life and *likely* to cause death, and that does in fact cause the death of another person. If both defendants fire to the house and store while the family was inside, and the victims died as a result of the fire, then the defendants are just as guilty of murder as if they were found to have stabbed, shot or bludgeoned the boys to death by their own hands. Serne's and Goldfinch's intent, if they ever had any, that all the family members escape unharmed is irrelevant if they started the fires. I say the verdict is not guilty.

No guilty.

People v. Phillips
Supreme Court of California, 414 P.2d 353 (1966)

FACTS

Linda Epping, an eight-year-old girl, suffered from a fast-growing cancer of the eye. Her parents were advised by a medical center to consent to the immediate removal of her eye to save or prolong the child's life. Instead of following the doctors' advice, her parents opted to follow the advice of a chiropractor, Defendant Phillips. Phillips told her parents that he could cure the child without surgery by administering a treatment designed "to build up her resistance" charging them $700 for the service. Linda died in about six months. Phillips was indicted for murder in the second degree. A tripartite instruction was given by the trial court to the jury on murder in the second degree. Part three of the instruction rested upon the felony murder rule. There, the trial judge told the jury that the unlawful killing of another person with malice aforethought but without the deliberate and premeditated intent to kill is murder in the second degree if "[t]he killing is done in the perpetration or attempt to perpetrate a felony such as Grand Theft. If a death occurs in the perpetration of a course of conduct amounting to Grand Theft, which course of conduct is a proximate cause of the unlawful killing of a human being, such course of conduct constitutes murder in the second degree, even though the death was not intended." Phillips appealed on the ground that this instruction was erroneous.

 Under California law, can a chiropractor be found guilty of felony murder when his so-called cure for his patient's cancer failed when based on his fraudulent act and/or misrepresentations?

 Under California law, in order to raise the felony murder rule, the prosecution must show that the felony the defendant committed was of a type "that is inherently dangerous to human life."

 Not every felony falls under the felony-murder rule when a death is involved. Under California law, a homicide committed during the perpetration of a fraud cannot be held to be a felony murder. Even if fraud is considered in the jurisdiction a felony, it [the felony] must be of a type "that is inherently dangerous to human life." Thus, the trial court erred in giving a felony murder instruction. In order to determine whether a felony is inherently dangerous to human life, California courts do not look to the "facts" of individual cases, but rather look to the elements of the felony in the abstract. The felony murder rule is narrowly construed and no prior case has held that the felony murder rule may be invoked where a death results from the perpetration of a fraud. The Attorney General argues us to create a novel type of felony and apply it to the case at bar. This new felony, "grand theft medical fraud," he urges, would involve an inherent danger to human life. We decline his invitation to do so. This would broaden the felony murder rule and conflict and cause confusion with respect to prior cases that have narrowed the application of the rule. The felony murder instruction was clearly erroneous and prejudicial because it

People v. Phillips
Supreme Court of California, 414 P.2d 353 (1966)

permitted the jury to convict Phillips without finding malice aforethought; substituting this required element for the crime charged [second degree murder] with a finding that Phillips had committed fraud only. The prosecution does not deny the proffered jury instruction brought about the possibility of a conviction of murder in the absence of a finding of malice; rather it argues that regardless of the instruction, the jury must have found that Phillips acted with a conscious disregard for human life and, therefore, acted with "malice aforethought" anyway. Such a finding, however, does not establish as a matter of law, the existence of the intent to commit, with the conscious disregard for human life, actions likely to result in the death of another. Alternatively, it is just as likely that Phillips could have just as easily passed on false information believing it to be true.

 Judgment reversed.

People v. Stewart
Supreme Court of Rhode Island, 663 A.2d 912 (1995)

FACTS

Defendant Tracey Stewart went on a crack cocaine binge for a few days during which time she neither fed nor cared for her infant son. She was charged with second-degree felony murder after her son died of dehydration. She was charged Stewart with "wrongfully permitting the child to be a habitual suffer" as codified by R.I. Gen L. §11-9-5, which was a felony in Rhode Island. As such, the prosecution argued that Stewart could be charged with second-degree murder under the felony murder rule because her acts were the result of neglect under the statute, not intentionally withholding food or care from the infant. Stewart, on the other hand, argued that the felony murder rule was inapplicable because her crime was not inherently dangerous "in the abstract."

Must a felony be inherently dangerous "in the abstract" in order to implicate the felony-murder rule?

Whether a felony is inherently dangerous is a determination made with reference to the facts and circumstances of the case by the trier of fact taking into consideration the circumstances in which the crime was committed.

Whether a felony is inherently dangerous is a determination made with reference to the facts and circumstances of the case by the trier of fact taking into consideration the circumstances in which the crime was committed. We reject the approach adopted by in California, which requires that a court determine whether a particular felony is inherently dangerous "in the abstract," if the felony murder rule is to apply. A number of felonies appear, at first glance, not be inherently dangerous, yet they may be committed in such a manner as to make them inherently dangerous to life. Escape from prison is not inherently dangerous, yet we have upheld a conviction under the felony murder rule when the escapee's accomplice killed a prison guard. For that reason, the jury instruction given by the trial court was proper. A jury should be allowed to determine whether the parental neglect was inherently dangerous to human life "in the manner of commission."

Affirmed.

Hines v. State

Supreme Court of Georgia, 578 S.E.2d 868 (2003)

FACTS

While hunting, Robert Lee Hines mistook his friend Steven Wood for a turkey and shot him dead. A jury convicted Hines of felony murder based on the underlying crime of possession of a firearm by a convicted felon. Hines contends that a convicted felon's possession of a firearm while turkey hunting cannot be one of the inherently dangerous felonies required to support a conviction of felony murder. A felony is inherently dangerous when it is "dangerous per se" or "by its circumstances" creates a foreseeable risk of death.

Can a convicted felon's possession of a firearm while turkey hunting considered one of the inherently dangerous felonies required to support a conviction of felony murder?

A convicted felon's possession of a firearm while turkey hunting can be considered as one of the inherently dangerous felonies required to support a conviction of felony murder.

Hines intentionally fired his shotgun intending to hit his target. He had been drinking before he went hunting and there was evidence he had been drinking while hunting. He knew that other hunters were in the area and was unaware of their exact location. He took an unsafe shot at dusk, through heavy foliage, at a target 80 feet away that he had not positively identified. Under these circumstances, we conclude that Hines's violation of the prohibition of a firearm created a foreseeable risk of death. Hines's violation of the prohibition against convicted felons possessing firearms was an inherently dangerous felony that could support a felony-murder conviction.

Judgment affirmed.

People v. Burton
Supreme Court of California, 491 P.2d 793 (1971)

FACTS

Defendant Bozzie Bryant Burton III, a 16-year-old minor was charged by information with two counts of murder and a third count of assault with intent to commit murder. After a jury trial he was found guilty as charged on two counts of murder in the first degree and guilty of assault, a lesser offense than that charged in the third count, but necessarily included therein. Defendant was sentenced to the term prescribed by law on the two counts of murder and to 180 days in county jail on the count of assault, each sentence to run concurrently. He appeals from the judgment of conviction. Defendant contends that his confession to the above charges was obtained in violation of the rules announced in *Miranda* v. *Arizona* (1966) 384 U.S. 436 and that its admission into evidence over his objection constitutes reversible error.

 Can a second degree felony-murder instruction be given when it is based upon a felony which is an integral part of the homicide and which the evidence produced by the prosecution shows to be an offense included *in fact* within the offense charged?

 In California, a second degree felony-murder instruction may not properly be given when it is based upon a felony which is an integral part of the homicide and which the evidence produced by the prosecution shows to be an offense included *in fact* within the offense charged.

 Defendant contends that his confession to the above charges was obtained in violation of the rules announced in *Miranda* v. *Arizona* and that its admission into evidence over his objection constitutes reversible error. We agree and, therefore, reverse the judgment. " ... a second degree felony-murder instruction may not properly be given when it is based upon a felony which is an integral part of the homicide and which the evidence produced by the prosecution shows to be an offense included *in fact* within the offense charged." *People* v. *Ireland*. Thus, we conclude that there is a very significant difference between deaths resulting from assaults with a deadly weapon, where the purpose of the conduct was the very assault which resulted in death, and deaths resulting from conduct for an independent felonious purpose, such as robbery or rape, which happened to be accomplished by a deadly weapon and therefore technically includes assault with a deadly weapon. Our inquiry cannot stop with the fact that death resulted from the use of a deadly weapon and, therefore, technically included an assault with a deadly weapon, but must extend to an investigation of the purpose of the conduct. In both *Ireland* and *Wilson* the purpose of the conduct which eventually resulted in a homicide was assault with a deadly weapon, namely the infliction of bodily injury upon the person of another. The desired infliction of bodily injury was in each case not satisfied short of death. Thus, there was a single course of conduct with a single purpose.

 The judgment is reversed.

State v. Canola

Supreme Court of New Jersey, 374 A.2d 20 (1977)

FACTS

Defendant Canola was in the process of robbing a jewelry store with three accomplices when the store owner and his employee resisted, gunfire erupted, and the store owner and one of the three accomplices were killed. The accomplice was killed by the store owner. Canola and the remaining two of his accomplices were indicted on two counts of murder, one count of robbery, and one count of armed robbery. Canola was found guilty on both murder counts and was sentenced to life imprisonment. The Appellate Division unanimously affirmed the conviction for the murder of the robbery victim and upheld the trial court's denial of a motion to dismiss the count of murder assigned to the killing of the accomplice. The New Jersey Supreme Court granted certiorari.

 Under New Jersey law, can a defendant be found guilty of felony murder when one of the robbery victims shoots one of the defendant's accomplices?

 The definition of felony murder will not be extended to include situations where the actions of a felon set in motion a chain reaction leading to the death of another co-felon.

 Conventional definitions of felony murder do not encompass situations such as the one in this case. Traditionally, the felony murder rule has only been invoked when the defendant himself killed the victim. The English courts never applied the felony murder rule to hold a felon guilty for the death of his co-felon at the hands of the intended victim. In United States, the general rule is that the felony murder rule may not be applied to homicides not attributable to the defendant. At one time, the proximate cause theory was espoused by the Pennsylvania Supreme Court. However, currently no court currently attaches liability under the felony murder rule to *any* death proximately caused by the perpetration of the felony. The theory of proximate causation holds that if a felon sets in motion a chain of events that could foreseeably lead to the death of another, he will be found guilty of the death. We reject this approach. Moreover, this case is not one of the so-called "shield" cases. In a shield case, the victim is fatally shot by police officers after the defendant, trying to escape after committing a felony, uses an innocent bystander as a human shield. Felony murder attaches in those case because, although the accused did not actually pull the trigger, his actions reveal "express malice;" a conscious disregard of the natural and probable consequences of his act [his choice to use an innocent person as a shield against the police].

 Judgment modified to strike the conviction and sentencing of Canola for the murder of his accomplice.

Gregg v. Georgia
Supreme Court of the United States, 428 U.S. 153 (1976)

FACTS

Defendant-petitioner Gregg was charged with committing armed robbery and murder for killing and robbing two men. At the trial stage of Georgia's bifurcated procedure, the jury found petitioner guilty of two counts of armed robbery and two counts of murder. At the penalty stage, the judge instructed the jury that it could recommend either a death sentence or a life prison sentence on each count; that it was free to consider mitigating or aggravating circumstances, if any, as presented by the parties; and that it would not be authorized to consider imposing the death sentence unless it first found beyond a reasonable doubt (1) that the murder was committed while the offender was engaged in the commission of other capital felonies, *viz.*, the armed robberies of the victims; (2) that he committed the murder for the purpose of receiving the victims' money and automobile; or (3) that the murder was "outrageously and wantonly vile, horrible and inhuman" in that it "involved the depravity of [the] mind of the defendant." The jury returned a sentence of death. The Georgia Supreme Court affirmed the convictions. After reviewing the trial transcript and record the court upheld the death sentences for the murders, but vacated the armed robbery sentences on the ground, *inter alia*, that the death penalty had rarely been imposed in Georgia for that offense. Petitioner challenges imposition of the death sentence under the Georgia statute as "cruel and unusual" punishment under the Eighth and Fourteenth Amendments. That statute, as amended, retains the death penalty for murder and five other crimes. Guilt or innocence is determined in the first stage of a bifurcated trial; and if the trial is by jury, the trial judge must charge lesser included offenses when supported by any view of the evidence. At least one of 10 specified aggravating circumstances must be found to exist beyond a reasonable doubt and designated in writing before a death sentence can be imposed. In jury cases, the trial judge is bound by the recommended sentence. In its review of a death sentence (which is automatic), the State Supreme Court must consider whether the sentence was influenced by passion, prejudice, or any other arbitrary factor; if the court affirms the death sentence it must include in its decision reference to similar cases that it has considered.

 Is Georgia's Statute, which imposes the death penalty under certain circumstances, constitutional?

 Georgia's Statute, which imposes the death penalty on murderers in certain circumstances, is constitutional because the death penalty is consistent with societal standards, is not an excessive punishment, and the statute provides sufficient safeguards to prevent it from being imposed in an arbitrary or capricious manner.

 The punishment of death for the crime of murder does not, under all circumstances, violate the Eighth and Fourteenth Amendments. The Eighth Amendment, which has been interpreted in a flexible and dynamic manner

Gregg v. Georgia

Supreme Court of the United States, 428 U.S. 153 (1976)

to accord with evolving standards of decency, forbids the use of punishment that is "excessive" either because it involves the unnecessary and wanton infliction of pain or because it is grossly disproportionate to the severity of the crime. Though a legislature may not impose excessive punishment, it is not required to select the least severe penalty possible, and a heavy burden rests upon those attacking its judgment. The existence of capital punishment was accepted by the Framers of the Constitution, and for nearly two centuries this Court has recognized that capital punishment for the crime of murder is not invalid per se. Legislative measures adopted by the people's chosen representatives weigh heavily in ascertaining contemporary standards of decency; and the argument that such standards require that the Eighth Amendment be construed as prohibiting the death penalty has been undercut by Congress and at least 35 States which have enacted new statutes providing for the death penalty. Retribution and the possibility of deterrence of capital crimes by prospective offenders are not impermissible considerations for a legislature to weigh in determining whether the death penalty should be imposed. Capital punishment for the crime of murder cannot be viewed as invariably disproportionate to the severity of that crime. Concerns that the death penalty not be imposed arbitrarily or capriciously can be met by a carefully drafted statute that ensures that the sentencing authority is given adequate information and guidance; concerns best met by a system that provides for a bifurcated proceeding at which the sentencing authority is apprised of the information relevant to the imposition of sentence and provided with standards to guide its use of that information. The Georgia statutory system is constitutional. The new procedures on their face satisfy these concerns, since before the death penalty can be imposed there must be specific jury findings as to the circumstances of the crime or the character of the defendant, and the State Supreme Court thereafter reviews the comparability of each death sentence with the sentences imposed on similarly situated defendants to ensure that the sentence of death in a particular case is not disproportionate. Petitioner's contentions that the changes in Georgia's sentencing procedures have not removed the elements of arbitrariness and capriciousness are without merit. The opportunities under the Georgia scheme for affording an individual defendant mercy - whether through the prosecutor's unfettered authority to select those whom he wishes to prosecute for capital offenses and to plea bargain with them; the jury's option to convict a defendant of a lesser included offense; or the fact that the Governor or pardoning authority may commute a death sentence - do not render the Georgia statute unconstitutional. Petitioner's arguments, that certain statutory aggravating circumstances are too broad or vague lacks merit because they [the statutes], need not be given overly broad constructions or have already been narrowed by judicial construction. One such provision was held impermissibly vague by the Georgia Supreme Court. Petitioner's argument that the sentencing procedure allows for arbitrary grants of mercy reflects a misinterpretation of Furman and ignores the reviewing authority of the Georgia Supreme Court to determine whether each death sentence is proportional to other sentences imposed for similar crimes. Petitioner also urges that the scope of the evidence and argument that can be considered at the pre-sentence hearing is too wide, but it is desirable for a jury to have as much information as possible when it makes the sentencing decision. The Georgia sentencing scheme also provides for automatic sentence review by the Georgia Supreme Court to safeguard against prejudicial or arbitrary factors. In this very case the court vacated petitioner's death sentence for armed robbery as an excessive penalty.

The judgment is affirmed.

Atkins v. Virginia

Supreme Court of the United States, 536 U.S. 304 (2002)

FACTS

Petitioner, Daryl Renard Atkins, was convicted of abduction, armed robbery, and capital murder, and sentenced to death. At approximately midnight on August 16, 1996, Atkins and William Jones, armed with a semiautomatic handgun, abducted Eric Nesbitt, robbed him of the money on his person, drove him to an automated teller machine in his pickup truck where cameras recorded their withdrawal of additional cash, then took him to an isolated location where he was shot eight times and killed. Jones and Atkins both testified in the guilt phase of Atkins' trial. Each confirmed most of the details in the other's account of the incident, with the important exception that each stated that the other had actually shot and killed Nesbitt. Jones' testimony, which was both more coherent and credible than Atkins' was obviously credited by the jury and was sufficient to establish Atkins' guilt. At the penalty phase of the trial, the State introduced victim impact evidence and proved two aggravating circumstances: future dangerousness and "vileness of the offense." To prove future dangerousness, the State relied on Atkins' prior felony convictions as well as the testimony of four victims of earlier robberies and assaults. To prove the second aggravator, the prosecution relied upon the trial record, including pictures of the deceased's body and the autopsy report. In the penalty phase, the defense relied on one witness, Dr. Evan Nelson, a forensic psychologist who had evaluated Atkins before trial and concluded that he was "mildly mentally retarded." The jury sentenced Atkins to death, but the Virginia Supreme Court ordered a second sentencing hearing because the trial court had used a misleading verdict form. The jury again sentenced Atkins to death. The Supreme Court of Virginia affirmed the imposition of the death penalty. Atkins did not argue before the Virginia Supreme Court that his sentence was disproportionate to penalties imposed for similar crimes in Virginia, but he did contend "that he is mentally retarded and thus cannot be sentenced to death." The majority of the state court rejected this contention, relying on our holding in *Penry*. The Court was "not willing to commute Atkins' sentence of death to life imprisonment merely because of his IQ score."

Is a death sentence violative of the Eighth amendment when the accused is a mentally retarded person who meets the law's requirements for criminal responsibility and is tried and sentenced when he commits those crimes?

Those mentally retarded persons who meet the law's requirements for criminal responsibility should be tried and punished when they commit crimes but should not be sentenced to death in violation of the Eight Amendment.

Those mentally retarded persons who meet the law's requirements for criminal responsibility should be tried and punished when they commit crimes. Because of their disabilities in areas of reasoning, judgment, and control of their impulses, however, they do not act with the level of moral culpability that characterizes the most serious adult criminal conduct. Moreover, their impairments can jeopardize the reliability and fairness of capital proceedings against mentally retarded defendants. Presumably for these reasons, in the 13 years since we decided *Penry* v. *Lynaugh*, 492 U.S. 302 (1989), the American public, legislators, scholars, and judges have deliberated over the question whether the death penalty should ever be imposed on a mentally retarded criminal. The consensus reflected in those deliberations informs our answer to the question presented by this case: whether such executions are "cruel and unusual punishments" prohibited by the Eighth Amendment to the Federal Constitution. Our independent evaluation of the issue reveals no reason to disagree with the judgment of "the legislatures that have recently addressed the matter" and concluded that death is not a suitable punishment for a mentally retarded criminal. We are not persuaded that the execution of mentally retarded criminals will measurably advance the deterrent or the retributive purpose of the death penalty. Construing and applying the Eighth Amendment in the light of our "evolving standards of decency," we therefore conclude that such punishment is excessive and that the Constitution "places a substantive restriction on the State's power to take the life" of a mentally retarded offender. *Ford*, 477 U.S., at 405.

 The judgment of the Virginia Supreme Court is reversed and the case is remanded for further proceedings not inconsistent with this opinion.

McCleskey v. Kemp

Supreme Court of the United States, 481 U.S. 279 (1987)

FACTS

In 1978, petitioner Warren McCleskey, a black man, was convicted in a Georgia trial court of armed robbery and murder, arising from the killing of a white police officer during the robbery of a store. Pursuant to Georgia statutes, the jury at the penalty hearing considered the mitigating and aggravating circumstances of petitioner's conduct and recommended the death penalty on the murder charge. The trial court followed the recommendation, and the Georgia Supreme Court affirmed. After unsuccessfully seeking post-conviction relief in state courts, petitioner sought habeas corpus relief in Federal District Court. His petition included a claim that the Georgia capital sentencing process was administered in a racially discriminatory manner in violation of the Eighth and Fourteenth Amendments. In support of the claim, petitioner proffered a statistical study (the Baldus study) that purports to show a disparity in the imposition of the death sentence in Georgia based on the murder victim's race and, to a lesser extent, the defendant's race. The study is based on over 2,000 murder cases that occurred in Georgia during the 1970's, and involves data relating to the victim's race, the defendant's race, and the various combinations of such persons' races. The study indicates that black defendants who killed white victims have the greatest likelihood of receiving the death penalty. Rejecting petitioner's constitutional claims, the court denied his petition insofar as it was based on the Baldus study, and the Court of Appeals affirmed the District Court's decision on this issue. It assumed the validity of the Baldus study but found the statistics insufficient to demonstrate unconstitutional discrimination in the Fourteenth Amendment context or to show irrationality, arbitrariness, and capriciousness under Eighth Amendment analysis. The U.S. Supreme Court granted certiorari.

Can a complex statistical study that shows a risk that capital sentencing is influenced by race prove that a specific death sentence is unconstitutional under the 8th or 14th Amendments?

A statistical study that shows a risk that capital sentencing in influenced by race does not prove that a specific sentence violates the 8th or 14th Amendment.

The Baldus study does not establish that the administration of the Georgia capital punishment system violates the Equal Protection Clause. To prevail under that Clause, petitioner must prove that the decision makers in his case acted with discriminatory purpose. Petitioner offered no evidence specific to his own case that would support an inference that racial considerations played a part in his sentence, and the Baldus study is insufficient to support an inference that any of the decision makers in his case acted with discriminatory purpose. This Court has accepted statistics as proof of intent to discriminate in the context of a State's selection of the jury venire. However, the nature of the capital sentencing decision and

McCleskey v. Kemp

Supreme Court of the United States, 481 U.S. 279 (1987)

the relationship of the statistics to that decision are fundamentally different from the corresponding elements in the venire-selection or Title VII cases. Petitioner's statistical proffer must be viewed in the context of his challenge to decisions at the heart of the State's criminal justice system. Because discretion is essential to the criminal justice process, exceptionally clear proof is required before this Court will infer that the discretion has been abused. There is no merit to petitioner's argument that the Baldus study proves that the State has violated the Equal Protection Clause by adopting the capital punishment statute and allowing it to remain in force despite its allegedly discriminatory application. For this claim to prevail, petitioner would have to prove that the Georgia Legislature enacted or maintained the death penalty statute because of an anticipated racially discriminatory effect. There is no evidence that the legislature either enacted the statute to further a racially discriminatory purpose, or maintained the statute because of the racially disproportionate impact suggested by the Baldus study. Petitioner's argument that the Baldus study demonstrates that the Georgia capital sentencing system violates the Eighth Amendment's prohibition of cruel and unusual punishment must be analyzed in the light of this Court's prior decisions under that Amendment. Decisions since *Furman v. Georgia* have identified a constitutionally permissible range of discretion in imposing the death penalty. First, there is a required threshold below which the death penalty cannot be imposed, and the State must establish rational criteria that narrow the decision maker's judgment. Second, States cannot limit the sentencer's consideration of any relevant circumstance that could cause it to decline to impose the death penalty. In this respect, the State cannot limit the sentencer's discretion, but must allow it to consider any relevant information offered by the defendant. Petitioner cannot successfully argue that the sentence in his case is disproportionate to the sentences in other murder cases. The Georgia Supreme Court found that his death sentence was not disproportionate to other death sentences imposed in the State. On the other hand, absent a showing that the Georgia capital punishment system operates in an arbitrary and capricious manner, petitioner cannot prove a constitutional violation by demonstrating that other defendants who may be similarly situated did not receive the death penalty. The opportunities for discretionary leniency under state law do not render the capital sentences imposed arbitrary and capricious. Because petitioner's sentence was imposed under Georgia sentencing procedures, it may be presumed that his death sentence was not "wantonly and freakishly" imposed, and thus that the sentence is not disproportionate within any recognized meaning under the Eighth Amendment. There is no merit to the contention that the Baldus study shows that Georgia's capital punishment system is arbitrary and capricious in application. The statistics do not prove that race enters into any capital sentencing decisions or that race was a factor in petitioner's case. The likelihood of racial prejudice allegedly shown by the study does not constitute the constitutional measure of an unacceptable risk of racial prejudice. The inherent lack of predictability of jury decisions does not justify their condemnation. At most, the Baldus study indicates a discrepancy that appears to correlate with race, but this discrepancy does not constitute a major systemic defect. Despite such imperfections, constitutional guarantees are met when the mode for determining guilt or punishment has been surrounded with safeguards to make it as fair as possible. The Constitution does not require that a State

McCleskey v. Kemp
Supreme Court of the United States, 481 U.S. 279 (1987)

eliminate any demonstrable disparity that correlates with a potentially irrelevant factor in order to operate a criminal justice system that includes capital punishment. Petitioner's arguments are best presented to the legislative bodies, not the courts.

 Affirmed.

People v. Acosta

Court of Appeal of California, 4th Appellate District, 284 Cal. Rptr. 117 (1991)

FACTS

At 10p.m. on March 10, 1987, Police officers Salceda and Francis of the Santa Ana Police Department's automobile theft division saw Defendant Vincent William Acosta in a stolen vehicle parked on the street. The officers approached Acosta and identified themselves. He sped away and led the police on a 48-mile chase on numerous streets and freeways through Orange County. During the chase, Acosta ran stop signs, red lights, and drove on the wrong side of the streets into oncoming traffic. Police helicopters from two different cities were summoned to assist. At some pointy, while the two helicopters were tracking Acosta's car below, they collided with one another, killing three people in one of the helicopters. In addition his other crimes, Acosta was charged with second degree murder. At trial, the defense called an aviation expert who testified that in his opinion, one of the helicopters violated certain FAA regulations prohibiting careless and reckless operation of an aircraft by failing to properly clear the area, not maintaining the proper communication with the other aircraft and for not maintaining line-of-sight with the other helicopter at all times. Acosta was subsequently convicted on three counts of second degree murder. He appeals his conviction arguing 1) that there was insufficient evidence that he was the proximate cause of the death of the occupants of the helicopter; 2) that it was not foreseeable that two *helicopters* would crash; 3) that the pilot's own conduct in violation of the FAA regulations was a superseding cause; and 4) that there was insufficient evidence of malice in order to convict him of the murder charge.

1) Was the defendant's act the "actual cause" of the victims' death 2) If so, was the defendant's act the proximate cause of the victims' death or did an intervening third party's negligence and recklessness relieve the defendant of liability?

Proximate cause can exist, even when a 3rd party's negligence and recklessness is an intervening cause, if the harm that results from the defendant's act is a likely consequence that might reasonably have been considered.

The threshold quest we must answer is whether the defendant's act was the "actual cause" of the victims' death. Unless the act is an actual cause of the injury, it will not be considered a proximate cause and our analysis stops here. That said, proximate cause can exist, even when a third party's negligence and recklessness is an intervening cause, if harm that results from defendant's act is a likely consequence that might reasonably have been considered. As we have said, "proximate cause" requires that an act be the "actual cause" of the injury. The applicable test for this is: but for the defendant's act would the injury have occurred? If the answer is "yes" it will be considered a proximate cause; if "no" it will not. Therefore, in order for Agosta to be held criminally liable for the victims' death, the deaths of the helicopter pilots must have been foreseeable. We believe that they were not. The standard for determining proximate cause excludes *extraordinary* results, and

People v. Acosta

Court of Appeal of California, 4th Appellate District, 284 Cal. Rptr. 117 (1991)

---

allows the trier of fact to determine the issue on the particular facts of the case using "the common sense of the common man as to common things." As with all other ultimate issues, appellate courts must give due deference to the trier of facts upon review. Here, but for Acosta's conduct of fleeing the police, the helicopters would never have been in position for the crash. Although a two helicopter crash is not known to have occurred, and no reported cases describe one, it was at least a possible consequence which reasonably might have been contemplated that one of the pursuers, in the heat of the chase, may act recklessly or negligently. Given these circumstances, a finding of proximate cause is appropriate. However, on the issue of malice, we find that there was not sufficient evidence to show that Acosta consciously disregarded the risk to the helicopter pilots.

 Therefore, the judgment is reversed.

People v. Arzon
Supreme Court, New York County, 401 N.Y.S.2d 156 (1978)

FACTS

Defendant Arzon was indicted for two counts of second degree murder after he allegedly intentionally set a fire to a couch on the fifth floor of an abandoned building on 358 East 8th Street in New York City. In an attempt to bring the fire under control, a fireman died after sustaining smoke-related injuries. A second, independent fire also broke out at the same time on the second floor, but there was no evidence that Arzon was responsible for it. Arzon was charged with murder in the second degree based upon a "depraved indifference to human life, recklessly engaged in conduct which created a grave risk of death to another person" and with felony murder. The third charge of the indictment is not at issue for purposes of the instant case. The smoke from the two fires created an extremely hazardous situation and contributed to the fireman's inability to safely escape the burning building shortly before his death. Arzon contends that the evidence before the grand jury is insufficient to support the first two charges in that murder requires a causal link between the underlying crime and death, which was lacking here.

 Must the defendant's conduct be the sole and exclusive factor in the victim's death in order to maintain the required causal link between the underlying crime and the resulting death, thus imparting criminal liability?

 A defendant's conduct need not be the sole and exclusive factor in the victim's death in order to maintain the required causal link between the underlying crime and the resulting death, so long as the conduct of a defendant is a sufficiently direct cause of the victim's death and the ultimate harm is something which should bee foreseen as being reasonably related to his act.

 A defendant's conduct need not be the sole and exclusive factor in the victim's death in order to maintain the required causal link between the underlying crime and the resulting death, thus imparting criminal liability. If the conduct of a defendant may be a sufficiently direct cause of the victim's death and the ultimate harm is something which should bee foreseen as being reasonably related to his acts, it is not necessary that the defendant's conduct be the sole and exclusive factor in the victim's death in order to maintain the required causal link between the underlying crime and the resulting death. In *People v. Kibbe*, an intoxicated robbery victim was abandoned by the side of the road by the thieves and was hit by a truck and died. In that case, there is a causal link in that the ultimate harm is something which should have been foreseen as being reasonably related to the acts of the accused. However, that is not to say that any obscure or merely probable connection between a defendant's conduct and another person's death is enough to support a charge of homicide. In *People v. Stewart*, a stabbing victim was operated on for the wound inflicted by the defendant, but the victim died from an unrelated hernia procedure performed by the surgeon after treating the stab wound. In that case, there

People v. Arzon
Supreme Court, New York County, 401 N.Y.S.2d 156 (1978)

---

is no causal link between the crime and the death, and the victim's estate must sue the doctor to recover. In the instant case, it did not matter that a second, intervening fire on the second floor contributed to the conditions which ultimately resulted in the death of the fireman. Certainly, it was certainly foreseeable that firemen would respond to the situation, thereby exposing them and others to the danger of death or severe injury. The fire set by the defendant formed an essential and indispensable link in the causal chain of events that resulted in the victim's death. Defendant is not absolved from criminal responsibility, motion to dismiss the murder counts of the indictment is denied.

Motion to dismiss denied.

People v. Warner-Lambert Co.

414 N.E.2d 660 (1980)

FACTS

Defendant Warner-Lambert Co. and several of its officers and employees were indicted for second degree manslaughter and criminally negligent homicide as a result of an explosion in a Warner-Lambert chewing gum factory. Warner-Lambert used two explosive substances, magnesium stearate (MS) and liquid nitrogen, in their manufacturing process. Warner-Lambert's insurance carrier issued a warning concerning the risk of explosion posed by high concentrations of magnesium stearate dust and other conditions, but the company failed to eliminate the hazards prior to the explosion. No firm cause of the explosion was evidenced, however, it was speculated that the explosion was triggered by a mechanical spark or by liquid nitrogen dripping onto the magnesium stearate and igniting under the impact of moving metal.

Does "but-for" causation [a/k/a legal causation] require that the defendant could have foreseen the immediate, triggering cause of the victim's injury or death?

The immediate, triggering cause of the injury must have been foreseeable to the defendant for his act to be considered the legal cause of the victim's injury or death.

The immediate, triggering cause of the injury must have been foreseeable to the defendant for his act to be considered the legal cause of the victim's injury or death. The People argue that the causal chain of physical events which started the explosion is extraneous; that it is enough that a defendant exposed his victim to the risk of death and that the victim in fact died. In essence, the People argue that all that is required to impose criminal liability on the defendant is but-for causation. We disagree. We have rejected the application of any such sweeping theory of culpability under our criminal law and hold that the defendant's actions must have been a sufficiently direct cause of the injury before there can be any imposition of criminal liability.

See Rule above.

People v. Campbell
Court of Appeals of Michigan, 335 N.W.2d 27 (1983)

FACTS

Defendant Campbell, who was drinking heavily with one Basnaw, encouraged the latter to commit suicide; Campbell was upset with Basnaw for having sex with his wife. Having been given Campbell's gun [by Campbell] and five shells, Basnaw later shot and killed himself. Consequently, Campbell was charged with murder in connection with the suicide. Campbell moved to quash the information and warrant and dismiss the proceedings on the ground that providing a weapon to one who uses it to commit suicide does not constitute murder, and, as such, he asserted that he should not be responsible for Basnaw's ensuing intentional act of suicide. The motion to quash was denied by the circuit court and the Court of Appeals granted leave for Campbell to appeal.

In order to extend criminal liability to a defendant for the murder of another, can the principle of foreseeability, used to establish causation, be applied to a situation where an 1) intentional, 2) subsequent, 3) human act 4) not of the defendant, is the cause of the victim's injury or death?

The principle of foreseeability is not to be used to establish causation where an 1) intentional, 2) subsequent, 3) human act 4) not of the defendant, is the cause of the victim's injury or death.

The principle of foreseeability is not to be used to establish causation where an intentional, subsequent, human act, not of the defendant, is the cause of the victim's injury or death. Homicide is defined at common law as "the killing of one human being by another." The prosecution urges that inciting one to commit suicide, coupled with an overt act, in this case furnishing the gun to an intoxicated person in a state of depression constitutes a "willful, deliberate and premeditated killing." We disagree and reject this argument because the term suicide excludes by definition a homicide, and the defendant here did not kill another person. We also find that there was no present intention to kill on the part of Campbell. He provided the gun and left, even though he unquestionably hoped that Basnaw would kill himself. The matter is reversed and case is remanded with instructions to quash the information and warrant and discharge Campbell.

Reversed and remanded.

People v. Kervorkian

Supreme Court of Michigan, 527 N.W.2d 714 (1994)

FACTS

Sherry Miller and Marjorie Wantz, two chronically ill women who were said to be in great pain, who gained the assistance of Defendant Dr. Jack Kevorkian in committing suicide by way of his "suicide machine." This machine essentially injects the user with lethal chemicals through IV tubing into the user's bloodstream when the *user* activates the machine. An IV needle needs to be manually inserted into the user's blood vessel for the device to work. Kevorkian successfully inserted the IV needle into one of the women, who did as instructed and died shortly thereafter. However, Kevorkian was unsuccessful in his attempts to inset the IV needle into the arm or hand of the other woman, so he instead strapped a mask onto her face which was connected to a cylinder of carbon monoxide and instructed her on how to release the gas by way of a lever he placed in her hand. The woman followed instructions and died of carbon monoxide poisoning. Kevorkian was subsequently indicted on two counts of murder, pled guilty and appealed.

Does the legal classification of murder included assisting another in a suicide?

The common law definition of murder does not include the intentional act of providing the means for another to commits suicide.

The common law definition of murder does not include the intentional act of providing the means for another to commits suicide. To convict a defendant of criminal homicide, it must be proven that the death occurred as a direct and natural result of the defendant's act. Few jurisdictions retain the common law view and many current statutes now treat assisted suicide as crime apart from murder. Recent decisions have drawn a distinction between active participation in the suicide and involvement in the events leading up to the suicide. Thus, defendant claims simply to have held the rifle while the decedent pulled the trigger. We agree with his position and hold that he may not be convicted of murder where he merely furnishes the weapon.

Remanded.

Stephenson v. State

Supreme Court of Indiana, 179 N.E. 633 (1932)

FACTS

Defendant Stephenson and several of his associates abducted the victim and subjected her to various acts of sexual perversion and physical torture over a period of several days. At some point, the victim was able to secretly buy and take six tablets of bichloride of mercury, a poison, in an effort to commit suicide and end her torment. Her attempt failed and she became violently ill. Defendant had her ingest milk and suggested that *he* take her to a hospital, *she* refused. Eventually he took her home where her parents sought medical attention for her. She died ten days later from a combination of shock, loss of food and rest, consumption of the poison, infection, and lack of early treatment. The jury convicted Stephenson of second-degree murder.

Does the deceased's own act of an intervening responsible agent [here her refusal to seek medical attention] break the causal connection between the defendant's act(s) [his abduction and torture] and her ultimate death, such that his act(s) were not the proximate cause of her death?

An intervening responsible agent breaks the causal connection between the defendant's act(s) and deceased ultimate injury or death, such that the defendant's act(s) are not the proximate cause of the deceased's injury or death thus precluding criminal liability unless a suicide or death follows either a physical or mental wound inflicted by the defendant and the victim was rendered irresponsible by such wound and as a natural result of it [in such a case his act is homicidal].

Stephenson contends that he cannot be guilty of murder since the victim's attempted suicide without his knowledge and of her own free will breaks the chain of causation between his acts and her death. Stephenson relies on *State v. Preslar,* where a husband was found not guilty of wife's murder where, following fight, the wife left their home and decided to spend the night outside her father's home until morning, but died later from exposure to the cold. The holding of this case is not controlling here. We conclude that when suicide follows either a physical or mental wound inflicted by the defendant, his act is homicidal if the victim was rendered irresponsible by such wound and as a natural result of it. Here, the victim was at all times enslaved by Stephenson and subjected to his custody, control, desire and will. She made many failed attempts to call for help and at the time she took the pills, she was very ill and weak due to her treatment at the hands of Stephenson and his associates. In light of the above, we simply cannot hold that there was no causal connection between the defendant's acts and the death of the victim. The record shows that it was Stephenson's own treatment of the victim which rendered her distraught and mentally irresponsible. Stephenson is guilty of murder in the second-degree as charged.

Judgment affirmed.

Commonwealth v. Root

Supreme Court of Pennsylvania, 170 A.2d 310 (1961)

FACTS

Defendant Root accepted a challenge by the deceased to race their respective automobiles. While both were racing, the deceased, in an attempt to overtake Root', crossed over the dividing line in a no-passing zone and drove on the wrong side of the highway at between 70 to 90 m.p.h. The deceased collided head-on with an oncoming truck and was killed. Both were exceeding the speed limit and driving recklessly. Root was found guilty of involuntary manslaughter for the death of his competitor and appeals his conviction on the ground that he did not cause the death of the decedent.

Do successive human conduct that is reckless and may result in possible harm or death break the chain of causation?

Subsequent human conduct that is reckless and may result in possible harm or death breaks the chain of causation.

If a person voluntarily chooses to engage in later conduct that is reckless and risky and may cause possible harm, injury or death to that person, the chain of causation will be broken and the defendant will not be criminally responsible for any harm to the individual. As such, hold that the proper standard to be applied in criminal cases is the direct causal connection, and not the proximate cause standard used in civil cases. In this case, in order to prove involuntary manslaughter, evidence must exist to prove that Root was driving in a reckless or unlawful manner and that his [Root's] unlawful or reckless conduct was the direct cause of the death of the decedent. There is clearly sufficient evidence to establish the first element; that Root was driving in a reckless or unlawful manner. However, the second element, that Root's unlawful or reckless conduct was the direct cause of the death of the decedent, has not been met. The conduct by the deceased was one brought upon by him alone. It was not forced upon him by Root. The deceased's own reckless conduct in driving his automobile is what brought about his death. Root's reckless conduct was not a sufficiently direct cause of the deceased's death to force upon him any criminally responsibility.

Reversed.

State v. McFadden

Supreme Court of Iowa, 320 N.W.2d 608 (1982)

FACTS

On a city street in Des Moines, Iowa in April of 1980, Defendant Michael Dwayne McFadden and Matthew Sulgrove were drag racing, the latter driver lost control of his car, swerved into oncoming traffic, collided with another vehicle and was killed. A six year old passenger in the oncoming vehicle was also killed in the collision. McFadden's car did not physically contact either vehicle. McFadden was charged with two counts of involuntary manslaughter and convicted on both counts. He appealed claiming proof of causation was lacking.

Does subsequent human conduct that is reckless and which risks future harm, break the chain of causation where the acts of both parties work to cause of the harm?

Subsequent human conduct that is reckless and which risks resulting harm does not break the chain of causation where the acts of both the defendant and the deceased were contributing and substantial factors in bringing about the deaths of the deceased or any others.

The fact that Sulgrove [the deceased] voluntary and recklessly participated in the drag race does not by itself relieve McFadden of criminal responsibility for his [Sulgrove's] death. The acts of McFadden were contributing and substantial factors in bringing about the deaths of others. Where the acts and omissions of two or more persons work concurrently to cause of an injury, each act is regarded as a proximate cause. We disagree with the defendant's contention that the trial judge erred in applying the civil standard of proximate cause to this case, rather than the direct causal connection used in *Commonwealth v. Root*. In *Root* the proximate cause principle was rejected in criminal cases in favor of more stringent direct causal connection standard. The element of proximate cause in criminal prosecutions serves as a requirement that there be a sufficient causal relationship between the defendant's conduct and a proscribed harm to hold him criminally responsible. We disagree with the defendant's contention that the trial court erred in applying a civil standard of proximate cause in a criminal prosecution. We simply do not see a justification for a different standard of proximate causation under criminal and civil matters – and the defendant has suggested no specific policy differences nor can we think of any. Proximate cause is based on the principle of foreseeability. The requirement of foreseeability encompassed within proximate cause, together with proof of recklessness, will prevent any harsh or unjust results in involuntary manslaughter cases.

Affirmed.

Commonwealth v. Atencio
Supreme Judicial Court of Massachusetts, 189 N.E.2d 323 (1963)

FACTS

On October 22, 1961, the deceased, one Stewart E. Britch, his brother Ronald and the defendants including Atencio (defendant-appellant) spent the day drinking in a rooming house in Boston. One of the individuals, Marshall, left the room only to return with a gun, from which he removed one bullet. Later that evening, the individuals played Russian Roulette. The gun was passed to one of the individuals and he pointed it at his head and pulled the trigger but nothing happened. The gun was given to Atencio and he did the same with the same result. However, when Atencio passed the gun to the deceased, who pulled the trigger, the gun fired and the deceased was killed. Atencio and others were convicted of manslaughter and thereafter motioned for directed verdicts. Their request was denied and they appealed.

 Does subsequent human conduct that is reckless and which risks future harm, break the chain of causation when the defendant participates in a joint enterprise with the victim or encourages, cooperates with or joins him in an activity which results in harm to the victim?

 Subsequent human conduct that is reckless and which risks future harm does not break the chain of causation when the defendant participates in a joint enterprise with the victim or encourages, cooperates with or joins him in an activity which results in harm to the victim.

 Subsequent human conduct that is reckless and which risks future harm does not break the chain of causation when the defendant participates in a joint enterprise with the victim or encourages, cooperates with or joins him in an activity which results in harm to the victim. We are of the opinion that the defendants could be properly found guilty of manslaughter based upon the existence of a mutual encouragement in a joint and reckless enterprise. The defendants were more than mere participants, and while they were under no duty to prevent the deceased from playing the game, there was a duty on their part not to cooperate or join with him in the game. Moreover, it is immaterial who took the gun and was the first to play the "game." Criminal responsibility would exist and attach had the deceased been the first one to play. The convicted defendants were much more than merely present at a crime. In Russian Roulette the outcome is certain, absent a misfire, if the chamber under the hammer happens to contain the one bullet loaded.

 Judgments affirmed.

Smallwood v. State
Maryland Court of Appeals, 680 A.2d 512 (1996)

FACTS

Defendant Smallwood was convicted by a non-jury trial of assault with intent to kill his rape victims based on the fact that he knew he was HIV positive and had been warned to practice safe sex. Smallwood challenged his conviction on the ground that just because he knew he was HIV positive and engaged in unprotected sex, without more, does not mean that it can be inferred that he also possessed a specific intent to kill. The most, he contended, that could be inferred from his conduct was that he acted with a reckless endangerment toward his victims. The State, on the other hand, argues that the facts of this case infer an intent to kill just as if he took aim and fired a loaded weapon at his victims. Smallwood appealed.

May the specific intent to kill be inferred from the defendant's conduct which poses a significantly heightened increase in the likelihood of death, though not a certain risk of death?

The specific intent required for a conviction for attempt may be inferred from the defendant's conduct <u>only</u> if the crime attempted was the natural and probable result of the defendant's conduct, and would have been achieved but for some impediment to its successful completion.

The specific intent to kill may not be inferred from the defendant's conduct which poses a significantly heightened increase in the likelihood of death, though not a certain risk of death. This is because the specific intent required for a conviction for attempt may only be inferred from the defendant's conduct if the crime attempted was the natural and probable result of the defendant's conduct, and would have been achieved but for some impediment to its successful completion. The State argues that Smallwood's conviction may stand based on *State v. Raines* which held that the intent to kill can be inferred from using a deadly weapon aimed at a vital part of the body. However, the *Raines* holding is misplaced as applied to the facts of this case. In Raines, the notion that death was the "natural and probable result of the defendant's conduct" was evident: defendant fired a pistol into the driver's side window of a tractor trailer and the shot killed the driver. The same inference cannot be made in this case when Smallwood risks infecting his victim with HIV because the virus may vastly increase the risk of death, but death is by no means certain to occur.

See Rule above.

People v. Rizzo
Court of Appeals of New York, 158 N.E. 888 (1927)

FACTS

Defendant-appellant Charles Rizzo and three others planned to rob Charles Rao of a payroll he was carrying to the bank valued at about $1,200. The four men, two of whom were armed, set out in an automobile to find Rao or the man who was carrying the payroll on that day. Rizzo claimed to be able to identify the man and was to point him out to the others who were to do the actual hold-up. They went to the bank and searched several buildings looking for Rao; but to no avail. By this time, they were watched and followed by two police officers. As When Rizzo jumped out of the car and went into a building, the four men were arrested. Neither Rao nor the man who was to actually carrying the payroll that day were in the building where the arrest took place; the four men neither saw nor found the man they intended to rob; no person carrying a payroll was present at any of the places where they had stopped; and no one had been pointed out or identified by Rizzo.

Do the various acts carried out by the accused constitute the crime of an attempt to commit robbery in the first degree?

For an act to constitute an attempt, it must come very near to the accomplishment of the crime.

How shall we apply this rule of immediate nearness to this case? To constitute the crime of robbery the money must have been taken from Rao by means of force or violence, or through fear. The crime of attempt to commit robbery was committed if Rizzo and the others did an act tending to the commission of this robbery. The target, Rao, was not found and those accused of the crime were still looking for him when they were arrested. No attempt to rob him could even be made until he came into sight. In short, Rizzo and the other men had planned to commit a crime and were looking around the city for an opportunity to commit it, but the opportunity never came.

Judgment of conviction of Rizzo must be reversed and a new trial granted.

McQuirter v. State

Alabama Court of Appeals, 63 So. 2d 388 (1953)

FACTS

Defendant-appellant McQuirter, a black man, was found guilty of attempt to commit an assault with intent to rape. The jury assessed a fine of $500. At about 8:00 p.m. on the night of June 29, 1951, McQuirter was sitting in his truck when Mrs. Ted Allen and her two children and a neighbor's child walked by. As they walked by, appellant said something unintelligible and got out and walked down the street behind them. Mrs. Allen stopped at a house along the way for ten minutes and waited for McQuirter to pass. After he did, she proceeded on and he came toward her from behind a telephone pole. She told her children to run to the Simmons' house and tell Mr. Simmons to come outside. When Simmons approached, McQuirter went down the street to an area across from Mrs. Allen's house. Mrs. Allen watched him there from the porch of the other house for thirty minuets, after which time he came back down the street and she went home. Chief of Police W.E. Strickland testified that McQuirter had confessed while in jail that he intended to rape Mrs. Allen. McQuirter denied making such statements and testified that he had merely been waiting for his friend, Bill Page, to return to the truck. He was convicted by a jury and subsequently appealed.

Can inferential evidence be used to prove an attempt to commit the underlying crime?

The intent to commit the underlying crime may be proven by inferential evidence to prove attempt.

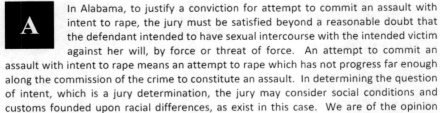

In Alabama, to justify a conviction for attempt to commit an assault with intent to rape, the jury must be satisfied beyond a reasonable doubt that the defendant intended to have sexual intercourse with the intended victim against her will, by force or threat of force. An attempt to commit an assault with intent to rape means an attempt to rape which has not progress far enough along the commission of the crime to constitute an assault. In determining the question of intent, which is a jury determination, the jury may consider social conditions and customs founded upon racial differences, as exist in this case. We are of the opinion that the evidence was sufficient to warrant the submission of the defendant's guilt to the jury, and there is ample evidence to sustain the judgment of conviction.

Affirmed.

United States v. Jackson
United States Court of Appeals, 560 F.2d 112 (2nd Cir. 1977)

FACTS

Beginning on June 11, 1976, Defendant Jackson, Scott, Allen and a female unindicted co-conspirator, Vanessa Hodges, planned the robbery of the Manufacturers Handover bank branch in Flushing, Queens, on June 14. After arriving at the bank on the specified date with masks and weapons, they aborted and rescheduled the heist for June 21 because they observed a number of bank patrons still inside the bank. Before the rescheduled date arrived, the female co-conspirator was arrested on unrelated charges and began cooperating with the Government. Hodges told them of the past, aborted attempt and the new date planned for the robbery. Lying in wait outside the bank on June 21, the police observed a car with three individuals which matched the descriptions given to them by the female informant. The car cased the street, and stopped for several minutes a few blocks away before finally parking closer to the bank. After thirty minutes, the car began moving closer towards the bank. At some point near the bank, the occupants of the car detected the FBI and police surveillance teams, but which overtaken by the law enforcement personnel before the three could exit the car and escape capture. All three, including Jackson, were arrested. A search of the car revealed two shotguns, a revolver, a pair of handcuffs, masks, and a license plate lying on the front floor of the car. Defendant Jackson, Scott and Allen were convicted of attempted robbery of a bank, as well as conspiracy. They appealed the convictions of attempted robbery on the ground that their conduct was mere preparation alone and did not rise to the level of attempt.

When does conduct which starts off as mere preparation for a crime cross the line and rise to the level of an attempt?

Conduct which constitutes a substantial step toward commission of the crime, and is strongly corroborative of the firmness of the defendant's criminal intent may establish attempt.

The trial judge found the appellants guilty as charged by applying the two-tiered inquiry of *United States v. Mandujano*: First, the defendant must have been acting with the kind of culpability otherwise required for the commission of the crime he is charged with attempting; and second, the defendant must have engaged in conduct which constitutes a substantial step toward commission of the crime which is strongly corroborative of the firmness of the defendant's criminal intent. The trial judge in this case concluded that on two occasions, Jackson and the others were seriously dedicated to the commission of a crime and would have assaulted the bank had they not been dissuaded by certain external factors: the breaking up of the weekend deposits and the number of bank patrons inside the bank on the first [June 14] attempt and detecting the FBI and the police on the second [June 21] attempt. The necessary weapons, handcuffs, mask and

United States v. Jackson
United States Court of Appeals, 560 F.2d 112 (2nd Cir. 1977)

other paraphernalia used in the commission of crimes were present on both occasions; material which could serve no lawful purpose other than to commit the intended crimes. Either type of conduct [taken from the two-tiered inquiry of *United States v. Mandujano,* above], standing alone, was sufficient as a matter of law to constitute a "substantial step" if it strongly corroboratedtheir criminal purpose. Here, both types of conduct, along with other elements, are strongly corroborative of the firmness of the appellants' criminal intents.

Affirmed.

State v. Davis
Supreme Court of Missouri, 6 S.W.2d 609 (1928)

FACTS

Defendant Davis was convicted of attempted first degree murder. The defendant and a married woman, one Alberdina Lourie, planned to kill the woman's husband in order to collect on his life insurance money. To facilitate the plane, Davis sought the help of one Earl Leverton, who in turn was to solicit an ex-convict to do the killing. Unfortunately for Davis and Lourie, Leverton told a police officer of the plot, and the officer decided to pose as the ex-convict. Davis paid the undercover officer money to kill the husband and discussed the plan for the killing, with Davis providing the undercover officer photographs, a drawing and partial payment. Davis was arrested at his home, was convicted and appealed. On appeal, he argued an insufficiency of evidence needed to sustain the conviction in that mere solicitation, without an act moving toward the commission of the intended crime, is not an overt act constituting an element of the crime of attempt.

 Does mere solicitation of a crime constitute attempt?

 Mere solicitation of a crime does not constitute attempt.

 The crime of attempt consists of 1) an endeavor or effort to do an act or accomplish a crime, 2) the performance of some act toward the commission of the crime 3) which carries beyond preparation, 4) but lacks execution. With respect to the second element, the physical overt act required for attempt is separate and apart from any solicitation or preparation; and the act must progress directly toward the commission of the completed offense. Solicitation is a crime is a separate crime from attempt such that merely soliciting one to commit a crime does not constitute an attempt. The State contends that the arrangement of the plan for accomplishment of the murder, together with the selection and hiring of the means to carry it out constitute overt act and not mere preparation. We disagree. The facts of the case do not show overt acts toward the commission of a crime. The verbal arrangement with the undercover police officer and the delivery of photographs, drawings and partial payment are simply acts of preparation; as were the acts of entering into a contract for hire and payment of money.

 Judgment reversed.

United States v. Church

29 Mil. J. Rptr. 679 (ct. Milit. Rev. 1989)

FACTS

Defendant-appellant Mr. Church, an airman stationed in North Dakota, began to talk about hiring a hit man to kill his wife after he realized he was unlikely to regain legal custody of his children. Alarmed, Church's associates reported his utterances to the authorities from the Office of Special Investigations (OSI). Thereafter, an undercover OSI agent posed a hit man and in a meeting between the two, Church provided the agent with a partial payment, expense money, maps, photos, approved the use of the specific type of weapon to be used [a .22 caliber pistol with a silencer] and all the information necessary to carry out the murder. After he was notified that his wife had been killed, Church met with the agent to tender the balance of the payment due. At that meeting, Church was then arrested, tried and convicted of attempted premeditated murder.

 May a person be convicted of an attempt to commit a crime when he solicits another to commit a crime?

 If the solicitation constitutes a substantial step toward commission of the crime, it may be punishable as an attempt.

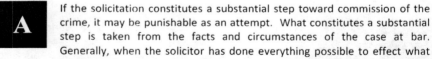 If the solicitation constitutes a substantial step toward commission of the crime, it may be punishable as an attempt. What constitutes a substantial step is taken from the facts and circumstances of the case at bar. Generally, when the solicitor has done everything possible to effect what he believes will be the commission of a crime, a substantial step has occurred. There is a split of authority in some jurisdictions as to what constitutes a substantial step. Some courts have held that the contracting out of a crime is mere preparation only, while others have upheld attempt convictions in cases involving crimes for hire. In this case, Church's hiring of the agent, his detailed participation in the planning of the crime, his approval of the type of weapon and method of execution, and his payment of the fee all constituted a substantial step toward commission of the crime. He was at the end, preparation had passed, all that was left to do was for the "hit man" to pull the trigger; there was nothing else Church could do to effect the murder of his wife.

 See Rule above.

People v. Jaffe
New York Court of Appeals, 78 N.E. 169 (1906)

FACTS

On October 6, 1902, Defendant Jaffe attempted to buy the property, consisting of 20 yards of cloth, believing it to have been stolen. However, when Jaffe actually attempted to buy it, the property had lost its status as stolen goods because it had been returned to its rightful owners and was being offered for sale to Jaffe through their authority and agency. Despite this, Jaffe was convicted of attempting to buy and receive stolen property. He appealed the conviction arguing that the completed act would not have constituted a crime and that he should not have been convicted of attempting to commit an act which would not have been criminal if completed. The Appellate Division affirmed the conviction and Jaffe appealed to New York's Court of Appeals.

Can the accused be convicted of an attempt to receive stolen property, believing the property to be stolen when it came into his possession, when in fact it was not?

A person cannot be convicted of an attempt to receive stolen property, believing the property was stolen when it came into his possession, when in fact it was not.

A person cannot be convicted of an attempt to receive stolen property, believing the property was stolen when it came into his possession, when in fact it was not. Some crimes, however, permit the accused to be convicted of an attempt even though certain facts were unknown to him which would have rendered the completed crime impossible. Examples include: Pickpockets who are convicted for attempt to commit larceny without the need to prove that there was anything in the pockets; and extortionists who are convicted even though they do not know that their intended victim is a decoy for the police, and thus could not be induced to pay the money by fear. What distinguishes these examples from the case at bar is the following: Here, the act would not have been a crime even if it had been consummated. Therefore, no matter what the defendant thought, or did, he could not commit the crime since the property itself was not stolen property. By contrast, if the pickpocket carried out the immediate act, it would have been criminal. Here, it does not matter if the act [of purchasing the goods] was carried out, it would still not have been criminal to do so. There simply can be no receiving of stolen good that have not been stolen. Here, his conviction cannot stand even though he possessed the requisite intent to commit a crime.

Judgment of the Appellate Division must be reversed.

People v. Dlugash

New York Court of Appeals, 363 N.E.2d 1155 (1977)

FACTS

On the night of December 21, 1973, Defendant Dlugash, Bush and Geller had been out drinking. On several occasions that evening, Geller demanded that Bush pay him $100 towards the rent because Bush had been staying at Geller's apartment. The drinking continued after they returned to Geller's apartment. Geller again made a demand for money from Bush, whereupon Bush aimed his .38 caliber pistol at Geller and shot him three times. After two to five minutes had passed, Dlugash took his own gun and shot Geller in the head and face approximately five times as Geller lay on the floor. Dlugash maintained that by the time he fired shots, it looked as if Geller was already dead. When questioned by the police, Dlugash initially maintained that he did not know why he shot Geller; he later remarked that it must have been because he was afraid of Bush. At trial, the prosecution sought to show that Geller was still alive at the time Dlugash shot him. However, there was conflicting medical testimony as to how long Geller lived after he was initially shot by Bush, if he was even still alive at the point Dlugash shot him. The trial court instructed the jury to decide whether Dlugash had either intentionally murdered Geller or had attempted to murder him. The jury found Dlugash guilty of murder. The Appellate Court reversed the conviction on the law and dismissed the indictment and held that the judgment could not be modified to reflect a conviction of attempted murder because there was evidence that Dlugash believed Geller to be dead at the time he shot him. The case was appealed to the New York Court of Appeals, the highest court in the state.

 Is a defendant guilty of attempted murder if he shoots his victim, believing him to be alive, when in fact he may have already died?

 In New York, a defendant is guilty of attempted murder if he shoots his victim, believing him to be alive, even though he may have already died.

 New York's statutory law does not recognize the defenses of legal and factually impossibility to the crime of attempt if the crime could have been committed had the circumstances been as the defendant believed them to be. Thus, under this statute, a person is guilty of an attempt when, with the intent to commit a crime, he engages in conduct which tends to effect the commission of the crime. Turning to the case at bar, if Dlugash believed Geller to be alive at the time he shot him, it is no defense that Geller may have already have been dead at the hands of Bush. The record shows that there is ample evidence from which the jury could have concluded that Dlugash believed Geller to be alive at the time he fired the shots into Geller's head. The jury convicted Dlugash of murder, so they necessarily must have found that he possessed the requisite intent to kill. Implicit within this finding is the conclusion that Dlugash believed that Geller was alive. It is immaterial whether or not Geller was actually alive that the point Dlugash shot him for the purposes of attempt; what matters is what Dlugash though at the time.

The Appellate Division erred in not modifying the judgment to reflect a conviction for attempted murder.

United States v. Berrigan
482 F.2d 171 (3rd Cir. 1973)

FACTS

Defendant Father Berrigan, a Roman Catholic priest and imprisoned Vietnam War resister, was convicted of attempting to violate a federal statute making it a crime to take anything in or out of prison "without the knowledge and consent" of the warden. At trial, the evidence showed that Berrigan had attempted to smuggle some letters out of the prison to one Sister McAlister through the use of a courier. Although Berrigan believed that the warden was unaware of his plan, the warden actually had prior knowledge of the scheme and agreed to let the courier pretend cooperation in the plan.

 Is legal impossibility a valid defense to a charge of attempt?

 The defense of legal impossibility pertains to a situation where the defendant intended to commit a criminal act, but the act committed is not illegal and does not amount to a criminal act.

 Legal impossibility is a valid defense to a charge of attempt. The defense of legal impossibility pertains to a situation where the defendant intended to commit a criminal act, but the act committed is not illegal and does not amount to a criminal act. Had the defendant attempted to send the letters through normal channels believing that it constituted a crime, he could not be punished because the proposed act was not a crime. If he attempted to send the letter without the knowledge and consent of the warden and the warden was oblivious to his plan, then Berrigan would be guilty of attempt. The facts of this case, however, are quite different. In this case, Berrigan intended to send a letter without the knowledge or consent of the warden, actually sent the letter, but unknown to him the letter was sent with the full knowledge and consent of the warden. The writing of the letter and their subsequent transmittal to the courier constituted the "Act." This "Act" is an indispensable component necessary for an attempt conviction. However, the statute also requires that the government prove that the warden lacked any knowledge of the letters and failed to give his consent for their transmittal by courier. Evidence of this so-called "objective component" was lacking in the government's case and they failed to prove otherwise. Without this evidence, there can be no violation of the statute.

 See Rule above.

United States v. Oviedo

525 F.2d 881 (5th Cir. 1976)

FACTS

Defendant Oviedo was approached by an undercover agent who asked to purchase heroin. At a later meeting between the two, Oviedo gave the agent what he claimed was heroin. The agent performed a field test which indicated the presence of heroin and Oviedo was arrested. Later on, when a second lab tests showed that the substance was not heroin but actually procaine hydrochloride, a <u>legal</u> substance, the prosecution charged Oviedo with <u>attempted</u> distribution of heroin. Oviedo claimed that he knew the substance was legal when he gave it to the undercover officer and was only trying to "rip him off." The jury, however, convicted him of the attempt charge.

May a defendant be convicted of an attempt to distribute what he believes are illegal drugs, but which in fact are legal?

In order for a defendant to be guilty of a criminal attempt, the objective acts performed, without any reliance on the accompanying *mens rea*, must indicate that the defendant's conduct was criminal in nature.

A defendant may not be convicted of an attempt to distribute what he believes are illegal substances, but which in fact are legal. In order for a defendant to be guilty of a criminal attempt, the objective acts performed, without any reliance on the accompanying *mens rea*, must indicate that the defendant's conduct was criminal in nature. Preliminarily, we reject the traditional distinction between factual and legal impossibility because it is not particularly helpful to the facts here, as it does nothing more than provide a different focus for the instant analysis. That is to say that Oviedo's acts can be framed as *either* involving factual impossibility or legal impossibility. For example, the defendant's acts implicate factual impossibility in that while the sale of heroin is illegal, his objective, the sale of the heroine, was not criminal only because he believed the substance was heroine when in fact it was not. This case can also be framed as one of legal impossibility because Oviedo's act of selling a legal substance was not a crime. When the defendant sells a substance which it actually heroin, it is reasonable to infer that he knew the physical nature of the substance. Thus, we place on him the burden of proving otherwise. However, where the substance is not in fact heroin, a major objective evidentiary element is eliminated, and we increase the risk of a mistaken conclusion that the defendant believed the substance to be heroin. Thus, we demand that in order for a defendant to be guilty of a criminal attempt, the objective acts performed, without any reliance on the accompanying *mens rea*, must indicate that the defendant's conduct was criminal in nature. Here, the acts do not implicate a criminal enterprise. Therefore, Oviedo's intent cannot form the sole basis of a conviction.

Conviction reversed.

The Case of Lady Eldon's French Lace
A hypothetical decision on a hypothetical state of Facts

FACTS

While traveling with her husband on the European continent, Defendant Lady Eldon bought what she thought was expensive French lace, subject to high duties if brought into England. In an attempt to smuggle it past English Customs, she hid the lace in a secret pocket. When she arrived at the English port of entry at Dover, a customs agent discovered the package. However, the lace was a fake, not French at all, but rather turned to be manufactured in England, of little value and not subject to duty.

Can an individual be convicted of the crime of attempt when she acts and believes she is committing a crime, even though her conduct under the circumstances does not amount to a crime?

A person can be convicted of attempt when her conduct *did not* constitute a crime under actual circumstances, but she believed that it did, and, but for her belief, what she set out to do would constitute a crime.

A person can be convicted of attempt when her conduct *did not* constitute a crime under the actual circumstances, but she believed that it did, and, but for her belief, what she set out to do would constitute a crime. We believe that Lady Eldon should be held criminally liable. We acknowledge that in some situations, a person's intent is determined by what they contemplated in their head and not by what they actually did. Hypothetically, had Lady Eldon actually purchased French lace believing it to be English face, she could not be found guilty of attempted smuggling because she would have lacked the requisite intent to smuggle *French* lace. So why shouldn't the same reasoning apply to the instant case? That is, judged by the same standard: what she believed she was doing, rather than what she actually did? The question may be answered as follows: innocent thoughts can exculpate, but a criminal mind should not inculpate. No legitimate purpose can be served by those who mean to act blamelessly, but society is served by punishing those who decide to commit a crime. However, here we are not punishing the bad thoughts of Lady Eldon because she both thought *and* acted – she *did* everything she *thought* was required to commit the crime. Thus, we conclude that Lady Eldon should be found guilty of attempt to smuggle. And while we concede that there are some genuine cases of legal impossibility whereby the defendant may validly raise the defense, no such situation exists here.

See Rule above.

Hicks v. United States

Supreme Court of the United States, 150 U.S. 442 (1893)

FACTS

Defendant John Hicks, a Cherokee Indian, was a friend to Andrew J. Colvard, a white man who was married to a Cherokee woman and lived in the Cherokee nation. On February 13, 1892, Hicks and Colvard were riding on horseback when they were confronted by Stand Rowe, another Cherokee Indian. During the conversation between the three, Stand Rowe was said to have twice raised his rifle at Colvard and to have twice lowered it. Witnesses said that they saw and heard Hicks laugh aloud each time Stand Rowe directed his rifle and aimed it at Colvard and also saw Hicks take off his hat, slap his horse with it, and say to Colvard, "Take off your hat and die like a man" at which point Stand Rowe then raised his rifle, took aim, and shot and killed Colvard. The witnesses further testified that they then saw Stand Rowe and John Hicks ride off together. Thereafter, Rowe was killed as officers tried to arrest him. Hicks was arrested, tried, and found guilty of the murder. At trial, Hicks testified in his own defense that he never encouraged or abetted Rowe to kill Colvard. Quite the contrary, he claimed to have tried to dissuade Rowe from shooting Colvard. Hicks also testified that he felt threatened by Rowe and that Rowe demanded Hicks show him the road Colvard traveled on; that after the murder he separated from the company of Rowe after a few minutes and never met with him again; and that he had never been in the company of Rowe for several weeks before the murder. The trial judge instructed the jury that it could convict the defendant if they found that the defendant's own words had the effect of enticing Rowe to kill Colvard. Hicks was convicted of murder and appealed to the United States Supreme Court.

 Can the accused be convicted of murder as an accomplice for speaking words that effectively encouraged the murder of another, even though the speaker lacked any intent to bring about such an effect?

 The accused cannot be convicted of murder as an accomplice for speaking words that effectively encouraged the murder of another when the speaker's words lacked any intent to bring about such an effect.

 The trial judge's instructions to the jury were in error. The judge's instruction was erroneous in two respects: 1) He failed to instruct the jury that any words or acts of Hicks must have been made with the intent of encouraging and abetting Stand Rowe; and 2) because the judge instructed the jury, in essence, that where an accomplice is present for the purpose of aiding and abetting in a murder, but refrains from doing so because it turned out not to be necessary for the accomplishment of the common purpose, he is equally guilty as if he did actively participate by acts or encouragements or words. With respect to the first erroneous part of the judge's instruction, we note that judge failed to instruct the jury that any words or acts of Hicks must have been made with the intent of encouraging and abetting Stand Rowe. The effect of Hicks' words devoid of any intent to kill on his

Hicks v. United States

Supreme Court of the United States, 150 U.S. 442 (1893)

---

part is immaterial. Thus, to be found guilty of murder, Hicks must have intended the words to have such an effect; however, Hick's alleged statement was ambiguous at best. According to his own testimony, Hicks claimed to have made the statement to Colvard, not to Rowe, because he [Hicks] feared for his life and was afraid that Rowe would shoot him. With respect to the second erroneous part of the instruction, we note that the judge's instruction would have been an otherwise proper instruction *if* there had been substantial evidence of a prior arrangement or conspiracy between Hicks and Rowe. The evidence does not indicate that there was. As actually instructed, the jury charge assumes that Hicks had a guilty intent, yet there was insufficient evidence that there was.

 The judgment of the Circuit Court below is reversed and the cause remanded for a new trial.

State v. Gladstone
Supreme Court of Washington, 474 P.2d 274 (1980)

FACTS

Douglas MacArthur Thompson, Robert Kent, and Defendant Bruce Gladstone were all students at the University of Puget Sound. Thompson was hired by the Tacoma Police Department to act as an informant to buy marijuana from Gladstone. Thompson visited Gladstone at his home, but Gladstone did not have any marijuana to sell him. Instead, Gladstone volunteered the name of another student, one Kent, as someone who had marijuana to sell. Gladstone gave Thompson Kent's address and drew him a map directing him to Kent's house. Thereafter, Thompson bought the marijuana from Kent. There was no evidence of any communication between Thompson and Kent concerning the marijuana. Subsequently, a jury found Gladstone guilty of aiding and abetting Kent in the sale of marijuana. Gladstone appealed.

Can a person be guilty of aiding and abetting where there is no nexus [connection or association] between the accused and the party he is charged with aiding and abetting in the commission of the crime?

A person cannot be guilty of aiding and abetting where there is no nexus [connection or association] between the accused and the party he is charged with aiding and abetting [the principal] in the commission of the crime.

The record contains no evidence whatsoever of an communication by word, gesture, or sign, before or after he drew the map, for which it can be inferred that he counseled, encouraged, hired, commanded, induced or procured Kent to sell the marijuana to Thompson. Gladstone was convicted based only on his conversation with Thompson regarding the possible sale of marijuana and nothing more. This evidence is insufficient; it does not establish that a crime was committed because a vital element, the so-called "nexus" between the accused and the party whom he is charged with aiding and abetting in the commission of a crime is missing. We emphasize that Gladstone was *not* charged with aiding or abetting *Thompson's* purchase of marijuana. An accomplice does not need to be physically present at the crime to be found as guilty as the principal so long as there is evidence that the accomplice in some way associated himself with the venture, or participated in it as in something that he wishes to bring about, or sought by his action to make it succeed. In this case, there is no such evidence of any association - Gladstone neither communicated with Kent before or after the sale expressing any indication that he would aid, encourage, or direct Kent in the sale of marijuana. Moreover, Gladstone is in no way the beneficiary of Kent-Thompson sale.

In light of the above, we reverse the judgment and remand with directions to dismiss.

People v. Luparello

California Court of Appeal, 231 Ca. Rptr. 832 (4th Cir. 1987)

FACTS

Defendant Luparello was devastated after his former lover, Teri, left him to marry someone else. Luparello thought he could discover her whereabouts from Mark Martin, who was a good friend of her current husband. To that end, Luparello enlisted the help of several of his friends to find Martin and to get the information about his former girlfriend's whereabouts at any cost. Luparello's friends paid Martin a visit, but they failed to get the requested information on her whereabouts. The next evening armed with a gun and a sword, Luparello's friends, without Luparello present, lured Martin outside and shot and killed him. Luparello was charged and convicted of first-degree murder based on aiding and abetting liability.

 Can an individual be convicted for murder for the unplanned and unintended act of his co-conspirators?

 An individual is liable for the unplanned and unintended acts of co-conspirators that are the natural, probable, and foreseeable consequences of his assistance.

 Luparello argues that the murder here was the unplanned and unintended act of a coconspirator and therefore not attributable to him. In support of this contention, he argues that the accomplice must share the perpetrator's intent in order to for the accomplice to be charged with the same offense. We disagree. The theory of accomplice liability does not require an identical intent, but "an equivalent *mens rea*." This is an important distinction defendant overlooks. The requirement of "an equivalent *mens rea*" allows liability to be expanded to include the actual crime committed, rather than the crime intended. The justification for this is grounded in the notion that an aider, abettor or co-conspirator should be held liable for the crimes that are the natural, probable, and foreseeable consequences of their acts. Thus, Luparello is vicariously liable and guilty not only of the offense he intended to facilitate, but also for any reasonably foreseeable offense committed by any person he aids and abets.

 The judgment is affirmed.

Roy v. United States
652 A.2d 1098 (D.C. Ct. App. 1995)

FACTS

Peppi Miller, a paid police informant, approached Defendant Roy in an attempt to make an undercover purchase of a handgun. Roy told Miller to return with $400.00, at which time Roy referred Miller to Ross, who he was told was the person who would sell him the gun. Ross gave Miller the gun, but then asked for it back, saying he changed his mind, and then robbed Miller of the $600 he was carrying. Roy was convicted as an accomplice to Ross's armed robbery. At trial, the judge instructed the jury that it could find Roy guilty if it concluded that the robbery was the natural and probably consequence of the illegal attempt to sell the gun, even if he [Roy] did not intend Ross to rob Miller. At the same time, however, the trial judge then invited the appellate court to review the issue. Roy was convicted and appealed his conviction.

If a person puts a criminal plan in motion, or intentionally assists in the commission of a crime, can the person be held responsible for the consequences of a second crime which could not be reasonably predicted from the first but was at least possible to occur?

A person may be held responsible for the criminal act of another, in an accessory liability context, when the criminal act was the natural and probable consequence of the crime; [the crime committed] must fall within a reasonably predictable range of possible outcomes, and likely to occur from the planned events without the interference of any intervening factors.

When a person puts a criminal plan in motion, or intentionally assists in the commission of a crime, he can the person be held responsible for the consequences of a second crime which could not be reasonably predicted from the first but was at least possible to occur. By invoking the "natural and probable consequences" theory, the government insists that we sustain Roy's convictions of armed robbery without requiring a showing that he intended to participate in the robbery of Miller. Armed robbery is a felony punishable by life imprisonment; selling a handgun is a misdemeanor of which Roy has been independently convicted. Were we to accept the government's application of the "natural and probable consequences" doctrine, we would thus allow the dramatic expansion of Roy's criminal liability even where he did not intend a crime of violence to be committed. This court has stated that "an accessory is liable for any criminal act which in the ordinary course of things was the natural and probable consequence of the crime that he advised or commanded, although such consequence may not have been intended by him." The phrase "in the ordinary course of things" refers to what may reasonably ensue from the planned events, not what might conceivably happen, and in particular suggests the absence of intervening factors. It is not enough for the prosecution to show that the accomplice knew or should have known that the principal might commit the offense which the accomplice is charged with aiding and abetting. More is required. A "natural and probable" consequence in the "ordinary course of

Roy v. United States
652 A.2d 1098 (D.C. Ct. App. 1995)

things" presupposes an outcome within a reasonably predictable range; not an outcome that is remote and attenuated. The evidence *might* support a finding that Roy should have known that the armed robbery was at least a possibility. However, the evidence was inadequate to prove that a robbery would follow in the "ordinary course of events," or that it was a "natural and probable consequence" of Roy actions.

Reversed.

State v. McVay

Supreme Court of Rhode Island, 132 A. 436 (1926)

FACTS

Defendants Kelley, McVay and Grant were crew members aboard the steamer *Mackinac,* a passenger ship. Kelley instructed the Captain, George W. McVay and engineer, John A. Grant, to depart despite his knowledge of the existence of a dangerous condition on board the vessel involving the ship's boilers. *En route* to Newport, the steamship's boilers exploded killing three people aboard. Grant and McVay were indicted for manslaughter, and Kelley as an accessory before the fact. Specifically, Kelly was indicted for "feloniously and maliciously aid, assist, abet, counsel, hire, command and procure" the captain and engineer to commit manslaughter. Kelley argued that a person could not be an accessory before the fact to manslaughter, because a manslaughter charge is "without malice" and "involuntary." His argument being that manslaughter is a sudden and unpremeditated crime, inadvertent and unintentional by its very nature and thus cannot be "maliciously" incited before the crime is committed. The issue was brought to the Rhode Island Supreme Court for certification before the trial began.

 May the accused be convicted of being an accessory before the fact to the crime of manslaughter arising through criminal negligence?

 A person may be convicted of being an accessory before the fact to the crime of manslaughter arising through criminal negligence.

 Kelley claims that because the captain and engineer were indicted on manslaughter charges without malice he cannot be incited indicted as an accessory before the fact for "feloniously and maliciously aid, assist, abet, counsel, hire, command and procure" the captain and engineer to commit manslaughter," a sudden and unpremeditated crime that is "inadvertent and unintentional." We cannot say that premeditation is inconsistent with every charge of manslaughter and not all charges of manslaughter involve unpremeditated acts - some include intentional unlawful acts that result in unintentional killing and some encompass an unintentional killing as a result of gross negligence stemming from lawful acts. There is no inherent reason why, prior to the commission of a crime, one may not aid, abet, counsel or command the doing of a lawful or unlawful act in a negligent manner. Here, the record alleges that Kelley intentionally directed and counseled the grossly negligent act that resulted in the crime. While he may not have consciously intended death to follow, the facts indicate that he knew the boiler was unsafe but negligently chose to disregard the risks and the possible results that could follow an explosion. The defendants' conduct was of a character that criminal intention could be inferred. It was both voluntary and intention in that the defendants exercised a choice among courses of conduct, with Kelley's participation, which resulted in the deaths of three persons.

State v. McVay
Supreme Court of Rhode Island, 132 A. 436 (1926)

The facts set forth in the indictment, if accurate, are such that a jury could find that Kelley acted with full knowledge of the possible danger to life and limb yet still ordered the captain and the engineer to operate the ship and take the risk that nothing would happen.

Thus, we answer in the affirmative the question certified on each indictment.

FACTS

On December 17, 1992, Defendant Russell and two other codefendants engaged in a gun battle on Center Mall in the Red Hook Housing Project in Brooklyn, New York. During the shootout, Patrick Daly, a public school principal and innocent bystander, was killed. The ballistics report was inconclusive as to which of the three defendants fired the fatal bullet that killed Daly. Consequently, the prosecution argued at trial that each of the three defendants acted with the mental culpability necessary for the commission of the crime, and that each intentionally aided the one who fired the fatal shot. All three defendants were convicted of second degree, depraved indifference murder; all three appealed on grounds of insufficient evidence necessary to sustain the conviction.

Where one than one defendant is engaged in a gun battle that results in the death of an innocent party, may the State hold each defendant individually responsible for the homicide when it is unclear which defendant's gun fired the single fatal shot?

When the evidence is sufficient to establish that each defendant acted with the mental culpability required for the commission of depraved indifference murder and that each defendant intentionally aided the defendant who fired the fatal shot, then prosecution is not required to prove which defendant fired the single fatal shot.

When the evidence is sufficient to establish that each defendant acted with the mental culpability required for the commission of depraved indifference murder and that each defendant intentionally aided the defendant who fired the fatal shot, then prosecution is not required to prove which defendant fired the fatal shot. Defendant Russell argues that the prosecution's evidence introduced at trial did not support a finding that all three defendants shared the "community of purpose" necessary for accomplice liability as they were adversaries in a deadly gun battle. We disagree. The fact that Russell and the others set out to injure or kill one another does not rationally preclude a finding that they intentionally aided each other to engage in the mutual combat that caused Daly's death. In *People v. Abbott,* the two defendants were drag racing and were later found guilty of criminally negligent homicide when an innocent man was killed by one of them during the race. The *Abbott* Court held that each defendant's intentional participation in an inherently dangerous activity mandates that they share culpability since the activity is not possible without the participation of each defendant. Here, in the present case, the jurors were instructed: "If you find that the People have proven beyond a reasonable doubt that defendants took up each other's challenge, shared in the venture and unjustifiably, voluntarily and jointly created a zone of danger, then each is responsible for his own acts and the acts of the others . . . [and] it makes no difference [whose bullet] penetrated Mr. Daly and caused his death." This was a proper instruction. There was adequate proof to justify the finding that the three defendants tacitly agreed to engage in a gun battle that placed the life of any innocent bystander at

People v. Russell
Court of Appeals of New York, 693 N.E.2d 280 (1998)

---

grave risk and ultimately killed Daly. Indeed, unlike an unanticipated ambush or spontaneous attack that might have taken defendants by surprise, the gunfight in this case only began after defendants acknowledged andaccepted each other's challenge to engage in a deadly battle on a public concourse. The evidence adduced at trial was also sufficient for the jury to determine that Russell and the other defendants acted with the mental culpability required for depraved indifference murder, and that they intentionally aided and encouraged each other to create the lethal crossfire that caused the death of Patrick Daly.

 Affirmed.

Wilcox v. Jeffery
King's Bench Division 1 All E.R. 464 (1951)

FACTS

Coleman Hawkins, an American citizen and celebrated professor of the saxophone, was invited by two gentlemen, Curtis and Hughes, to perform a concert at a jazz club in England. Curtis and Hughes applied for permission for Hawkins to "land" (permission allowing travel or passage; permission to be in the country) as required by law, which was refused, but Hawkins nevertheless went to England with four other musicians. Defendant Wilcox, who had no part in bringing the musicians to England, was at the airport when they arrived and was to report their arrival for the jazz magazine he wrote for. Wilcox, along with many others, bought a ticket and attended the concert. He then wrote a most admiring description of the concert in his magazine.

 Can the accessed by charged and successfully prosecuted for the crime of aiding and abetting by merely being present at an illegal concert performance?

 Physical presence and payment to attend an illegal performance can constitute aiding and abetting the criminal act.

 Wilcox was not present at the concert accidentally. He paid for at ticket and went to go to went there because he wanted to report it for his magazine. Hawkins was playing performing the concert illegally; and Wilcox clearly knew of that fact. Since Wilcox had gone there to hear Hawkins and to report on the concert, his (Wilcox's) presence and payment to attend provided encouragement for Hawkins to be there and perform. Wilcox must, therefore, be held to have been present, taking part, concurring or encouraging. He went there to make use of the performance to help sell his magazine. Under these circumstances there was evidence on which the magistrate could find that Wilcox aided and abetted.

 For the above reasons, I am of the opinion that the appeal fails.

State ex. rel. Attorney General v. Tally, Judge
102 Ala. 25 (1894)

FACTS

Ross seduced Defendant Judge Tally's sister-in-law. The sister-in-law's brothers, the Skelton brothers, followed Ross to the nearby town of Stevenson to kill him. While at the local telegraph office, Tally learned that one of Ross's relatives telegrammed him warning him of the impending danger. In response, Tally sent his own telegram to the telegraph Operator in Stevenson, who he knew, telling him not to deliver the telegram to Ross. The operator did not deliver the warning and Ross was killed. The court found Tally to be an accomplice to murder and removed him from the bench. Judge Tally appealed.

 Can a defendant be convicted as an accomplice to a crime when, but for the defendant's intervention, the crime may not have been committed?

 A defendant who assists a murder by destroying an opportunity for the victim to escape harm is guilty as an accomplice; and will still be held guilty as an accomplice even if 1) he facilitated the harm that would have occurred without his intervention; or 2) he renders it easier for the principal actor to accomplish the harm but it was later found that the victim would not have escaped and the death would have resulted anyway.

 It must be shown that his Judge Tally's actions to prevent Ross from being warned aided the Skelton brothers in killing Ross, thus contributing to his death, before the Judge can be found guilty of aiding and abetting the murder of Ross. The assistance given, however, need not contribute to the criminal result in the sense that but for it the result would not have ensued. It is quite sufficient if it facilitated a result that would have transpired without it. It is quite enough if the aid merely renders it easier for the principal actor to accomplish the end intended by him and the aider and abettor, though the end would have been attained without it. If the aid in homicide can be shown to have put the deceased at a disadvantage, to have deprived him of a single chance of life, he who furnishes such aid is guilty though it cannot be known or shown that the dead man, in the absence thereof, would have availed himself of that chance. If the aid can be shown to have put the deceased at a disadvantage or if the aid destroyed an opportunity for the victim to escape which he might otherwise have had, that facilitator will be guilty as an accomplice even though it may be found that the victim would not have escaped the principal and his death would have resulted anyway.

 Affirmed.

State v. Hayes

Supreme Court of Missouri, 16 S.W. 514 (1891)

FACTS

Defendant Hayes proposed to one Hill that the two rob a general store. Unknown to Hayes, Hill actually happened to be a relative of the store's owners. Hill feigned cooperation with Hayes, but warned the store's owners about the plan. On the night of the planned burglary, the store's owners arrived at their store, Hayes opened a window and helped Hill inside the building at which point Hill picked up a side of bacon and handed it out to Hayes. Afterward, they were arrested. Hayes was convicted of burglary and larceny, and he appealed.

 Can an accomplice be held criminally liable if the principal lacked criminal intent?

 An accomplice cannot be held criminally liable if the principal lacked criminal intent.

 The trial court charged the jury in its instruction to find Hayes guilty of burglary if he possessed a felonious intent and assisted and aided Hill to enter the building, irrespective of Hill's own intent. This instruction was erroneous. Hill did not enter the store with an intent to steal; his intent was intent to entrap Hayes. Hill's act was not a criminal act, yet it became criminal when it was attributed to Hayes because of Hayes's felonious intent. Hill's act was may have been a criminal act if he [Hill] was a passive and submissive agent who was acting under the control and compulsion of Hayes. However, Hill was working with Hayes on his own free will, as an active agent, with the intent to entrap Hayes and have him captured. Hayes did not commit the crime of burglary because he did not enter the building and because both parties did not share the same intent. To make Hayes responsible for Hill's breaking and entry, both defendants must have had a "common motive and scheme." They did not. In fact, their motives were not only distinct and dissimilar, but antagonistic. The court should instruct the jury that if Hill broke into and entered the warehouse with a felonious intent, and Hayes was present aiding him but with no intent to steal and without entering the room himself, then he [Hayes] cannot be guilty of burglary and larceny as charged.

 The judgment is reversed, and the case remanded for a new trial.

Vaden v. State
768 P.2d 1102 (Alaska 1989)

FACTS

After receiving a tip that Defendant Vaden, a local guide, was promoting illegal hunting to his customers, Fish and Wildlife Protection officers send an undercover agent, John Snell, to pose as a hunter and commission Vaden's services. Snell sought Vaden's assistance in illegally hunting foxes. Vaden agreed. As part of the hunt, Vaden piloted a helicopter from which Snell shot four foxes. Vaden was convicted as an accomplice to the illegal taking of foxes from an aircraft and as an accomplice for hunting during closed season, in violation of Alaska law. Vaden appealed arguing that he could not be an accomplice because his action was justified in light of the needs of law enforcement (the "public authority justification defense" - which justifies the actions of a law enforcement officer who commits a crime).

 Can the public authority justification defense be used by an accomplice as a valid defense arguing that, in essence, no criminal action occurred for which he could be convicted of?

 The public authority justification defense is personal to law enforcement officers and cannot be used by an accomplice to argue that no crime was committed thereby precluding criminal liability.

 Under the "public authority justification defense," the fact that a party's actions are justified in light of the needs of law enforcement does not mean that no criminal action transpired to which accomplice liability can be imposed. Here, we feel that Snell's actions were not, in fact, justified. However, even if they were, the defense is not available to him because the justification would be personal to *Snell* and not personal to law enforcement.

 Affirmed.

New York Central Hudson R.R. Co. v. United States

Supreme Court of the United States, 212 U.S. 481 (1909)

FACTS

Fred L. Pomeroy, an employee of Defendant New York Central and Hudson River Railroad Company paid illegal rebates to the American Sugar Refining Company for using railroad company's lines to ship its sugar. Under this arrangement, the railroad company would ship the sugar between New York and Detroit at a "reduced rate" instead of the published rate. These rebates were illegal under the Elkins Act, a federal statute. As a consequence, the railroad and Pomeroy were convicted under the statute. The railroad company appealed the conviction arguing that the statute was unconstitutional because a corporation cannot be held criminally liable for the actions of its employees.

 Can a corporation be held criminally liable for the acts of its employees?

 A corporation can be held criminally liable for the acts of its employees.

A The railroad company argues that the statute is unconstitutional because by holding a corporation liable for criminal prosecution, any punishment imposed would actually punish innocent stockholders and deprive them of their property in violation of due process of law. We disagree. While the common law held that corporations were excluded from criminal liability, the modern authority, so far as we know, states the contrary. It recognizes that corporations commit crime and allows for their punishment. It is now well established that a corporation can be held liable in tort for the damages caused by the acts of one or more of its agents acting within the scope of his employment. Since a corporation acts by its officers and agents, their purposes, motives, and intent are just as much a part of the corporation as those things done. The logic is as follows: If the officer or agent is acting to benefit the principal, and the principal here is a corporation, then if the conduct is criminal, the corporation must be held criminally liable for the acts. The record indicates that payment of rebates by its agents and officers benefited the corporation, that such rebates were illegal, and that because the statute can be effectively enforced against the agents and officers, so may the corporation be held liable. We find "no valid objection in law, and every reason in public policy" why a corporation cannot be held liable for the actions and intent of its agents who were authorized to act on behalf of the corporation and who actions monetarily benefited the corporation. Thus, to give corporations immunity would virtually take away the only means of effectually controlling the subject matter and correcting the abuses aimed at.

R Judgment affirmed.

United States v. Hilton Hotels Corp.

U.S. Court of Appeals, 467 F.2d 1000 (9th Cir. 1972)

FACTS

Operators of hotels, restaurants, and hotel and restaurants supply companies ("suppliers"), including Defendant-appellant Hilton Hotels Corporation ("Hilton"), organized an association in Portland, Oregon to attract conventions to their city. To finance the association, hotel members allegedly agreed to give preferential treatment to and buy their supplies from suppliers who paid contributions to the association and curtail purchases from those suppliers who did not contribute. In return, the suppliers agreed to contribute an amount equal to 1% of their sales to hotel members. This agreement was a *per se* violation of the Sherman Antitrust Act. Hilton's president testified that such boycotts were contrary to the policy of the corporation and Hilton's manager of the Portland hotel testified that supply purchases were made solely on the basis of quality, price, and service. Hilton's purchasing agent confirmed the receipt of these instructions but nevertheless admitted threatening a supplier with a boycott unless the supplier paid the association's assessment "because of [his] anger and personal pique toward the individual representing the supplier." The court instructed the jury that a corporation can be held liable for the acts and statements of its agents, made within the scope of employment on behalf of the corporation regardless, even if the agent's conduct was in violation of specific instructions or the corporation's stated policies. Hilton was convicted under the Sherman Act (the"Act") and appealed.

Can a corporation be held liable for the acts of its agents, acting within the scope of their employment, even if the corporation's policy and specific instructions prohibited such acts?

A corporation can be held liable for the acts of its agents, acting within the scope of their employment, even if the corporation's policy and specific instructions prohibited such acts.

Congress may constitutionally impose criminal liability on a corporation for the acts of its agents acting within the scope of their employment. Liability may attach without proof that the conduct was within agent's actual authority even though the actions may have been contrary to express instructions. The text of the Sherman Act does not expressly address this issue, however, we believe that the construction of the act that best achieves its purpose is that a corporation is liable for the acts of its agents within the scope of their authority even when don against company orders. Since violations of the Sherman Act are predominantly commercial violations, motivated by the desire to maximize profits, they often involve large and highly decentralized corporate business practices which are delegated. Under such a structure, it is often difficult to identify specific corporate agents who violated the Act and their conviction and punishment is particularly ineffective as a deterrent. Moreover, a violation of the Act usually means that the corporation, and not the individual agents, will have realized the profits stemming from

United States v. Hilton Hotels Corp.

U.S. Court of Appeals, 467 F.2d 1000 (9th Cir. 1972)

the illegal activity such that conviction and punishment of the business entity itself is likely to be both appropriate and effective. For these reasons, we conclude that as a general rule a corporation can be liable under the Sherman Act for the acts of its agents within the scopeof their employment even when the corporation has a stated policy and has given instructions to the employees opposing the acts they were accused of violating.

Judgment affirmed.

Commonwealth v. Beneficial Finance Co.
Supreme Judicial Court of Massachusetts, 275 N.E.2d 33 (1971)

FACTS

Three defendants, two employees of Beneficial Finance Company ("Beneficial") as well as the company itself were held criminally liable for bribery and conspiring to bribe state banking officials in order to receive favorable treatment from the State Small Loans Regulatory Board. One of the employees, Farrell, was an officer and director of a wholly owned subsidiary of Beneficial; while the other employee, Glynn, was a lower level employee of another wholly owned subsidiary of Beneficial but reported to Farrell. Beneficial argued that the corporation should not be held criminally liable for their acts unless their conduct was "performed, authorized, ratified, adopted or tolerated by the corporation's directors, officers or other 'high managerial agents' who are sufficient high in the corporate hierarchy to [impart liability to the corporation]." The trial court instructed the jury to find Beneficial guilty if it had placed the employees in a position where they had enough authority and responsibility to act for and on behalf of the corporation in handling the particular corporate matter and committed the criminal act in furtherance of that particular corporate matter. All three defendants were found guilty of bribery and conspiring to bribe. Beneficial appealed.

 Can a corporation be held criminally responsible for the acts of its agents or officers, if either or both have the authority to act for and on behalf of the corporation and either or both committed a crime(s) while engaged in corporate business?

 A corporation can be held criminally liable for the acts of its agents if it is shown that the corporation placed the agent in a position where he has enough authority and responsibility to act for and on behalf of the corporation in handling the particular corporate business, operation or project in which he was engaged at the time he committed the criminal act.

 Beneficial argues that corporate criminal liability should be determined under the standard set by the Model Penal Code (the "MPC"), where the criminal acts of agents can be imputed to the corporation if the conduct was "performed, authorized, ratified, adopted or tolerated by the corporation's directors, officers or other 'high managerial agents.'" By contrast, the trial court instructed the jury that liability may be found if Beneficial placed its employees in a position where they had enough authority and responsibility to act for and on behalf of the corporation in handling the particular corporate matter and committed the criminal act in furtherance of that particular corporate matter. We note the differences: The MPC approach refers to a "high managerial agent" and imposes liability when it appears that its directors or high managerial agents "authorized ... or recklessly tolerated" the allegedly criminal acts. The judge's instructions, on the other hand, focus on the authority of the corporate agent in relation to the particular corporate business in which the agent was engaged. In either case, the key issue is whether the acts and intent of the corporation's agents can be treated as the acts and intent of the corporation itself. It is our opinion that the Model Penal Code approach inadequately

Commonwealth v. Beneficial Finance Co.

Supreme Judicial Court of Massachusetts, 275 N.E.2d 33 (1971)

handles the evidentiary problems associated with proof needed to establish the guilt of directors or officers. Evidence of the authorization or ratification of criminal acts is often easily concealed. Moreover, in large corporations, lower ranking corporate employees are often delegated considerable authority to deal with specific matters within their sphere of expertise as it relates to the everyday operations of the corporation. In such a situation, a high ranking officer or agent may have not authority or involvement in such a corporate activity precisely because the activity is specialized and/or deals with the everyday operations of the company by a lower-ranking employee. In consideration of these issues, we conclude and propose the following test: A corporation can be held criminally liable for the acts of its agents if it is shown that the corporation "placed the agent in a position where he has enough authority and responsibility to act for and on behalf of the corporation in handling the particular corporate business, operation or project in which he was engaged at the time he committed the criminal act." In this case, the judge's instruction was proper; there was sufficient evidence to support a finding that the employees of the corporation had sufficient authority to act on behalf of company in dealing with the state officials who were bribed and the judge correctly stated that this standard does not depend upon the responsibility or authority which the agent has with respect to the *entire* corporate business, but only to his position with relation to the *particular* business in which he was serving the corporation.

Judgment affirmed.

Gordon v. U.S.

U.S. Court of Appeals, 203 F.2d 248 (10th Cir. 1953)

FACTS

Defendant Gordon was one partner in a sewing machine and appliance business and was convicted of violating the Defense Production Act, a federal law which prohibited the sale of sewing machine on credit terms prohibited by the act and according to the regulations issued thereunder. Unknown to the defendant, certain salespersons of his made sewing machine sales without collecting a down payment. Consequently, Gordon and his partners, along with the salespersons directly involved with the sale, were charged with violating the statute. At trial, the jury was instructed that it may find Gordon and his partners guilty on the theory that the knowledge of any one partner, agent or employee was "imputable, attributable and chargeable" to Gordon and his partners personally. Gordon and his partners were convicted; they subsequently appealed.

 Can an employer, without knowledge of the act of his employee(s), be held criminally liable for the latter's willful criminal act committed within the course and scope of his [the employee's] employment?

 An employer, even without knowledge of the acts of his employee(s), can be held criminally liable for the latter's willful criminal act committed during the course and scope of employment.

 Willfulness is a specific prerequisite to guilt, such that the statute before us and at issue requires willfulness as an element of the offense. The concept of *men rea*, or guilty mind, here "willfulness" is an indispensable element of any punishable offense deeply rooted in our criminal jurisprudence. Here, the trial court charged the employers with indirect responsibility, so-called constructive knowledge of the illegal acts; sometimes referred to as vicarious responsibility. The defendant-partners, including Gordon, had a duty and a responsibility to run their business lawfully placed upon them by the law. This duty does not exist in isolation, but extends to their employees as well, such that their [the partners] constructive knowledge of the illegal acts [of the employees] could be construed by a trier of fact as voluntary and deliberate, hence intentional or as negligent, inadvertent, thus excusable. Since the jury instructions were proper, this is an issue properly left to the jury.

 Judgment affirmed.

United States v. Park
Supreme Court of the United States, 421 U.S. 658 (1975)

FACTS

Acme Markets, Inc. (Acme), a large national food chain, and Defendant-respondent John Park, its President and CEO, were charged with violating 301(k) of the Federal Food, Drug, and Cosmetic Act (Act) alleging that they had caused interstate food shipments being held in Acme's Baltimore warehouse to be exposed to rodent contamination. Acme pleaded guilty; Park pleaded not guilty. At his trial respondent conceded that providing sanitary conditions for food offered for sale to the public was something that he was "responsible for in the entire operation of the company," and that it was one of the many phases of the company that he assigned to "dependable subordinates." Evidence was admitted over respondent's objection that he had received a Food and Drug Administration (FDA) letter in 1970 concerning unsanitary conditions at Acme's Philadelphia warehouse. Respondent conceded that the same individuals were largely responsible for sanitation in both Baltimore and Philadelphia, and that as Acme's president he was responsible for any result that occurred in the company. The trial court, *inter alia*, instructed the jury that although respondent need not have personally participated in the situation, he must have had "a responsible relationship to the issue." Respondent was convicted, but the Court of Appeals reversed, reasoning that although this Court's decision in *United States v. Dotterweich*, had construed the statutory provisions under which respondent had been tried to dispense with the traditional element of "'awareness of some wrongdoing,'" the Court had not construed them as dispensing with the element of "wrongful action." The Court of Appeals concluded that the trial court's instructions "might well have left the jury with the erroneous impression that [respondent] could be found guilty in the absence of 'wrongful action' on his part," and that proof of that element was required by due process. The court also held that the admission in evidence of the 1970 FDA warning to respondent was reversible error. The U.S. Supreme Court granted certiorari.

Can a corporate officer be held criminally liable predicated solely upon a showing that he was the President of the offending corporation and without proof of the "responsible relationship" requirement of *United States v. Dotterweich?*

A corporate officer can be held criminally liable, without proof of any wrongful act on his part, if the officer was in a position of authority and responsibility to prevent or correct the criminal violation.

The Act imposes upon persons exercising authority and supervisory responsibility vested in them by a business organization not only a positive duty to seek out and remedy violations, but also a duty to implement measures that will insure that violations will not occur. In order to make food distributors "the strictest censors of their merchandise," *Smith v. California*, the Act punishes "neglect where the law requires care, or inaction where it imposes a duty," *Morissette v. United States*. Viewed as a whole and in context, the trial court's

United States v. Park
Supreme Court of the United States, 421 U.S. 658 (1975)

instructions were not misleading and provided a proper guide for the jury's determination. The charge adequately focused on the issue of respondent's authority respecting the conditions that formed the basis of the alleged violations, fairly advising the jury that to find guilt it must find that respondent "had a responsible relation to the situation"; that the "situation" was the condition of the warehouse; and that by virtue of his position he had "authority and responsibility" to deal therewith. The admission of testimony concerning the 1970 FDA warning was proper rebuttal evidence to respondent's defense that he had justifiably relied upon subordinates to handle sanitation matters.

 Judgment of the court of appeals is reversed.

United States v. MacDonald & Watson Waste Oil Co.
United States Court of Appeals, 933 F.2d 35 (1st Cir. 1991)

FACTS

Defendant Eugene K. D'Allesandro was the president of the MacDonald & Watson Waste Oil Company, (the "Company"), a small waste disposal and transportation corporation. The Company, also a defendant in this case, operated a disposal facility which was authorized to dispose of *liquid* wastes only. The Company was hired to remove some *solid* waste from the Grounds of the Master Chemical Company. An employee of the Company supervised the transportation of that material [the solid waste] to the disposal facility in violation of the Resource Conservation and Recovery Act (RCRA), §3008(d)(1). This section of the Act provides penalties to those who knowingly transport, or cause to be transported, hazardous waste to a facility without a permit. The government charged D'Allesandro and the Company with violating RCRA, and presented evidence that D'Allesandro was not only the President and owner of the Company, but that he was a "hands-on" manager; that his subordinates had contracted for the transportation and disposal of the solid waste and that D'Allesandro was guilty of violating §3008(d)(1) whether he had actual knowledge of it or not because he was the responsible corporate officer and was in a position to ensure compliance but failed to do so even after he had been warned on two prior occasions that other shipments of the same type of solid waste had been disposed of without the proper permit. The jury was instructed, inter alia, that they could convict D'Allesandro without finding that he had actual knowledge of the transportation of the sold waste in violation of the statute. The Company and D'Allesandro were both convicted of violating the statute. The Company appealed.

Can a corporate officer be held criminally liable under the responsible corporate officer doctrine when the statute is devoid of any applicable strict liability requirement?

A corporate officer cannot be held criminally liable under the responsible corporate officer doctrine if the statute is devoid of a strict liability requirement; however, he can be convicted based on the *mens rea* requirement of the statute.

We agree with the defendant that the jury instructions were in error when they allowed the jury to convict D'Allesandro without finding that he had actual knowledge of the illegal transportation of solid waste. In *Dotterweich* and *Park*, the Court dispensed with a scienter requirement and established criminal liability for the violation of a statute could be found without a showing of express knowledge. However, those cases involved misdemeanor charges and dealt with public welfare statutes. No such precedent for ignoring a scienter requirement exists here - where Congress has expressly included one in a criminal statue. Moreover, this is especially relevant where the crime is a felony carrying the possibility of imprisonment of 5 years and for a second offense, 10 years, as we see here. The trial court's jury instruction was correct with respect to the inference of knowledge; that is,

United States v. MacDonald & Watson Waste Oil Co.
United States Court of Appeals, 933 F.2d 35 (1st Cir. 1991)

---

that the jury may infer "willful blindness" based on the circumstantial evidence of the case. Its instruction was also correct in that the jury may find that D'Allesandro's was a "responsible corporate officer" and that definitive proof that he had the "knowledge" required for conviction under the statute was sufficient. However, simple knowledge is not an adequate substitute for direct and circumstantial proof of knowledge as an express element, as required by the Act.

 The conviction is vacated and remanded for a new trial.

Krulewitch v. United States
Supreme Court of the United States, 336 U.S. 440 (1949)

FACTS

Krulewitch and a woman defendant were indicted by a federal district court which charged in three counts that they had (1) induced and persuaded another woman to go on October 20, 1941, from New York City to Miami, Florida, for the purpose of prostitution, in violation of 18 U.S.C. 399 (now 2422); (2) transported or caused her to be transported from New York to Miami for that purpose, in violation of 18 U.S.C. 398 (now 2421); and (3) conspired to commit those offenses in violation of 18 U.S.C. 88 (now 371.) Tried alone, the petitioner was convicted on all three counts of the indictment. The Court of Appeals affirmed. The U.S. Supreme Court granted certiorari limiting our review to consideration of alleged error in admission of certain hearsay testimony.

May hearsay evidence be admitted at trial when it relates to an alleged, implied, but uncharged conspiracy to avoid criminal punishment?

A statement made in furtherance of an implied conspiracy to conceal a conspiracy, is not admissible under the hearsay rule.

Although the Government recognizes that the chief objective of the conspiracy, the transportation of the complaining witness to Florida for prostitution, had ended before the reported conversation took place, it nevertheless argues for admissibility of the hearsay declaration as one in furtherance of a continuing objective of the conspiracy. Specifically, the Government argues that conspirators about to commit crimes always expressly or implicitly agree to collaborate with each other to conceal facts in order to prevent detection, conviction and punishment. Thus, they contend, even after the central criminal objectives of a conspiracy have succeeded or failed, an implicit subsidiary phase of the conspiracy always survives, the phase which has concealment as its sole objective. We cannot accept this contention. The Government, in essence, asks us to expand a narrow exception to the hearsay rule and hold admissible a declaration, not made in furtherance of the alleged criminal transportation conspiracy charged, but made in furtherance of an alleged implied but uncharged conspiracy aimed at preventing detection and punishment. The Government contention does find some support in state court opinions; but in none of them does there appear to be recognition of any such broad exception to the hearsay rule as they urge us to adopt here. We are not persuaded to accept the Government's implicit conspiracy theory which would automatically create in all criminal conspiracy cases a further breach of the general rule against the admission of hearsay evidence. It is contended that the statement attributed to the alleged co-conspirator was merely cumulative evidence, that without the statement the case against petitioner was so strong that we should hold it error harmless. Yet in the case before us, the Florida District Court grand jury failed to indict.

Krulewitch v. United States

Supreme Court of the United States, 336 U.S. 440 (1949)

And after indictment in New York, petitioner was tried four times with the following results: mistrial; conviction; mistrial; conviction with recommendation for leniency. These results make it difficult to believe that a jury convinced of a strong case against him would have recommended leniency. There was corroborative evidence of the complaining witness on certain phases of the case. But as to all vital phases, such as those involving the sordid criminal features, the jury was compelled to choose between believing the petitioner or the complaining witness. The record persuades us that the jury's task was difficult at best. We cannot say that the erroneous admission of the hearsay declaration may not have been the weight that tipped the scales against petitioner.

Reversed.

Pinkerton v. United States
Supreme Court of the United States, 328 U.S. 640 (1946)

FACTS

Defendant-petitioners Walter and Daniel Pinkerton (Daniel) are brothers who live a short distance from each other on Daniel's farm. They were indicted for violations of the Internal Revenue Code. The indictment contained ten substantive counts and one conspiracy count. The jury found Walter guilty on nine of the substantive counts and on the conspiracy count. It found Daniel guilty on six of the substantive counts and on the conspiracy count. Walter was fined $500 and sentenced generally on the substantive counts to imprisonment for thirty months. On the conspiracy count he was given a two year sentence to run concurrently with the other sentence. Daniel was fined $1,000 and sentenced generally on the substantive counts to imprisonment for thirty months. On the conspiracy count he was fined $500 and given a two year sentence to run concurrently with the other sentence. The judgments of conviction were affirmed by the Circuit Court of Appeals. The U.S. Supreme Court granted certiorari because one of the questions presented involved a conflict between the decision below and *United States v. Sall*, decided by the Circuit Court of Appeals for the Third Circuit.

Is participation in a conspiracy enough to sustain a conviction for the substantive offense ass well?

Participation in the conspiracy is enough to sustain a conviction for the substantive offense in furtherance of the conspiracy.

In the instant case, a single conspiracy was charged and proved. Some of the overt acts charged in the conspiracy count were the same acts charged in the substantive counts and each of the substantive offenses found was committed pursuant to the conspiracy. In light of the above, petitioners therefore contend that the substantive counts merged into the conspiracy count, and that only a single sentence provided by the conspiracy statute could be imposed. Alternatively, petitioners contend that each of the substantive counts became a separate conspiracy count, and since only a single conspiracy was charged and proved, only single sentence for conspiracy could be imposed. Yet the common law rule that the substantive offense, if a felony, merges into the conspiracy has little vitality in this country. It has been long and consistently recognized by the Court that the commission of the substantive offense and a conspiracy to commit it are separate and distinct offenses. The power of Congress to separate the two and to affix to each a different penalty is well established. And where is no evidence to show that Daniel participated directly in the commission of the substantive offenses on which his conviction has been sustained, there was evidence to show that these substantive offenses were in fact committed by Walter in furtherance of the unlawful agreement or conspiracy existing between the brothers. Daniel relies on *United States v. Sall*, which held that

Pinkerton v. United States
Supreme Court of the United States, 328 U.S. 640 (1946)

participation in the conspiracy was not itself enough to sustain a conviction for the substantive offense even though it was committed in furtherance of the conspiracy. The court held that, in addition to evidence that the offense was in fact committed in furtherance of the conspiracy, evidence of direct participation in the commission of the substantive offense or other evidence from which participation might fairly be inferred was necessary. We take a different view. We have here a continuous conspiracy. There is here no evidence of the affirmative action on the part of Daniel which is necessary to establish his withdrawal from it. Since the offense has not been terminated or accomplished, he is still offending. And so long as the partnership in crime continues, the partners act for each other in carrying it forward. Thus, a scheme to use the mails to defraud, which is joined in by more than one person, is a conspiracy. Yet all members are responsible, though only one did the mailing. And while an overt act is an essential ingredient of the crime of conspiracy, if it can be supplied by the act of one conspirator, we fail to see why the same or other acts in furtherance of the conspiracy are likewise not attributable to the others for the purpose of holding them responsible for the substantive offense. A different case would arise if the substantive offense committed by one of the conspirators was not in fact done in furtherance of the conspiracy, did not fall within the scope of the unlawful project, or was merely a pat of the ramifications of the plan which could not be reasonably foreseen as a necessary or natural consequence of the unlawful agreement. But as we read this record, that is not this case.

 Judgment affirmed.

State v. Bridges
New Jersey Supreme Court, 628 A.2d 270 (1993)

FACTS

At a birthday party for a 16 year old friend, Defendant Bridges got into an argument with another guest, Andy Strickland. Angry, Bridges left the party yelling he would return with some of his "friends." Thereafter, he returned with Bing and Rollie, each of whom was armed with a gun, as defendant expected a confrontation. The plan was that Bing and Rollie would hold the crowd at bay with the guns as Bridges fought Strickland. At the party, Bridges began fighting with one of Strickland's friends. At some point during the fight, Bing was hit in the face by a member of the crowd. After getting hit, Bing and Rollie, fired their guns into the air and then into the crowd. An onlooker was killed as a result. Bridges was tried and convicted of conspiracy to commit aggravated assault and of the substantive crime of murder and sentenced to life imprisonment with the possibility of parole after serving thirty years. Bridges appealed, and the Appellate Division held that the defendant could not be held responsible for the murder because he did not share the same intent and purpose of his co-conspirators. The State appealed.

When a crime is committed by one member of the conspiracy, not originally planned but nonetheless committed during the commission of the conspiracy, can other co-conspirators be held liable for the unplanned crime?

A co-conspirator may be liable for the commission of substantive criminal acts that are not within the scope of the conspiracy if they are reasonably foreseeable as the necessary or natural consequences of the conspiracy.

The provision of the New Jersey Code of Criminal Justice that imposes criminal liability on the basis of participation in a conspiracy is silent with respect to its culpability requirement. It provides that "A person is legally accountable for the conduct of another person when ... He is engaged in a conspiracy with such other person." The Appellate Division read N.J.S.A. 2C:2-6b(4), which provides that involvement in a conspiracy can be the basis for criminal liability for the commission of substantive crimes, as requiring a level of culpability and state of mind that is identical to that required of accomplice liability. As such, the Appellate Division held that a conspirator is vicariously liable for the substantive crimes committed by co-conspirators <u>only</u> when the conspirator had the same intent and purpose as the co-conspirator who committed the crimes. The Appellate Division's reading of the Code thus contemplated "complete congruity" between accomplice and vicarious conspirator liability, reasoning that *Pinkerton* mandates that a crime must have been within a co-conspirator's contemplation when he entered into the agreement. This understanding of *Pinkerton* is not supported. While *Pinkerton* did impose vicarious liability on each conspirator for the acts of others based on an objective standard of reasonable foreseeability, it was understood that the liability of a co-conspirator under the

State v. Bridges
New Jersey Supreme Court, 628 A.2d 270 (1993)

objective standard of reasonable foreseeability would be broader than that of an accomplice, where the defendant must actually foresee and intend the result of his or her acts. Although conspirator liability is restricted by the requirement of a close causal connection between the conspiracy and the substantive crime, that standard concededly is less strict than that defining accomplice accountability. Accordingly, we conclude that a co-conspirator maybe liable for the commission of substantive criminal acts that are not within the scope of the conspiracy *if they are reasonably foreseeable as the necessary or natural consequences of the conspiracy.* Turning to the record of the case before us, we note that the objective of the Bridges conspiracy was not murder; however, the conspiratorial plan did contemplate bringing loaded guns to keep a large crowd at bay and it is reasonably foreseeable that one or more of the guns might be fired into the crowd. Thus, a jury may conclude that a reasonably foreseeable risk and a probable and natural consequence of carrying guns and using them to hold back a crowd might be that persons in the crowd might get shot or be killed. Under the circumstances, such conduct would be sufficiently connected to the original conspiratorial plan to prove a just basis for a determination of guilt for that substantive offense.

 Reversed.

United States v. Alvarez
United States Court of Appeals, 755 F.2d 830 (11ᵗʰ Cir. 1985)

FACTS

In a run-down hotel in Miami, Florida, undercover ATF (Alcohol, Tobacco, and Firearms) agents arranged a $147,000 cocaine buy from Alvarez and some of his associates as part of an ongoing and lengthy sting operation. After the arrival of the cocaine and some other agents following the buy, a gun battle erupted in the hotel room and an ATF agent was killed and two were seriously wounded. All of the dealers were convicted of conspiracy to commit various drug offenses. Two, including Alvarez, were convicted of first-degree murder, and three other defendants (Portal, Concepcion, and Hernandez) were convicted of second-degree murder, even though they played no part in the shooting: Defendant Portal was armed at the time of the buy but served as a lookout in front of the hotel at the time of the buy; Defendant Concepcion was present at the time of the shootout and introduced the agents to Alvarez, and Defendant Hernandez owned the hotel and acted as a translator during the meeting between the agents and the dealers. These three defendants appealed, contending that their convictions were based on an improper extension of *Pinkerton* in that the murder of the ATF agent was not a reasonably foreseeable consequence of a drug conspiracy, and therefore their convictions should be reversed.

Can co-conspirators who play a "minor role" in a conspiracy be held criminal liable for reasonably foreseeable but originally unintended crimes substantive carried out during the course of the conspiracy?

Co-conspirators who play a "minor role" in a conspiracy or who and actual knowledge of at least some of the circumstances and events culminating in the reasonably foreseeable but originally unintended substantive crime may be held criminally liable for the acts of their con-conspirators carried out during the course of the conspiracy.

Co-conspirators who play a "minor role" in a conspiracy or who and actual knowledge of at least some of the circumstances and events culminating in the reasonably foreseeable but originally unintended substantive crime may be held criminally liable for the acts of their con-conspirators carried out during the course of the conspiracy. Although our decision today extends the *Pinkerton* doctrine to cases involving reasonably foreseeable but originally unintended substantive crimes, we emphasize that we do so only with narrow confines. Our holding is limited to conspirators that played more than a "minor role" in the conspiracy or who and actual knowledge of at least some of the circumstances and events culminating in the reasonably foreseeable but originally unintended substantive crime. The three defendants argue that the murder was not the objective or intended purpose of the conspiracy, and that their individual roles were sufficiently minor, such that they should not be held responsible for the murder. We disagree. All three were more than minor participants in the drug conspiracy. Each had actual knowledge of at least some of the circumstances and events leading up to the murder. The evidence that Portal was

United States v. Alvarez
United States Court of Appeals, 755 F.2d 830 (11th Cir. 1985)

carrying a weapon demonstrated that he anticipated the possible use of deadly force to protect the conspirators' interests. Moreover, both Concepcion and Hernandez were present when Alvarez stated that he would rather die than go back to prison, indicating that they too were aware that deadly force might be used to prevent apprehension by law enforcement agents.

Affirmed.

Interstate Circuit Inc. v. United States

Supreme Court of the United States, 306 U.S. 208 (1939)

FACTS

This case involves the alleged conspiracy between two movie theater chains who dominated the market for playing films in the cities where their theaters were located and the eight independent corporations that distributed the films to them. Defendant Interstate Circuit ("Interstate") and Defendant Texas Consolidated Theaters ("Consolidated") entered into contractual agreements with eight film distributors who were responsible for releasing 75% of all first run films in the United States. The contracts restricted the distributors from 1) releasing second run films in theaters that charged an admission price of less than $0.25 and 2) restricted the distributors from releasing its first run films on a double bill with another feature film. These agreements were pursuant to an Interstate manager's demand to each of the eight distributors that they comply with 1) and 2) above as a condition of Interstate's continued exhibition of that distributor's films. All eight distributors complied with Interstate's demands. The government charged the two defendant-move chains with violations of the Sherman Antitrust Act. Since each distributor had entered into a separate contract with the two defendants, and the letter addressed and identified all eight distributors, it was the only evidence of the existence of the conspiracy. The trial court drew the inference of the illegal agreement from the nature of the proposals made on behalf of the defendants; the substantial unanimity of action taken by the distributors after the alleged agreement; and the fact that appellants did not call as witnesses any of the parties that negotiated the contracts on behalf of the defendants who would have knowledge of the existence or non-existence of any such agreement. Subsequently, the trial court held that the evidence was sufficient to support a conviction of conspiracy in violation of the Sherman Antitrust Act. Both defendants appealed.

Can evidence of the existence of a conspiracy be based on inferences drawn from the conduct of the parties?

Evidence of a conspiratorial agreement can be based on inferences drawn from the conduct of the alleged conspirators.

Proof of an alleged conspiracy as evidenced by direct testimony that the conspirators entered into an agreement is rare. Therefore, in order to prove such an agreement, it is proper for the government "to rely on inferences drawn from the course of conduct of the alleged conspirators." The trial court did just that when it drew an inference of the illegal conspiracy from 1) the manner which the proposal was, from the "substantial unanimity" of the distributor's conduct after the proposal was made, and the fact that the defendants did not call as witnesses any of the superior officials who negotiated the distributor agreements. The linchpin of the government's case, the letter written by the Interstate

Interstate Circuit Inc. v. United States
Supreme Court of the United States, 306 U.S. 208 (1939)

manager and sent to all eight distributors, addresses all eight distributors. Each distributor knew that the other distributors were considering the proposal and each distributor also knew that, without substantial unanimous group participation, there was a risk of a loss of business. Thus, compliance with the defendants' demands coupled with a concerted action on their [the distributors] part meant the likelihood of increased profits. The acceptance of the agreement involved a "radical departure from the media's business practices of the industry" and a drastic increase in theater admission prices. Lastly, there was a risk that without near-uniform agreement, a multiplicity of action would follow.

 Judgment affirmed.

United States v. Alvarez

United States Court of Appeals, 625 F.2d 1196 (5th Cir. 1981)

FACTS

Undercover DEA Agent Martinez arranged to import 110,000 lbs. of marijuana into the United States from Columbia by plane with the help of Alvarez, Cifarelli and Cruz, as part of a sting operation. According to the government's evidence, Agent Martinez met the three at the Opa-Locka airport in the U.S. Alvarez drove up in a pickup truck loaded with household appliances in which Cruz and Cifarelli were riding. The DEA agent asked Cifarelli who Alvarez was and his response was that Alvarez "would be at the off-loading site in the United States." The agent also spoke with Alvarez in Spanish and asked him if he planned to be at the unloading site. Alvarez smiled and nodded his head, signifying "yes." Alvarez thereafter unloaded the household appliances from the pickup truck. Afterwards, the agent spoke with Cruz and after Cruz outlined his plans for the arrival of the plan and its unloading, all three were arrested. Alvarez was convicted as a co-conspirator, but is conviction was reversed on appeal by a three-judge panel finding that a defendant does not join a conspiracy merely by participating in a substantive offense, or by associating with persons who are members of a conspiracy. The 5th Circuit Court of Appeals granted a rehearing *en banc*.

Can the conduct of a defendant together with the totality of the facts and circumstances at hand be used to infer that the defendant knew that criminal activity was afoot, thereby inferring guilt of his participation in a conspiracy?

The conduct of a defendant together with the totality of the facts and circumstances at hand can be used to infer that the defendant knew that criminal activity was afoot, thereby inferring guilt of his participation in a conspiracy.

The government is not required to prove that Alvarez had knowledge of all the details of the conspiracy provided that the prosecution established his knowledge of the conspiracy. A defendant will not be permitted to escape criminal liability upon proof that he joined the conspiracy until well after its inception or because he simply played a "minor" role in the scheme. In this case, we find that the aggregate of the evidence is sufficient to infer that Alvarez knew that criminal activity was afoot. There is direct evidence showing that Alvarez intended to be at the off-loading site [a jury may conclude that his intended presence manifested a prior agreement to assist in the unloading]. Also, when the agent asked Alvarez if he would be present at unloading and Alvarez nodded in the affirmative. Lastly, a reasonable jury could have concluded that only a person with knowledge of the scheme would agree "to be on hand at a remote and unlikely area for the unloading of cargo." The outcome might have been different had *not* Cifarelli and Cruz assured the DEA agent that Alvarez would be at hand at the designated time and place.

The conviction is affirmed.

People v. Lauria
California District Court of Appeal, 59 Cal. Rptr. 628 (1967)

FACTS

During an investigation into prostitution, the police focused their attention on three prostitutes, each of whom used Lauria's telephone service.   As part of their investigation, an undercover policewoman, Stella Weeks, signed up for Lauria's services. Weeks hinted that she was a prostitute, and wanted to assurances that Lauria's services were discrete, especially from the police. Lauria assured her that his service was both secret and safe. A few weeks later, Weeks called Lauria and complained that she had lost two "clients" because of his service. Lauria claimed that her "clients" probably lied about leaving messages for her.   Weeks hinted to Lauria that she needed more customers, but he did not respond other than to invite her over to "his place." Two months later, Lauria and the three prostitutes under investigation were arrested. Lauria testified before the Grand Jury that kept records for known or suspected prostitutes for his convenience and that of the police. He claimed that "so long as they paid their bills we tolerate them." Lauria admitted having personal knowledge that some of his customers were prostitutes.   Lauria and the three prostitutes were indicted for conspiracy to commit prostitution. The trial court set aside the indictment as having been brought without a showing of reasonable or probable cause. The Government appeals claiming that a conspiracy did in fact exist and argues a sufficient showing of an unlawful agreement to further prostitution was made.

Can a supplier of goods and/or services the supplier knows will assist another in an illegal enterprise, be criminally liable for conspiracy?

With respect to <u>misdemeanors</u>, the positive knowledge of a supplier that his products will be used for illegal activities does not in itself establish intent to participate in the misdemeanor; with respect to <u>all felonies</u>, knowledge of criminal use alone may justify an inference of intent such that the intent of a supplier who knows his supplies will be put to criminal use may be established by (1) direct evidence that he intends to participate, or (2) through an inference that he intends to participate based on (a) his special interest in the activity, or (b) the felonious nature of the crime itself.

To establish agreement, the Government need show no more than an implied mutual understanding, between coconspirators, to accomplish an unlawful act. The question for us becomes, therefore, under what circumstances does a supplier of goods and services he knows are to be used buy the buyer for illegal purposes become part of the conspiracy? The two leading cases on this point aim in opposite directions. In *United States v. Falcone,* the court held that a seller's knowledge of the illegal use of the goods was insufficient to make the seller a participant in the conspiracy. By contrast, the court in *Direct Sales Co. v. United States* held that the conviction on federal narcotics laws of a drug wholesaler was affirmed on a showing that the company had actively promoted the sale of morphine. In both cases, however, the element of knowledge of the illegal use of the goods or services and the element of intent to further that use must be present in order to make the supplier a participant in a criminal conspiracy. In the instant case, Lauria admitted he knew that some of his customers were prostitutes and probably knew that some of his customers were using his service in order to further their trade. The Government argues that this knowledge serves as a basis for concluding that Lauria intended to participate in the criminal activities. We disagree. Intent may be inferred from knowledge when 1) the purveyor of the legal goods for illegal use has acquired a stake in the venture; 2) when no legitimate use for the goods or services exists; and 3) when the volume of business with the buyer is grossly disproportionate to any legitimate demand. From the record before us, we note that Lauria had no stake in the venture, and was not charging higher prices to the prostitutes. Moreover, nothing in the furnishing of telephone service implies that it will be used for prostitution, since all sorts of persons might use the service for completely legal activities. Finally, no evidence suggests any unusual volume of Lauria's business was with prostitutes. Thus, with respect to misdemeanors, we conclude that positive knowledge of a supplier that his products will be used for illegal activities does not in itself establish intent to participate in the misdemeanor. However, with respect to felonies, we hold that in all felony cases, knowledge of criminal use alone may justify an inference of intent such that the intent of a supplier who knows of the criminal use to which his supplies are put to participate in the criminal activity connected with the use of his supplies may be established by (1) direct evidence that he intends to participate, or (2) through an inference that he intends to participate based on (a) his special interest in the activity, or (b) the felonious nature of the crime itself. Here, Lauria was charged with a misdemeanor. The evidence indicates that Lauria took no *direct action* to further the activities of the prostitutes. There is no evidence of a special interest in the prostitutes' activities. Thus the charges of conspiracy against Lauria fail.

The order is affirmed.

Kotteakos v. United States

Supreme Court of the United States, 328 U.S. 750 (1946)

FACTS

Defendant-petitioner Simon Brown was the president of Brownie Lumber Co. and was also a loan broker who arranged loans, on a 5% commission basis, for those seeking to modernize and renovate under the National Housing Act (NHA). One of his clients was Defendant Kotteakos. Brown knew that these loans were not going to be used for the purposes stated in the applications, a clear violation of the NHA. The record showed that Brown's other clients, the other defendants, were unaware of one other and that there was no evidence showing any connection between them, save for the fact that they had all transacted business with Brown. Thirty-two persons were indicted for the illegal loans; 19 were brought to trial; 13 were submitted to the jury. At trial, the trial court instructed the jury that there was only one conspiracy. Consequently, of the original 13 that were submitted to the jury, two were acquitted and the jury disagreed as to 4; the remaining 7 were found guilty. Brown was the only one of the group of 7 that pled guilty. Kotteakos and other convicted defendants thus appealed. The Court of Appeals found that there was not a single conspiracy, but at least eight separate conspiracies, maybe more, between the individual defendants and Brown. The government described the pattern as "separate spokes meeting at a common center" but, as the Court added, "without the rim of the wheel to enclose the spokes." The Court of Appeals found that the trial judge erred in finding a single, common conspiracy, but also found that the error was not prejudicial and harmless. The defendants appealed again to the U.S. Supreme Court.

 Can multiple defendants be guilty of a single conspiracy if they each dealt independently with a common central figure though each defendant was unaware of and had no connection with to any other co-defendant?

 Multiple defendants cannot be found guilty of a single conspiracy if each defendant dealt independently with a common central figure and each defendant was unaware of and had no connection to any other co-defendant.

 The trial judge's jury instruction was erroneous in two respects: Evidence of a single conspiracy is unfounded and the jury is not allowed to use the acts or statements of any of the defendants against all of the defendants. Had all the defendants been part of single conspiracy existed, which is not the case here, this instruction would have been proper.

 Judgment is reversed.

United States v. Bruno

United States Court of Appeals, 105 F.2d 921 (2nd Cir. 1939)

FACTS

Defendant-appellants Bruno and Iacono were indicted along with 86 other defendants for a single conspiracy to import, sell, and possess narcotics. The object of the conspiracy was to smuggle narcotics into the Port of New York and distribute them to addicts in New York, Louisiana and Texas by way of local retailers. Some defendants were convicted and some were acquitted; Bruno and Iacono were found guilty of a single conspiracy and appealed. Specially, the defendants argue that there were at least four groups of persons and at least three separate conspiracies by and between them: There were smugglers that imported the drugs; middlemen who paid the smugglers and distributed them to retailers; and two groups of retailers, one in New York and another in Texas and Louisiana. The defendants claim to have been involved in the smuggling phase of the distribution chain and there was no evidence that any cooperation or communication occurred between the smugglers and the retailers or between the two groups of retailers themselves. The U.S. Court of Appeal for the 2nd Circuit heard the defendant-petitioners' appeal.

Can multiple defendants be convicted of a single conspiracy when each was aware of the acts of the other [defendants] but neither of them ever cooperated or communicated with any other [defendant]?

Multiple defendants can be convicted of a single conspiracy when each was aware of the acts of the other even though neither of them ever cooperated or communicated with any other [defendant]?

While it is true that the evidence revealed no cooperation or communication between the smugglers [defendant-petitioners here] and either group of retailers or between the two groups of retailers themselves, there is evidence that the conspirators "at one end of the chain" knew what the conspirators at the other end of the chain were doing. That being true, a jury may find that a single conspiracy existed. The reasoning for this finding can be found in the maxim that "the success of one part was dependent upon the success of a whole." And while the argument that two separate conspiracies still existed can be made, i.e., one including the New York retailers and the other including the Texas and Louisiana retailers, such an argument is fallacious. This is because the smugglers didn't care whether the middlemen sold to one or more groups so long as they paid the middlemen for the drugs and provided a market to keep the distribution flowing. So too of any retailer; so long as he was getting the drugs from someone to sell, he was happy. Yet both groups were aware of the link and were as much parts of a single enterprise as two salesmen in the same shop.

Judgment affirmed.

United States v. McDermott

United States Court of Appeals, 245 F.3d 133 (2nd Cir. 2001)

FACTS

Defendant James J. McDermott appeals from a judgment entered against him in the United States District Court for the Southern District of New York following a jury trial before Kimba Wood, <u>Judge</u>, convicting him of conspiracy to commit insider trading in violation of 18 U.S.C. § 371 and of insider trading in violation of 15 U.S.C. §§ 78(j)(b) and 78ff and of 17 C.F.R. § 240.10b-5. On appeal, McDermott contends principally that (1) the evidence was insufficient as a matter of law to support his convictions; (2) he was unfairly prejudiced as a result of variance between the indictment and the proof at trial; and (3) the district court abused its discretion under Federal Rule of Evidence 403.

Can a conspiracy be committed if there was a there was a unitary purpose rather than by the agreement of its members to that purpose?

A conspiracy is committed by the agreement of its members to a specific purpose.

We agree that there is insufficient evidence to support the conspiracy count, although sufficient evidence exists to support McDermott's conviction on the substantive offenses. Nevertheless, because of the variance between the single conspiracy charged in the indictment and the proof adduced at trial, we find that McDermott was prejudiced to the point of being denied a fair trial. Accordingly, we reverse the conspiracy count and remand for a new trial on the substantive counts. "[I]n order to prove a single conspiracy, the government must show that each alleged member agreed to participate in what he knew to be a collective venture directed toward a common goal. The coconspirators need not have agreed on the details of the conspiracy, so long as they agreed on the essential nature of the plan." *United States v. Maldonado-Rivera*. We have frequently noted that the "essence of conspiracy is the agreement and not the commission of the substantive offense." Additionally, it is a long-standing principle of this Court's law of conspiracy that "[n]obody is liable in conspiracy except for the fair import of the concerted purpose or agreement as he understands it; if later comers change that, he is not liable for the change; his liability is limited to the common purposes while he remains in it." *United States v. Peoni*. Despite this well-settled law, the government here asks us to redefine a conspiracy by its purpose, rather than by the agreement of its members to that purpose. The government argues that from the perspective of Gannon and Pomponio, albeit not from McDermott's perspective, there was a unitary purpose to commit insider trading based on information furnished by McDermott. According to the government, therefore, McDermott was part of the conspiracy even though he did not agree to pass information to both Gannon and Pomponio. Accordingly, we hold that, as a matter of law, no rational jury could find McDermott guilty beyond a reasonable doubt of a single conspiracy with Pomponio to commit insider trading. The government has failed to show the most basic element of a single conspiracy, namely, an agreement to pass insider information to Gannon and possibly to another person, even if unknown. We therefore reverse the judgment of conviction on that count.

We reverse the conspiracy count and remand for a new trial on the substantive counts.

Gebardi v. United States

Supreme Court of the United States, 287 U.S. 112 (1932)

FACTS

Defendant-petitioners Gebardi and a woman agreed that Gebardi would transport her across state lines for the purpose of having sexual intercourse. Both petitioners, the man and woman, who were not yet husband and wife, were indicted in the District Court for Northern Illinois, for conspiring together, and with others not named, to transport the woman from one state to another for the purpose of engaging in sexual intercourse with the man. At the trial without a jury there was evidence from which the court could have found that the petitioners had engaged in illicit sexual relations in the course of each of the journeys alleged; that the man purchased the railway tickets for both petitioners for at least one journey; and that in each instance the woman, in advance of the purchase of the tickets, consented to go on the journey and did go on it voluntarily for the specified immoral purpose. There was no evidence supporting the allegation that any other person had conspired. The trial court overruled motions for a finding for the defendants, and in arrest of judgment, and gave judgment of conviction, which the Court of Appeals for the Seventh Circuit affirmed on the authority of *United States v. Holte*.

May a woman who consents to transportation across state lines for illicit purposes be convicted of conspiracy to violate the substantive offense of transporting herself across state lines?

A woman cannot be held criminally liable for conspiring to transport herself across state lines for illicit purposes, even where she consents to the substantive offense.

The only question which we need consider here is whether the evidence was sufficient to support the conviction. We do not have to consider what would be necessary to constitute the substantive crime under the Mann Act, or what evidence would be required to convict a woman under an indictment like this. We need only to decide whether it is impossible for the transported woman to be guilty of a crime in conspiring as alleged. To that end, we must apply the law to the evidence; the very inquiry which was said to be unnecessary to decision in *United States v. Holte*. We first note that the exceptional circumstances set forth in *Holte* as possible instances in which the woman might violate the act itself are clearly not present here. There is no evidence that petitioner purchased the railroad tickets or that hers was the active force in conceiving or carrying out the transportation. The proof shows no more than that she went willingly upon the trip for the purposes alleged. Section 2 of the Mann Act, violation of which is charged by the indictment here as the object of the conspiracy, imposes the penalty upon "any person who shall *knowingly* transport or cause to be transported, or aid or assist in obtaining transportation for, or in transporting, in interstate or foreign commerce . . . any woman or girl for the purpose of prostitution or debauchery, or for any other immoral purpose .

Gebardi v. United States

Supreme Court of the United States, 287 U.S. 112 (1932)

. ." The Act does not punish the woman for transporting herself; it contemplates two persons-one to transport and the woman or girl to be transported. For the woman to fall within the ban of the statute she must, at the least, "aid or assist" some one else in transporting or in procuring transportation for herself. But such aid and assistance must be more active than mere agreement on her part to the transportation and its immoral purpose. In applying this criminal statute we cannot infer that the mere acquiescence of the woman transported was intended to be condemned by the general language of the statute. The penalties of the statute are too clearly directed against the acts of the transporter as distinguished from the consent of the subject of the transportation. This conclusion was intimated in *Holte*, and this conclusion is not disputed by the government here. Next, we come to the main question in the case: whether she may be convicted of a conspiracy with the man to violate the Act. As was said in *Holte*, an agreement to commit an offense may be criminal, though its purpose is to do what some of the conspirators may be free to do alone. Incapacity of one to commit the substantive offense does not necessarily imply that one may, with impunity, conspire with others who are able to commit it.   But in this case we are concerned with something more than an agreement between two persons for one of them to commit an offense which the other cannot commit. There is the added element that the offense planned, the criminal object of the conspiracy, involves the agreement of the woman to her transportation by the man, which is the very conspiracy charged. Congress set out in the Mann Act to deal with cases which frequently involve consent and agreement on the part of the woman to the forbidden transportation. In every case in which she is not intimidated or forced into the transportation, the statute assumes she consented willingly. Yet this acquiescence was not made a crime under the Mann Act itself, so we take it as evidence that Congress meant to leave her acquiescence unpunished. On the evidence before us the woman has not violated the Mann Act, and is not guilty of conspiracy to do so. On the evidence before us the woman petitioner has not violated the Mann Act and, we hold, is not guilty of a conspiracy to do so. As there is no proof that the man conspired with anyone else to bring about the transportation, the convictions of both petitioners must be reversed.

Convictions of both petitioners must be reversed.

Garcia v. State

Supreme Court of Indiana, 394 N.E.2d 106 (1979)

FACTS

Defendant Garcia contacted Allen Young with regard to certain martial problems she was having with her husband. Specifically, Young was told that Garcia's husband constantly beat her and their children and that she wanted him killed. After a few more conversations with her, Young discussed the matter with two police detectives. Young offered to call the defendant and have the police listen in. The police thereafter recorded several conversations between Young and Garcia regarding the latter's request to help her find someone to kill her husband. The police then asked Young to set up a meeting between Young, Garcia, and an undercover detective pretending to be a gunman for hire. Young introduced the two and Garcia gave the detective a $200 down payment, a picture of her husband, and a record of his daily routine. She was arrested and convicted of conspiracy to commit murder. She appealed arguing that she cannot be guilty of a conspiracy because she conspired with someone who only pretended to go along with the scheme.

Can a person be found guilty of conspiracy when her co-conspirator only pretended to go along with the scheme and cannot legally be prosecuted for the conspiracy [the so-called "unilateral" concept]?

A person is guilty of conspiracy even if the other co-conspirator cannot be prosecuted for the conspiracy.

The bilateral concept of conspiracy is the traditional view and is derived from the common law. It requires that two or more persons agree to commit a crime, each with an intent to do so. Where one of the parties [in a two party conspiracy] feigned his acquiesce to the plan, courts have generally held no conviction because of an absence of a "conspiratorial agreement." If three persons, for example, were involved in a conspiracy and one was feigned his acquiesce to the plan, a conspiracy may still be found between the two not feigning acquiesce. The Model Penal Code, however, adopts a "unilateral" approach in which a defendant's culpability is unaffected by the culpability of the co-conspirators. In 1976, Indiana adopted a statute that follows the unilateral MPC approach. It provides the defendant with no defense if the co-conspirator "cannot be prosecuted for any reason."

This new statute controls in our State so the judgment is affirmed.

United States v. Elliott
U.S. Court of Appeals, 571 F.2d 880 (5th Cir. 1978)

FACTS

An indictment charged Defendant James Elliott and five other co-defendants with conspiring with each other, with 37 unindicted co-conspirators, and with "others to the grand jury known and unknown," to violate Section 1962, subsection (c) of the Racketeer Influenced and Corrupt Organizations Act (RICO). The essence of the conspiracy charge was that Elliott and the others agreed to participate, directly and indirectly, in the conduct of the affairs of an enterprise whose purposes were to commit thefts, fence stolen goods, illegally traffic in narcotics, obstruct justice, and engage in "other criminal activities." While the Government proved the existence of a criminal enterprise composed of at least five of the defendants, at no time did more than three of the defendants participate in any specific criminal endeavor, with the exception of one person, J.C. Hawkins, who was linked to all of the crimes. All the defendants, except defendant Foster, argue that while the indictment alleged but one conspiracy, the government's evidence at trial proved the existence of several conspiracies, resulting in a variance that substantially prejudiced their rights, mandating reversal. The U.S. Court of Appeals now reviews the convictions of the six persons accused of conspiring to violate RICO; two of whom were convicted of substantive RICO violations.

Does RICO allow the Government to charge numerous smaller conspiracies in a single count?

RICO allows the Government to charge numerous smaller conspiracies in a single count.

In *Kotteakos v. United States,* the Court held that proof of multiple conspiracies under an indictment alleging a single conspiracy constituted a material variance requiring reversal where a defendant's substantial rights had been affected. However, the impact of *Kotteakos* was soon limited by the Court in *Blumenthal v. United States,* where the chain conspiracy rationale was created. In *Blumenthal,* the Court reasoned that since the plan, which is the object of the conspiracy, must depend on the successful operation of each "link" in the chain, an individual associating himself with this type of conspiracy knows that for the crime to succeed, he must become an indispensable cog in the machinery with the other members of the conspiracy, through which the illegal scheme could be effectuated. Thus, the essential element of the conspiracy, allowing persons known to each other and never before in to be jointly prosecuted as co-conspirators, is interdependence. This rationale applies only insofar as the alleged agreement has a common end or single unified purpose. The rationale fails, however, where the remote members of the alleged conspiracy are not truly interdependent or where the various activities sought to be tied together cannot reasonably be said to constitute a unified scheme. Applying the

United States v. Elliott
U.S. Court of Appeals, 571 F.2d 880 (5th Cir. 1978)

Chain Conspiracy Rational (a *pre-RICO* conspiracy theory) to the instant facts of this case, we doubt that a single conspiracy could be demonstrated. The activities allegedly embraced by the illegal agreement in this case are simply too diverse to be tied together on the theory that participation in one activity necessarily implied awareness of others. Then along came RICO. Congress enacted RICO because it felt that found that the remedies available to the Government are unnecessarily limited in scope and impact thus allowing organized crime to continue to grow. One of the express purposes of the Act was to seek "eradication of organized crime by establishing new penal prohibitions, and by providing enhanced sanctions and new remedies to deal with the unlawful activities of those engaged in organized crime." In light of this Congressional intent, we are convinced that in enacting RICO, Congress deliberately allowed for the single prosecution of a multi-faceted, diversified conspiracy by replacing the inadequate Chain Conspiracy Rational. This new rational is called The Enterprise Conspiracy theory. Under the RICO Act, it is irrelevant that each defendant participated in the enterprise's affairs through different, even unrelated crimes, so long as we may reasonably infer that each crime was intended to further the enterprise's affairs. To be convicted as a member of an enterprise conspiracy, an individual, by his words or actions, must have objectively manifested an agreement to participate, directly or indirectly, in the affairs of an enterprise through the commission of two or more predicate crimes. Here, it is clear that the essential nature of the plan was to associate for the purpose of making money from repeated criminal activity. That risk is greatly compounded when the conspirators contemplate not a single crime but a career of crime. However, the evidence does not support a conclusion by the jury that Elliott agreed to participate, directly or indirectly, in the affairs of an enterprise through a pattern of racketeering activity. At best, the evidence shows he became peripherally involved in a stolen meat deal, which is not enough to prove that he knowingly and intentionally joined the broad conspiracy to violate RICO. Elliott agreed to participate in the affairs of the enterprise, but not through a *pattern* of racketeering activity, hence, not in violation of the Act.

Conviction must be reversed.

United States v. Peterson

U.S. Court of Appeals, 483 F.2d 1222 (D.C. Cir. 1973)

FACTS

Defendant-appellant Bennie L. Peterson was indicted for 2nd degree murder and convicted by a jury of manslaughter as a lesser included offense. The facts are as follows: Peterson came out of his house and into the alley behind his house to protest the fact that Keitt (accompanied by two friends) was removing the windshield wipers off the former's wrecked car. After a verbal exchange, Peterson went into his house to get a pistol, which he loaded yelling at Keitt not to move. In the meantime, Keitt and company were already in Keitt's car about to leave. Peterson walked to a point in the yard slightly inside the gate in the rear fence, holding his pistol, and said, "If you come in here I will kill you." Keitt got out of his car, walked toward Peterson and said, "What the hell do you think you are going to do with that?" He then walked back to his car and got a lug wrench. With the wrench in a raised position, he advanced toward Peterson who stood with the pistol pointed at him. Peterson warned Keitt not to "take another step," which Keitt did, and Peterson shot him in the face from a distance of about ten feet. Death was apparently instantaneous. Peterson was charged with second-degree murder and convicted of manslaughter. He appeals, arguing that two jury instructions were improper. Specifically, he refers to the alleged twice erred instructions that 1) the jury might consider whether he was the aggressor in the altercation that immediately preceded the homicide and 2) a failure by Peterson to retreat might be considered circumstantial evidence bearing on the question whether he was justified in using the amount of force which he did.

Can the initial aggressor in a conflict claim self defense after he commits a killing in order to save himself?

The initial aggressor in a conflict resulting in the death of another cannot justifiably rely on the right of self-defense.

Self-defense, the doctrine legally exonerating the taking of a human life, is a law of necessity. There must be a threat, actual or apparent, and the use of deadly force against the defendant. The threat must have been unlawful and immediate and the reaction to a threat must be proportional to the threat itself. The defender must have honestly believed that he was in immediate threat of death or serious bodily harm, and that his response was necessary to save himself. Such a belief is measured objectively. If a person incites, encourages, or otherwise promotes the circumstances that lead up to his killing another, that person is the aggressor and is not entitled to the claim of self-defense. The exception being if the aggressor communicates to his opponent his intent to withdraw and in good faith attempts to do so, he may claim self-defense. While we acknowledge that in the majority of jurisdictions, one may stand his ground and use deadly force whenever it

United States v. Peterson

U.S. Court of Appeals, 483 F.2d 1222 (D.C. Cir. 1973)

seems reasonably necessary to save himself, we do not follow this rule in our state. Turning to the facts of the instant case, we note that Peterson returned to the yard with a pistol just as Keitt was about to leave the scene. At this point, Keitt was not the aggressor. Peterson was not in any danger of bodily harm or death at this point in time; and prior to this instant, only verbal threats had been exchanged and a misdemeanor was in progress (deadly force may not be used in defense of property). After Peterson returned to the yard, he loaded his pistol, walked toward Keitt, told him not to come in, and threatened to kill him if he did. Peterson may not assert self-defense under these circumstances because he was the person who created the dangerous situation. He could have simply walked away, but did not. Peterson argues he was not required to retreat. Yet, as we have already stated, the right of self-defense is not available to the party who provokes the conflict. Under the instant facts, the jury instructions were proper.

 Judgment of the trial court for conviction affirmed.

People v. Goetz
Court of Appeals of New York, 497 N.E.2d 41 (1986)

FACTS

On December 22, 1984, Defendant-appellee Bernhard Goetz boarded a subway car in Manhattan and sat down toward the rear section of the same car occupied by, among others, four youths from the Bronx. Two of the youths had screwdrivers inside their coats. One of the youths asked Goetz how he was, to which Goetz responded "fine." One or two of the other youths walked over to Goetz and stated "give me five dollars." Goetz responded by taking out his unlicensed .38 caliber pistol and firing, in rapid succession, one youth in the chest, another in the back, a third in the arm. According to Goetz's statement, he shot at, but missed, one of the youths after which he said to him, "you seem to be all right, here's another," and fired another shot at him, this time hitting the youth and severing his spinal chord. According to Goetz's statement, "if I was in a little more under self-control... I would have put the barrel against his forehead and fired." Goetz stated that he purchased the gun in 1981 after he had been injured in a mugging. He also stated he successfully warded off two other assailants simply by displaying the gun in 1981 and 1984. Although he was certain none of them had guns, he was afraid they were going to "maim" him. A grand Jury indicted defendant on attempted murder, assault and other charges. Subsequently, the lower court held that the objective test submitted to the grand jury to determine the defense of justification was in error and that a subjective test should have been used. The charges of attempted murder, assault, and weapons possession were dismissed. The Court of Appeals of New York reversed the lower court's dismissal holding that the correct test of reasonableness under New York's law is an objective test, and thus reinstated the charges against defendant.

Does a defendant's claimed "justified" use of deadly force turn on whether the defendant reasonably believed such deadly force was necessary and that a "reasonable man" in his situation would find the use of deadly force necessary?

Before a defendant can prevail on a self-defense defense, he must show his belief regarding the use of force was both reasonable and necessary and comports with the "reasonable man" objective standard.

New York's law regarding the defense of justification is embodied in Penal Law article 35. Penal Law § 35.15(1) sets forth the general principles: "[a] person may... use physical force upon another person when and to the extent he reasonably believes such to be necessary to defend himself or a third person from what he reasonably believes to be the use or imminent use of unlawful physical force by such other person." However, "a person may not use deadly physical force upon another person under circumstances specified in subdivision one unless (a) He reasonably believes that such other person is using or about to use deadly physical force... or (b) He reasonably believes that such other person is committing or attempting to commit a kidnapping, forcible rape, forcible sodomy or robbery." The

People v. Goetz
Court of Appeals of New York, 497 N.E.2d 41 (1986)

entire case, indeed the critical issue before us, turns on the definition of the phrase "reasonably believes." The State (prosecutor) instructed the grand jury that an objective test was to be used in determining whether Goetz reasonably believed the youths were using or about to use deadly force or were committing or about to commit one of the enumerated felonies. The prosecutor told the grand jury they were to consider the circumstances of the incident and determine "whether the defendant's conduct was that of a reasonable man in the defendant's situation." However, the lower court held that because the law as written explicitly states "he reasonably believes," the correct test is a subjective test. That is, whether the defendant's beliefs and reactions were reasonable *to him*. We hold that the lower court was incorrect with respect to the application of the correct test and that the prosecutor's objective test is the correct test under New York law. If we were to apply a subjective test to the case at bar, or to any similar circumstance, any jury would have to acquit a man who claimed he felt his actions were warranted and reasonable. This would be an undesired result for obvious reasons. The application of an objective standard, however, avoids this result but would not foreclose a jury from considering the circumstances facing a defendant, including, but not limited to 1) the action taken by the alleged assailant, 2) the physical characteristics of all persons involved, 3) defendant's relevant knowledge about the assailant, and 4) any prior experiences of the defendant which would provide a reasonable basis for believing that another's intentions were to harm or rob the accused or that the use of deadly force was necessary under the circumstances.

The Appellate Division is reversed and the dismissed charges of the indictment reinstated.

State v. Kelly
Supreme Court of New Jersey, 478 A.2d 364 (1984)

FACTS

Defendant-appellant Gladys Kelly's husband, Ernest, beat her frequently. After one beating, Kelly stabbed him with a pair of scissors. He died shortly thereafter at a hospital. She was indicted for murder and at trial, asserted self-defense fearing that her husband would hurt her or her daughter. She also called an export witness on battered-woman's syndrome to show that she lived in constant fear of beating but was unable to leave her husband. The expert testified that battered-woman's syndrome comprised of various stages and consists of a complex psychological pattern which makes battered women believe they are unable to escape abusive relationships, because any attempt to resist is futile. As such, they gradually accept violence as normal, believe the battering will stop, and become completely demoralized. The prosecution, on the other hand, argued that Kelly started the fight and chased her husband before stabbing him. At the close of trial, the court ruled the expert's testimony inadmissible on the self-defense issue. She was convicted of reckless manslaughter and thereafter appealed.

On the issue of self-defense, is expert testimony on battered woman's syndrome admissible?

Expert testimony on battered woman's syndrome is admissible to prove a defendant's state of mind - to show that she honestly believed she was faced with an imminent danger of death or serious bodily injury but is *not* admissible to show her belief's objective reasonableness.

Expert testimony on battered woman's syndrome is admissible to prove a defendant's state of mind, that is, to show that she honestly believed she was faced with an imminent danger of death or serious bodily injury but is *not* admissible to show her belief was objectively reasonable. In New Jersey, forcible self-defense is justifiable "when the actor reasonably believes that such force is immediately necessary for the purpose of protecting himself against the use of unlawful force by such other person on the present occasion." Deadly force is only justified when the actor "reasonably believes that such force is necessary to protect himself against death or serious bodily harm." In the instant case, the defendant claimed self-defense claiming that she was in imminent danger of death. Under such conditions, the expert testimony is relevant to show *honesty* of her fear of imminent death and to suggest that Kelly's fear of death or injury was *objectively* reasonable. The testimony cannot be used to show that a battered woman might subjectively believe her life in danger where a reasonable person would not, since the self-defense must be objectively reasonable to be justified. The difficulty with the expert's testimony is that it *sounds* like something the jury knows very well, that is, the reasonableness of a person's fear of imminent serious danger. Yet that is not at all what this testimony is *directly* aimed at. It is aimed at an area where the supposed common knowledge of the jury may be very much mistaken, an area where jurors' logic, drawn from their own experience, may lead to an entirely erroneous conclusion. After hearing the expert, the

State v. Kelly

Supreme Court of New Jersey, 478 A.2d 364 (1984)

---

jury could conclude that her failure to leave was an essential part to life as a battered wife. The expert testimony has its limits on the issue of reasonableness - It would not be proper for the expert to suggest Kelly's belief at the time was reasonable, not because this is an ultimate issue in the case, but because the area of the expert's knowledge relates only to the reasons for her failure to leave her husband.

Conviction reversed; remanded for hearing on admissibility of expert's testimony.

State v. Norman
Supreme Court of North Carolina, 378 S.E.2d 8 (1989)

FACTS

Defendant Judy Norman and decedent John Thomas "J.T." Norman (Norman) were married for 25 years and had four living children. Starting five years into the marriage, Norman began to drink and beat his wife. When Judy was pregnant with their youngest child, Norman kicked her down a flight of stairs, causing the baby to be born prematurely the next day. Norman required Judy to prostitute herself in order to support him. Norman often threatened to kill Judy and often referred to Judy as "dogs," "whores," and "bitches." He often required her to eat cat or dog food from dog bowls, and to sleep on the concrete floor. He often beat Judy with whatever was in his hand, an ashtray, a flyswatter, a beer bottle. He threw food at Judy, refused to let her eat, put cigarettes out on her skin and required her to bark like a dog sometimes to "show off" for other people. Various witnesses testified that on June 10, 1985, Norman forced Judy to prostitute herself at a truck stop on Interstate 85 and that later that day he arrived intoxicated at the truck stop and began to hit Judy, slammed the car door into her, and threw hot coffee on her. On the way home, he was stopped by police and arrested for driving under the influence. The next morning, Norman was extremely angry after being released from jail and beat Judy throughout the day. Twice, he told her to make him a sandwich. When she brought him the sandwiches, he threw them to the floor telling her to put something on her hands because he didn't want her to touch the bread. She made the third sandwich using paper towels to cover her hands to avoid touching the bread. For this, he smeared the third sandwich on her face. That evening police responded to a domestic quarrel at the Norman residence. Judy was bruised and crying, but refused to take out a warrant on her husband because she was afraid if she did, Norman would kill her. Later that evening, the police were dispatched to the Norman residence again. This time, Norman was interfering with emergency personnel who had been called because Judy took an overdose of "nerve pills." After being treated at the hospital, Judy spent the night at her grandmother's house as advised by the therapist at the hospital. The next day, on June 12, a friend of Norman's asked Norman to drive with him to a nearby town to pick up his paycheck. Norman went to his friend's house and Judy drove the two. During the trip, Norman slapped Judy for following a truck too closely and kicked her in the side of the head while she was driving. He told her he would "cut her breast off and shove it up her rear end." Later that day, one of their children informed Judy's mother that Norman was beating Judy again. Judy's mother called the sheriff's department, but no one arrived. Norman again threatened to kill Judy. He smashed a doughnut on her face and put out a cigarette on her chest. In the afternoon, Norman laid down in the bedroom to take a nap. One of their children came into the room and asked if Judy could baby sit one of their grandchildren. Norman said Judy could do so. When the baby began to cry, Judy took the baby to her mother's house because she was afraid the crying would wake Norman. She found an automatic pistol at her mother's house, took the pistol back to her house, loaded it, and shot Norman twice in the head while he slept.

Did the defendant proffer sufficient evidence to require the trial court to instruct the jury on self defense?

State v. Norman

Supreme Court of North Carolina, 378 S.E.2d 8 (1989)

R A reasonable fear of *imminent* death or great bodily harm must exist on the part of the defendant before she is entitled to a jury instruction on self-defense.

A The Court of Appeals granted a new trial, citing as error the trial court's refusal to submit a possible verdict of acquittal by reason of self-defense. We conclude, however, that the evidence introduced in this case would not support a finding that the defendant killed her husband due to a reasonable fear of *imminent* death or great bodily harm. According we conclude that the evidence here would not support such a finding. An imminent threat is defined as an "immediate danger" which must be instantly met and cannot be avoided by calling for the assistance of others, including the protection of the law. In the instant case, all the evidence tended to show that Judy had ample time and opportunity to find other ways to prevent future abuse by Norman. The expert testimony simply showed that Judy felt very threatened, but that such a speculative belief concerned a remote and indefinite future. This was still true even though she believed her life would, at some point, end due to the abuse. What the evidence did not show was that Judy killed Norman believing that he posed an *imminent* threat of death or great bodily harm. Stretching the law of self-defense to fit the facts of this case would require changing the "imminent" requirement. Such a change would allow the killing of abusive husbands by their wives solely on the basis of the wives' testimony supported by conjecture as to the likelihood of future assaults by such men.

C See Rule above.

State v. Abbott
Supreme Court of New Jersey, 174 A.2d 881 (1961)

FACTS

A dispute arose between Defendant Abbott and Nicholas Scarano, two neighbors who shared a common driveway, after the latter hired a contractor to pave their portion. The dispute quickly escalated into a fistfight. Though Abbott managed to land the first punch, Nicholas came at Abbott with a hatchet and Nicholas's mother Mary Scarano, allegedly followed, armed with a carving knife and large fork. After a struggle and in the end, the Scaranos were all struck with the hatchet. Nicholas received sever head injuries which Abbott claimed were inflicted accidentally. Nevertheless, the prosecutor charged Abbott with atrocious assault and battery against the Scaranos. At trial, the judge gave jury instructions on the duty to retreat, and the jury convicted Abbott of atrocious assault and battery against Nicholas Scarano only. Abbott appealed, alleging tnat the jury instructions were erroneous in that its ambiguity confused the jury. The case now comes before the New Jersey Supreme Court for review.

 When the accused is confronted with an unlawful force, does he have a duty to retreat first before resorting to deadly force himself against his aggressor?

 Under the retreat rule [a/k/a the retreat doctrine] those confronted with force must attempt to retreat first before resorting to deadly defensive force if they knew [subjective standard] they could have retreated unharmed with complete safety.

 In jurisdictions that have adopted the retreat rule, those confronted with force must attempt to retreat first before resorting to deadly defensive force, if they knew they could have retreated with complete safety. The question is not whether in retrospect it can be found that the person, here the defendant, could have retreated unharmed. Rather the question is whether he knew the opportunity was there; a subjective inquiry. The rule has been accepted and adopted by our appellate court and the Model Penal Code. Today, we uphold its use because it preserves lives if reasonably limited to circumstances where one could have retreated unharmed with complete safety. Turning now to the case before us, we hold that the jury should have been instructed that Abbott was allowed to stand his ground when Nicholas came at him with his fists, and also when Mary Scarano came at him with the knife and fork, and that the question of retreat could arise only if Abbott intended to use deadly force against the Scaranos. If, however, Abbott was confronted with deadly force and *knew* at the time that he *could* retreat safely, the jury may find that his duty was breached and rightfully impose criminal liability on him.

 Here, the judge's instructions to the jury were ambiguous and confusing. Conviction reversed.

United States v. Peterson

U.S. Court of Appeals, 483 F.2d 1222 (D.C. Cir. 1973)

FACTS

Defendant-appellant Bennie L. Peterson was indicted for 2nd degree murder and convicted by a jury of manslaughter as a lesser included offense. The facts are as follows: Peterson came out of his house and into the alley behind his house to protest the fact that Keitt (accompanied by two friends) was removing the windshield wipers off the former's wrecked car. After a verbal exchange, Peterson went into his house to get a pistol, which he loaded yelling at Keitt not to move. In the meantime, Keitt and company were already in Keitt's car about to leave. Peterson walked to a point in the yard slightly inside the gate in the rear fence, holding his pistol, and said, "If you come in here I will kill you." Keitt got out of his car, walked toward Peterson and said, "What the hell do you think you are going to do with that?" He then walked back to his car and got a lug wrench. With the wrench in a raised position, he advanced toward Peterson who stood with the pistol pointed at him. Peterson warned Keitt not to "take another step," which Keitt did, and Peterson shot him in the face from a distance of about ten feet. Death was apparently instantaneous. Peterson was charged with second-degree murder and convicted of manslaughter. He appeals, arguing that two jury instructions were improper. Specifically, he refers to the alleged twice erred instructions that 1) the jury might consider whether he was the aggressor in the altercation that immediately preceded the homicide and 2) a failure by Peterson to retreat might be considered circumstantial evidence bearing on the question whether he was justified in using the amount of force which he did.

Can the initial aggressor in a conflict claim self defense after he commits a killing in order to save himself?

The initial aggressor in a conflict resulting in the death of another cannot justifiably rely on the right of self-defense.

Self-defense, the doctrine legally exonerating the taking of a human life, is a law of necessity. There must be a threat, actual or apparent, and the use of deadly force against the defendant. The threat must have been unlawful and immediate and the reaction to a threat must be proportional to the threat itself. The defender must have honestly believed that he was in immediate threat of death or serious bodily harm, and that his response was necessary to save himself. Such a belief is measured objectively. If a person incites, encourages, or otherwise promotes the circumstances that lead up to his killing another, that person is the aggressor and is not entitled to the claim of self-defense. The exception being if the aggressor communicates to his opponent his intent to withdraw and in good faith attempts to do so, he may claim self-defense. While we acknowledge that in the majority of jurisdictions, one may stand his ground and use deadly force whenever it seems reasonably necessary to save himself, we do not follow this rule in our state. Turning to the facts of the instant case, we note that Peterson returned to the yard with a pistol just as Keitt was about to leave the scene. At this point, Keitt was not the aggressor. Peterson was not in any danger of bodily harm or death at this point in time; and prior to this instant, only verbal threats had been exchanged and a misdemeanor was in progress (deadly force may not be used in defense of property). After Peterson returned to the yard, he loaded his pistol, walked toward Keitt, told him not to come in, and threatened to kill him if he did. Peterson may not assert self-defense under these circumstances because he was the person who created the dangerous situation. He could have simply walked away, but did not. Peterson argues he was not required to retreat. Yet, as we have already stated, the right of self-defense is not available to the party who provokes the conflict. Under the instant facts, the jury instructions were proper.

 Judgment of the trial court for conviction affirmed.

People v. Ceballos

Supreme Court of California, 526 P.2d 241 (1974)

FACTS

Don Ceballos lived in a small home with the living quarters above the garage, though Ceballos sometimes slept in the garage and had about $2,000 worth of property. In March of 1970, Ceballos noted that some tools had been stolen from his home. In May he noticed that the lock on his garage door was bent and that there were pry marks on the door. The next day he mounted a loaded .22 pistol in the garage, aimed at the center of the garage doors and connected by a wire to one of the doors so that the pistol would fire a shot if the door were opened several inches. Two boys, Stephen, aged 16, and Robert, aged 15 came to Ceballos house while he was away. Neither was armed. Stephen removed the lock with a crowbar, and as he pulled open the door, was shot in the face with a bullet. Stephen testified that he was not sure if he was going to steal anything, but wanted to go in the garage and look around. Ceballos testified that he felt he should set some kind of trap to protect himself and his property. When initially questioned by police, Ceballos stated that he wanted to protect what he did have. The jury found Ceballos guilty of assault with a deadly weapon. Ceballos appealed, contending that had he been present, he would have been justified in shooting Stephen under Penal Code section 197.

Can the use of a mechanical device which causes the death of another be justified to protect property against a non-violent burglary?

An injury or killing using a deadly mechanical device is not justified where the device injures a person in response to a non-violent burglary.

A A person may be held criminally liable for injuries or death resulting from a deadly mechanical device that he sets on his property. However, an exception to the rule exists where the defendant would have been justified in taking the life or inflicting the injury with his own hands. The reasoning behind the restriction stems from the fact that allowing persons to employ deadly mechanical devices imperils fireman, police officers and children. If the actor is present, he may realize that deadly force is not necessary, but deadly mechanical devices are without mercy or discretion – "silent instrumentalities of death." What's more, even if the use of deadly mechanical devices were applied here, Ceballos would not be justified in shooting Stephen because a killing in defense of property is warranted, among other things, when committed against one who clearly intends to commit a "atrocious" felony such as murder, mayhem, rape or robbery. The crime of burglary can be included as a forcible and atrocious crime, but only where it creates "a reasonable fear of great bodily harm." This was not the case here; it did not threaten death or serious bodily harm. We similarly reject defendant's contention that Penal Code section 197 justifies the homicide since it was committed while attempting to apprehend a felon. However, defendant's own testimony indicates that the intent of the killing was to prevent a burglary, not to apprehend a felon. Lastly, under the common law, we note the exception to the foregoing principle that "extreme force could be used to prevent dispossession of a dwelling house, or against burning of a dwelling." Yet as we have already stated, the intent of the accused was to prevent a burglary; he was not concerned with dispossession or a burning. Thus, we conclude as a matter of law that the exception to the rule of liability for injuries inflicted by a deadly mechanical device does not apply here.

Judgment affirmed.

Durham v. State
Supreme Court of Indiana, 159 N.E. 145 (1927)

FACTS

Defendant Durham, a deputy game warden, arrested Long for illegal fishing. With intent to escape, Long jumped into his boat and fled; Durham pursued. When Durham caught Long, the latter resisted arrest and beat Durham about the head with an oar. In response, Durham shot Long in the arm. Durham was charged with assault and battery for using excessive force in arresting Long. At trial, the judge instructed the jury that, if Long resisted arrest for a misdemeanor, Durham was not authorized to use deadly force to apprehend him. Durham was convicted of assault and battery. He appealed, arguing that the judge's jury instruction did not correctly state the law. Specifically, Durham argues that the jury's instruction should have stated that deadly force against suspects is allowed when the suspects offer deadly resistance.

 Does the law allow a peace officer use deadly force to arrest a misdemeanor suspect even when the suspect offers deadly resistance?

 Peace officers may use deadly force to arrest felony suspects and any suspects who offer deadly resistance; otherwise they may use only non-deadly force to arrest misdemeanor suspects not offering deadly resistance.

 Peace officers may use deadly force to arrest felony suspects and any suspects who offer deadly resistance; otherwise they may use only non-deadly force to arrest misdemeanor suspects not offering deadly resistance. In *Plummer v. State,* the court held that peace officers may not use more force than is necessary to arrest. And if they do use excessive force, suspects are justified in resisting arrest forcibly. However, if a suspect forcibly resists a proper arrest, the arresting officer may use any force necessary to arrest him, including deadly force. However, in other jurisdictions, courts have limited the amount of force which may be used to arrest one charged with a misdemeanor, as distinguished from a felony. The general rule of those cases is that an officer making a misdemeanor arrest may not use deadly force to make the arrest, and may not use deadly force against a misdemeanor offender who is fleeing but not resisting. If the suspect resists, the officer need not retreat, but may use any non-deadly force necessary to make the arrest. The officer may not use deadly force unless the suspect first attempts deadly force in resisting arrest. If in doing so the officer is absolutely obliged to seriously wound or kill in order to prevent the accused from seriously wounding or killing him [the peace officer] he will be justified. In the instant case, the jury instruction was misstate. It failed to state that Durham was justified in using deadly force to arrest a misdemeanor offender who offered deadly resistance.

 Conviction reversed and remanded for retrial.

Tennessee v. Gardner
Supreme Court of the United States, 471 U.S. 1 (1985)

FACTS

A Tennessee statute provides that if, after a police officer has given notice of an intent to arrest a criminal suspect, the suspect flees or forcibly resists, "the officer may use all the necessary means to effect the arrest." Acting under the authority of this statute, Memphis Police Officers Elton Hymon shot and killed appellee-respondent Garner's son as, after being told to halt, the son fled over a fence at night in the backyard of a house he was suspected of burglarizing. The officer used deadly force despite being "reasonably sure" the suspect was unarmed and thinking that he was 17 or 18 years old and of slight build. Garner's father then brought this action in the Federal District Court for the Western District of Tennessee, seeking damages under 42 U.S.C. 1983 for asserted violations of Garner's constitutional rights. The complaint alleged that the shooting violated the Fourth, Fifth, Sixth, Eighth, and Fourteenth Amendments of the United States Constitution. After a 3-day bench trial, the District Court entered judgment for all defendants. It then concluded that Hymon's actions were authorized by the Tennessee statute, which in turn was constitutional. Hymon had employed the only reasonable and practicable means of preventing Garner's escape. Garner had "recklessly and heedlessly attempted to vault over the fence to escape, thereby assuming the risk of being fired upon." The Court of Appeals for the Sixth Circuit affirmed with regard to Hymon, finding that he had acted in good-faith reliance on the Tennessee statute and was therefore within the scope of his qualified immunity. It remanded for reconsideration of the possible liability of the city, however, in light of *Monell v. New York City Dept. of Social Services*, which had come down after the District Court's decision. The District Court was directed to consider whether a city enjoyed a qualified immunity, whether the use of deadly force and hollow point bullets in these circumstances was constitutional, and whether any unconstitutional municipal conduct flowed from a "policy or custom" as required for liability under *Monell*. The District Court concluded that *Monell* did not affect its decision. While acknowledging some doubt as to the possible immunity of the city, it found that the statute (and Hymon's actions) were constitutional. Given this conclusion, it declined to consider the "policy or custom" question. The Court of Appeals reversed and remanded. It reasoned that the killing of a fleeing suspect is a "seizure" under the Fourth Amendment, and is therefore constitutional only if "reasonable." The State of Tennessee, which had intervened to defend the statute, appealed to the U.S. Supreme Court which noted probable jurisdiction in the appeal and granted the petition.

Is the Fourteenth Amendment implicated when deadly force is used to prevent the escape of an apparently unarmed suspected and fleeing felon?

The 4th Amendment reasonableness requirement prohibits officers from using deadly force to arrest a fleeing felon *unless* it is necessary to prevent his escape *and* the officer has probable cause to believe that the suspect poses a significant threat of death/serious bodily injury to himself or

Tennessee v. Gardner

Supreme Court of the United States, 471 U.S. 1 (1985)

others.

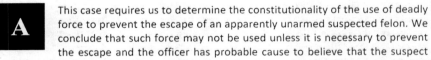

A This case requires us to determine the constitutionality of the use of deadly force to prevent the escape of an apparently unarmed suspected felon. We conclude that such force may not be used unless it is necessary to prevent the escape and the officer has probable cause to believe that the suspect poses a significant threat of death or serious physical injury to the officer or others. The Tennessee statute is unconstitutional insofar as it authorizes the use of deadly force against, as in this case, an apparently unarmed, non-dangerous fleeing suspect; such force may not be used unless necessary to prevent the escape and the officer has probable cause to believe that the suspect poses a significant threat of death or serious physical injury to the officer or others. Apprehension by the use of deadly force is a seizure subject to the Fourth Amendment's reasonableness requirement. To determine whether such a seizure is reasonable, the extent of the intrusion on the suspect's rights under that Amendment must be balanced against the governmental interests in effective law enforcement. This balancing process demonstrates that, notwithstanding probable cause to seize a suspect, an officer may not always do so by killing him. The use of deadly force to prevent the escape of all felony suspects, whatever the circumstances, is constitutionally unreasonable. The Fourth Amendment, for purposes of this case, should not be construed in light of the common-law rule allowing the use of whatever force is necessary to effect the arrest of a fleeing felon. Changes in the legal and technological context mean that that rule is distorted almost beyond recognition when literally applied. Whereas felonies were formerly capital crimes, few are now, or can be, and many crimes classified as misdemeanors, or nonexistent, at common law are now felonies. Also, the common-law rule developed at a time when weapons were rudimentary. And, in light of the varied rules adopted in the States indicating a long-term movement away from the common-law rule, particularly in the police departments themselves, that rule is a dubious indicium of the constitutionality of the Tennessee statute. There is no indication that holding a police practice such as that authorized by the statute unreasonable will severely hamper effective law enforcement. While burglary is a serious crime, the officer in this case could not reasonably have believed that the suspect - young, slight, and unarmed - posed any threat. Nor does the fact that an unarmed suspect has broken into a dwelling at night automatically mean he is dangerous.

C Affirmed and remanded.

People v. Unger
Supreme Court of Illinois, 362 N.E.2d 319 (1977)

FACTS

Defendant Francis Unger, a 22 year old, 155 lb. inmate, was serving a one to three-year term for auto theft. On February 23, 1972, defendant was transferred to the prison's minimum security "honor farm." Prior to his transfer, Unger testified that a fellow inmate had brandished a six-inch knife in an attempt to force him to engage in homosexual activities. At the honor farm, Unger was sexually attacked by three inmates whom he named at trial. On March 7, 1972, Unger walked off of an honor farm after receiving death threats and threats of homosexual attacks by other inmates. He was caught two days later in a motel room in St. Charles, Illinois. Unger testified that on the day he walked off the honor farm he received a telephone call in which an unidentified person threatened him with death because the caller believed Unger had reported the assaults to prison officials. At no time did Unger report any of the incidences to the proper authorities. Unger said he left the honor farm to save his life and that he planned to return once he found someone who could help him. Defendant's first trial for escape resulted in a hung jury. The jury in the second trial returned a verdict after a five hour deliberation. A jury instruction (People's Instruction No. 9) was given by the trial court over defendant's objection. The appellate court found the instruction to be reversible error. This appeal followed.

Was is in error for the trial court to instruct the jury that it must disregard the reasons given for the defendant's escape and to conversely refuse to instruct the jury on the statutory defenses of compulsion (duress) and necessity?

The instructions given were in error; an escaped prisoner may assert the defense of necessary if he can set forth facts that would tend to show that his choice to escape was the lessor of two evils - either escape or remain and be subjected to repeated sexual assault.

The trial court submitted the following jury instruction (People's Instruction No. 9) over the defendant's objection: "The reasons, if any, given for the alleged escape are immaterial and not to be considered by you as in any way justifying or excusing, if there were in fact such reasons." The trial court refused to submit jury instructions relating to the affirmative defenses of necessity and duress. We agree with the appellate court's finding that People's Instruction No. 9 constituted reversible error and also hold as reversible error the trial court's omission of instructions relating to the defense of necessity. Several recent decisions have recognized the defenses of duress and necessity in prison escape situations. In *People v. Harmon*, the defense of duress was held to apply in a case where the defendant alleged that he escaped in order to avoid repeated homosexual attacks by fellow inmates. In *People v. Lovercamp*, a limited defense of necessity was held to be available to two defendants whose escapes were allegedly motivated by fear of homosexual attacks. In the instant case, if Unger's testimony is to be believed, he was forced to choose

People v. Unger
Supreme Court of Illinois, 362 N.E.2d 319 (1977)

between two admitted evils: 1) a situation which arose from actual or threatened homosexual assaults and 2) fears of reprisal. Unger's complete and unabridged testimony was thus sufficient to justify the giving of a necessity instruction by the court. The State, however, would have us apply a more stringent test to prison escape situations and insists that the following test from *Lovercamp* is the appropriate test to follow in order to decide if a necessity instruction is proper. Those conditions are whether: (1) the prisoner is faced with a specific threat of death, forcible sexual attack or substantial bodily injury in the immediate future; (2) there is no time for a complaint to the authorities or there exists a history of futile complaints which make any result from such complaints illusory; (3) there is no time or opportunity to resort to the courts; (4) there is no evidence of force or violence used towards prison personnel or other 'innocent' persons in the escape; and (5) the prisoner immediately reports to the proper authorities when he has attained a position of safety from the immediate threat. All of these conditions are *relevant factors* to be considered in assessing a claim of necessity; however, each condition is not, *as a matter of law*, absolutely necessary to establish a successful necessity defense such that the absence of one or more of the conditions listed would not necessarily bar the defendant from asserting the defense of necessity.

 We affirm the judgment of the appellant court.

Commonwealth v. Leno
616 N.E.2d 453 (1993)

FACTS

The State of Massachusetts is one of 10 states that prohibit the distribution of hypodermic needles without a prescription. Defendant Leno and other defendants operated a needle exchange program in order to combat the spread of AIDS. Consequently, Leno and the others were charged and convicted of unauthorized 1) possession and 2) distribution [two distinct crimes] of instruments to administer controlled substances. On appeal, Leno argued that the judge erroneously refused to instruct the jury on the defense of necessity.

In order to raise the defense of necessity, must the danger be clear and imminent?

In order to claim the defense of necessity, the danger must be clear and imminent and not debatable and speculative.

Leno and the other defendants did not show that the danger they sought to avoid was clear and imminent, rather than debatable or speculative. Specifically, the danger they sought to avoid, the spread of aids through dirty needles, was debatable or speculative because great minds may differ as to the best course of action to take to avoid the spread of AIDS. No one public policy is the correct and only policy with respect to the AIDS crisis. Leno argues that the prescription requirement for possession and distribution of hypodermic needles and syringes is both ineffective and dangerous. However, it is up to the Legislature and not the courts, to determine how it wants to control the distribution of drug-related paraphernalia and their use in the consumption of illegal drugs. Leno's argument that their needle exchange program will eventually will result in an over-all reduction in the spread of HIV and that their actions constitute an effective means of combating the problem. Defendants' argument raises the issue of jury nullification, not the defense of necessity. We reject the idea that jurors have a right to nullify the law on which they are instructed by the judge.

Affirmed.

United States v. Schoon

U.S. Court of Appeals, 971 F.2d 193 (9th Cir. 1992)

FACTS

On December 4, 1989, thirty people, including Defendant-appellant Schoon and two other appellants, entered an IRS office in Tucson, Arizona, to protest the U.S. involvement in El Salvador. They chanted "Keep America's tax dollars out of El Salvador," splashed fake blood on the walls, counters, and carpeting, and obstructed the office's operation. At trial, Schoon offered evidence of the conditions in El Salvador as the motivation for their conduct and attempted to assert a necessity defense, arguing that acts in protest of American involvement in El Salvador were necessary to avoid further bloodshed in that country. The district court precluded the necessity defense, relying on Ninth Circuit precedent. Specifically, the court noted that (1) the requisite immediacy was lacking; (2) the actions taken would not abate the evil; and (3) other legal alternatives existed.

Can the necessity doctrine be validly raised as a defense to charges arising from protests of congressional policies?

Indirect civil disobedience, including protests of congressional polices, can never meet all the requirements of the necessity doctrine, thus making the necessity defense unavailable in such cases.

We conclude that the elements of the necessity defense are lacking in *indirect* civil disobedience cases. This is a case of indirect civil disobedience. Indirect civil disobedience involves violating a law or interfering with a government policy which is not, itself, the object of protest. Direct civil disobedience, on the other hand, involves violating a law or interfering with a government policy which is, itself, the object of protest. Necessity is a utilitarian defense which justifies criminal acts taken to avert a greater harm, where the social benefits of the crime outweigh the social costs of failing to commit the crime. In order to invoke the necessity defense, the defendants must show that: 1) they were faced with a choice of evils and chose the lesser evil; 2) they acted to prevent imminent harm; 3) they reasonably anticipated a direct causal relationship between their conduct and the harm to be averted; and 4) they had no legal alternatives to violating the law. Analyzing the actions of the protestors, we see that defendants cannot meet all of the necessity defenses four elements. With respect to element 1) above, there can be no aversion of harm by the protest, since the most immediate "harm" this form of protest targets is the existence of the law or policy. However, the mere existence of a constitutional law or policy cannot be deemed a cognizable harm. We do not rely upon the immanent harm prong of the defense because we believe there can be indirect civil disobedience cases where the protested harem is immanent. With respect to 3) above, in political necessity cases involving indirect civil disobedience, the act alone is unlikely to abate the evil precisely because the action is indirect. The IRS obstruction is unlikely to abate the killings in El Salvador, or immediately change Congress policy. Thus, there is no substantial causal relationship between the criminal conduct and the harm to be averted. With respect to 4), in indirect civil disobedience cases the legal alternatives will never be deemed exhausted when the harm can be mitigated by congressional action. Prior federal cases assumed that the "possibility" that Congress can change its mind at any time in response to citizen protest, such that petitioning Congress was sufficient in the context of the democratic process to make lawful political action a reasonable legal alternative. Thus, there can never be an absence of legal alternatives where congressional action is the protest's aim. In sum, indirect protests of congressional policies can never meet all the requirements of the necessity doctrine.

Judgment affirmed.

Regina v. Dudley and Stevens
Queen's Bench Division, 14 Q.B.D. 273 (1884)

FACTS

Defendants Thomas Dudley (Dudley) and Edward Stephens (Stephens) were indicted for the murder of Richard Parker on the high seas on July 25, 1884. On July 5th, 1884, defendants, one Brooks, and Richard Parker (Parker) (a young seventeen or eighteen-year-old English boy) set out to sea on a yacht. Not long afterward, they were cast away in a storm at sea, 1,600 miles away from the Cape of Good Hope, and were compelled to put into an open boat belonging to the yacht. For three days, the four individuals only had two 1-lb. tins of turnips and no water to subsist upon. On the fourth day, they caught a small turtle, which was entirely consumed after twelve days. For eight days after, they had nothing to eat, and no fresh water, except for rain water they were able to catch in their oilskin capes. On July 24th, Dudley proposed to Stephen and Brooks, but not to Parker, that lots should be cast to see who should be put to death and be used for food to save the rest. Brooks refused and no lots were drawn. The next day, July 25th, when no vessel appeared to save them, Dudley and Stephens agreed to kill Parker, despite dissent by Brooks. Dudley offered a prayer asking for forgiveness. Dudley, with the assent of Stevens, approached the young boy, and cut his throat thus killing him. The men fed upon the boy, and were rescued by a passing vessel four days after the act. Dudley and Stephens were tried and convicted of murder.

Is a killing out of necessity grounds for punishment and subsequent conviction for murder?

A person may be punished and convicted of murder, even if the killing was done out of necessity.

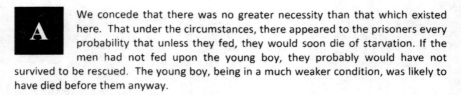

We concede that there was no greater necessity than that which existed here. That under the circumstances, there appeared to the prisoners every probability that unless they fed, they would soon die of starvation. If the men had not fed upon the young boy, they probably would have not survived to be rescued. The young boy, being in a much weaker condition, was likely to have died before them anyway.

If upon the whole matter the Court finds that the killing of Richard Parker be felony and murder, then the jurors say that Dudley and Stephens were each guilty of felony and murder as alleged in the indictment.

Public Committee Against Torture v. State of Israel

Supreme Court of Israel, H.C. 5100/94 (Sept. 6, 1999)

FACTS

Israel's General Security Service (GSS) investigates persons suspected of committing crimes against Israel's security. Administrative directives authorize investigators to use of physical means during interrogations; the justification of which is that it is deemed immediately necessary for saving lives. "Physical means" include forceful shaking, sleep deprivation, and forcing the suspect to wait in painful positions. The Public Committee Against Torture (plaintiff), a group representing suspects arrested and interrogated, sought an order prohibiting the use of these physical means during interrogations. The State of Israel (defendant) argued that it should be permitted to use physical means based upon the defense of necessity in order to foil and prevent terrorist attacks upon the State.

May the necessity defense be invoked to support directives that permit the use of "physical means" during interrogations as a way of combating and/or thwarting present/future violence against the State?

The necessity defense may not be used to support directives that permit the use of "physical means" during interrogations as a way of combating and/or thwarting present/future violence against the State.

We hold that the necessity defense may not be used to support directives that permit the use of "physical means" during interrogations as a way of combating and/or thwarting present/future violence against the State.

While "a reasonable investigation is likely to cause discomfort," the GSS's general mandate to conduct interrogations does not encompass the authority to use physical means under both Israeli law and International law. Thus, ordinary cases of interrogation must be free of torture, free of cruel, inhuman treatment and free of degrading handling whatsoever. There are no exceptions and no room for balancing. The State asserts that physical interrogation should be permitted in exceptional situations based upon the criminal law defense of necessity; that the State therefore argues that GSS investigators are authorized to apply physical means during interrogations in the appropriate circumstances, in order to prevent serious harm to human life or body, in the absence of other alternatives. Israel's Penal Law recognizes the necessity defense and we agree that in appropriate circumstances, GSS investigators may use the necessity defense *if indicted for criminal wrongdoing during interrogation of suspects.* However, that is not the case here - we are not addressing the potential criminal liability of a GSS investigator. Consequently, we declare that the GSS does not have the authority to "shake" a man, hold him in the "Shabach" position or deprive him of sleep in a manner other than that which is inherently required by the interrogation.

See Rule above.

Cruzan v. Director, Missouri Dept. of Health

Supreme Court of the United States, 497 U.S. 261 (1989)

FACTS

Defendant-petitioner Nancy Cruzan is incompetent, having sustained severe injuries in an automobile accident, and now lies in a Missouri state hospital in what is referred to as a persistent vegetative state: generally, a condition in which a person exhibits motor reflexes but evinces no indications of significant cognitive function. The State is bearing the cost of her care. Hospital employees refused, without court approval, to honor the request of Cruzan's parents, her co-petitioners, to terminate her artificial nutrition and hydration, since that would result in death. A state trial court authorized the termination, finding that a person in Cruzan's condition has a fundamental right under the State and Federal Constitutions to direct or refuse the withdrawal of death-prolonging procedures, and that Cruzan's expression to a former housemate that she would not wish to continue her life if sick or injured unless she could live at least halfway normally suggested that she would not wish to continue on with her nutrition and hydration. The State Supreme Court reversed. While recognizing a right to refuse treatment embodied in the common-law doctrine of informed consent, the court questioned its applicability in this case. It also declined to read into the State Constitution a broad right to privacy that would support an unrestricted right to refuse treatment and expressed doubt that the Federal Constitution embodied such a right. The court then decided that the State Living Will statute embodied a state policy strongly favoring the preservation of life, and that Cruzan's statements to her housemate were unreliable for the purpose of determining her intent. It rejected the argument that her parents were entitled to order the termination of her medical treatment, concluding that no person can assume that choice for an incompetent in the absence of the formalities required by the Living Will statute or clear and convincing evidence of the patient's wishes. The U.S. Supreme Court granted certiorari to determine whether Nancy Cruzan has a right under the U.S. Constitution to require the hospital to withdraw life-sustaining treatment under these circumstances.

 I — Does an incompetent person have a Constitutional right to withdraw life-sustaining treatment?

R — Competent adults have a Constitutional right to refuse or discontinue life-sustaining treatment; incompetent persons have the same Constitutional right *provided* that they expressed a clear intent to die under the circumstances while they were competent - if not, states may require life support to continue on the incompetent absent such a clear showing.

A — The United States Constitution does not forbid Missouri to require that evidence of an incompetent's wishes as to the withdrawal of life-sustaining treatment be proved by clear and convincing evidence. Most state courts have based a right to refuse treatment on the common law right to informed consent or on both that right and a constitutional privacy right. In addition to

Cruzan v. Director, Missouri Dept. of Health

Supreme Court of the United States, 497 U.S. 261 (1989)

relying on state constitutions and the common law, state courts have also turned to state statutes for guidance. However, these sources are not available to this Court, where the question is simply whether the Federal Constitution prohibits Missouri from choosing the rule of law which it did. A competent person has a liberty interest under the Due Process Clause in refusing unwanted medical treatment. However, the question whether that constitutional right has been violated must be determined by balancing the liberty interest against relevant state interests. For purposes of this case, it is assumed that a competent person would have a constitutionally protected right to refuse lifesaving hydration and nutrition. This does not mean that an incompetent person should possess the same right, since such a person is unable to make an informed and voluntary choice to exercise that hypothetical right or any other right. While Missouri has in effect recognized that, under certain circumstances, a surrogate may act for the patient in electing to withdraw hydration and nutrition and thus cause death, it has established a procedural safeguard to assure that the surrogate's action conforms as best it may to the wishes expressed by the patient while competent. It is permissible for Missouri, in its proceedings, to apply a clear and convincing evidence standard, which is an appropriate standard when the individual interests at stake are both particularly important and more substantial than mere loss of money. Here, Missouri has a general interest in the protection and preservation of human life, as well as other, more particular interests, at stake. It may legitimately seek to safeguard the personal element of an individual's choice between life and death. The State is also entitled to guard against potential abuses by surrogates who may not act to protect the patient. Similarly, it is entitled to consider that a judicial proceeding regarding an incompetent's wishes may not be adversarial, with the added guarantee of accurate factfinding that the adversary process brings with it. The State may also properly decline to make judgments about the "quality" of a particular individual's life, and simply assert an unqualified interest in the preservation of human life to be weighed against the constitutionally protected interests of the individual. It is self-evident that these interests are more substantial, both on an individual and societal level, than those involved in a common civil dispute. The clear and convincing evidence standard also serves as a societal judgment about how the risk of error should be distributed between the litigants. Missouri may permissibly place the increased risk of an erroneous decision on those seeking to terminate life-sustaining treatment. An erroneous decision not to terminate results in the maintenance of the status quo, with at least the potential that a wrong decision will eventually be corrected or its impact mitigated by an event such as an advancement in medical science or the patient's unexpected death. However, an erroneous decision to withdraw such treatment is not susceptible of correction. Although Missouri's proof requirement may have frustrated the effectuation of Cruzan's not-fully-expressed desires, the Constitution does not require general rules to work flawlessly. The State Supreme Court did not commit constitutional error in concluding that the evidence adduced at trial did not amount to clear and convincing proof of Cruzan's desire to have hydration and nutrition withdrawn. The trial court had not adopted a clear and convincing evidence standard, and Cruzan's observations that she did not want to live life as a "vegetable" did not deal in terms with withdrawal of medical treatment or of hydration and nutrition. The Due Process Clause does not

Cruzan v. Director, Missouri Dept. of Health

Supreme Court of the United States, 497 U.S. 261 (1989)

---

require a State to accept the "substituted judgment" of close family members in the absence of substantial proof that their views reflect the patient's. This Court's decision upholding a State's favored treatment of traditional family relationships may not be turned into a constitutional requirement that a State must recognize the primacy of these relationships in a situation like this. Nor may a decision upholding a State's right to permit family decisionmaking be turned into a constitutional requirement that the State recognize such decisionmaking. Nancy Cruzan's parents would surely be qualified to exercise such a right of "substituted judgment" were it required by the Constitution. However, for the same reasons that Missouri may require clear and convincing evidence of a patient's wishes, it may also choose to defer only to those wishes, rather than confide the decision to close family members.

Judgment affirmed.

Washington v. Glucksberg
Supreme Court of the United States, 521 U.S. 702 (1997)

FACTS

It has always been a crime to assist a suicide in the State of Washington. The State's present law makes "[p]romoting a suicide attempt" a felony, and provides: "A person is guilty of [that crime] when he knowingly causes or aids another person to attempt suicide." Plaintiff-Respondent Glucksberg and four Washington physicians who occasionally treat terminally ill, suffering patients, declare that they would assist these patients in ending their lives if not for the State's assisted suicide ban. Respondents, along with three gravely ill plaintiffs who have since died, and a nonprofit organization that counsels people considering physician assisted suicide, filed this suit against petitioners, the State and its Attorney General, seeking a declaration that the ban is, on its face, unconstitutional. They assert a liberty interest protected by the Fourteenth Amendment's Due Process Clause which extends to a personal choice by a mentally competent, terminally ill adult to commit physician assisted suicide. Relying primarily on *Planned Parenthood of Southeastern Pa. v. Casey*, and *Cruzan v. Director, Mo. Dept. of Health*, the Federal District Court agreed, concluding that Washington's assisted suicide ban is unconstitutional because it places an undue burden on the exercise of that constitutionally protected liberty interest. The *en banc* Ninth Circuit affirmed. The State of Washington (defendant) petitioned the United States Supreme Court.

 Does the Due Process Clause's liberty interest include a right to assist another in committing suicide?

 The Due Process Clause's liberty does not include a right to assist another in committing suicide because the asserted "right" is not a fundamental liberty interest protected by the Due Process Clause

 Washington's prohibition against "caus[ing]" or "aid[ing]" a suicide does not violate the Due Process Clause. An examination of our Nation's history, legal traditions, and practices demonstrates that Anglo American common law has punished or otherwise disapproved of assisting suicide for over 700 years; that rendering such assistance is still a crime in almost every State; that such prohibitions have never contained exceptions for those who were near death; that the prohibitions have in recent years been reexamined and, for the most part, reaffirmed in a number of States; and that the President recently signed the Federal Assisted Suicide Funding Restriction Act of 1997, which prohibits the use of federal funds in support of physician assisted suicide. In light of that history, this Court's decisions lead to the conclusion that respondents' asserted "right" to assistance in committing suicide is not a fundamental liberty interest protected by the Due Process Clause. The Court's established method of substantive due process analysis has two primary features: First, the Court has regularly observed that the Clause specially protects those fundamental rights and liberties which are, objectively, deeply rooted in this Nation's history and

Washington v. Glucksberg
Supreme Court of the United States, 521 U.S. 702 (1997)

tradition. Second, the Court has required a "careful description" of the asserted fundamental liberty interest. The Ninth Circuit's and respondents' various descriptions of the interest here at stake - e.g., a right to "determin[e] the time and manner of one's death," the "right to die," a "liberty to choose how to die," a right to "control of one's final days," "the right to choose a humane, dignified death," and "the liberty to shape death"- run counter to that second requirement. Since the Washington statute prohibits "aid[ing] another person to attempt suicide," the question before the Court is more properly characterized as whether the "liberty" specially protected by the Clause includes a right to commit suicide which itself includes a right to assistance in doing so. This asserted right has no place in our Nation's traditions, given the country's consistent, almost universal, and continuing rejection of the right, even for terminally ill, mentally competent adults. To hold for respondents, the Court would have to reverse centuries of legal doctrine and practice, and strike down the considered policy choice of almost every State. Respondents' contention that the asserted interest is consistent with this Court's substantive due process cases, if not with this Nation's history and practice, is unpersuasive. The constitutionally protected right to refuse lifesaving hydration and nutrition that was discussed in *Cruzan* was not simply deduced from abstract concepts of personal autonomy, but was instead grounded in the Nation's history and traditions, given the common law rule that forced medication was a battery, and the long legal tradition protecting the decision to refuse unwanted medical treatment. And although Casey recognized that many of the rights and liberties protected by the Due Process Clause sound in personal autonomy, it does not follow that any and all important, intimate, and personal decisions are so protected. The constitutional requirement that Washington's assisted suicide ban be rationally related to legitimate government interests is unquestionably met here. These interests include prohibiting intentional killing and preserving human life; preventing the serious public health problem of suicide, especially among the young, the elderly, and those suffering from untreated pain or from depression or other mental disorders; protecting the medical profession's integrity and ethics and maintaining physicians' role as their patients' healers; protecting the poor, the elderly, disabled persons, the terminally ill, and persons in other vulnerable groups from indifference, prejudice, and psychological and financial pressure to end their lives; and avoiding a possible slide towards voluntary and perhaps even involuntary euthanasia. The relative strengths of these various interests need not be weighed exactly, since they are unquestionably important and legitimate, and the law at issue is at least reasonably related to their promotion and protection. We therefore hold that the state's statute banning assisted suicide does not violate the Fourteenth Amendment's Due Process Clause.

 Reversed and remanded.

State v. Toscano
Supreme Court of New Jersey, 378 A.2d 755 (1977)

FACTS

Defendant Joseph Toscano, a chiropractor was charged and convicted with other individuals of conspiring to defraud insurance companies by staging accidents and settling for fictitious injuries. Toscano admitted that he aided in the fabrication of the false claims but claimed to have done so while under duress. Specifically, he claimed that his co-conspirator, Leonardo, a bookie who he owed gambling debts to had threatened him and that to escape these threats, Toscano moved to a new address, changed his number, applied for a gun permit, and discussed the situation with coworkers. At trial, the judge instructed the jury to disregard Toscano's claims of duress, holding when the peril is not imminent, as required under the duress doctrine, one cannot invoke the defense. The judge instructed the jury further stating that Toscano had time to call for police help, so the danger was no immanent. Toscano was subsequently convicted and fined $500 and appealed. The appellate court affirmed Toscano's conviction on appeal and the Supreme Court of New Jersey granted certification to consider the status of duress as an affirmative defense to a crime.

Under the law of New Jersey, may a criminal defendant raise the common law defense of duress if he alleges he was intimidated with the threat of future harm?

Under New Jersey law, duress is a valid defense to all crimes except for murder, if the defendant committed the crime because he was threatened with the use or threat of future force against himself or another which he was unable to resist, as judged by an objective [reasonable man] standard.

Under New Jersey law, duress is a valid defense to all crimes except for murder, if the defendant committed the crime because he was threatened with the use or threat of future force against himself or another which he was unable to resist, as judged by an objective [reasonable man] standard. Since New Jersey has no applicable statute defining the defense of duress, we are guided only by common law principles and contemporary notions of justice and fairness. At common law, duress was recognized only when the coercion is alleged to involve threats of "present, imminent and pending" harm "of such a nature as to induce a well grounded apprehension of death or serious bodily injury if the act is not done" and was permitted as a defense to prosecution for many serious offenses less the killing of an innocent person. Thus, under the Model Penal Code and a New Jersey statute currently in draft form, defendants threatened with future harm can invoke the defense of duress if they could prove the threats impressed upon them would force a reasonable person to acquiesce; the so-called objective standard. Under the Model Penal Code, duress can be an affirmative defense even to murder, but the New Jersey draft statute omits this exception. In the instant case, Toscano's testimony could allow a jury to find Toscano and his wife were threatened with violence if they did not assist in the fraudulent scheme, and that such threats were reasonable. Exercising our authority to revise

State v. Toscano

Supreme Court of New Jersey, 378 A.2d 755 (1977)

---

common law, we now adopt this approach as the law of New Jersey. Hereinafter, duress shall be a defense to crimes other than murder if the defendant committed a crime because he was coerced by the use or threat of unlawful force, against himself or another, which a reasonable person in the situation would be unable to resist.

Judgment reversed; remanded for retrial.

People v. Hood
Supreme Court of California, 462 P.2d 370 (1969)

FACTS

Defendant Hood, who was heavily intoxicated when arrested by a police officer, resisted, and in the course of doing so, seized the officer's gun and shot him in the legs. The officer was wounded but not killed. Consequently, Hood was convicted of assaulting a peace officer with a deadly weapon and for assault with intent to commit murder. Hood appealed.

Is *voluntary* intoxication a valid defense to a charge of assault?

Under the law of California, *voluntary* intoxication is no defense to assault.

California law does not recognize *voluntary* intoxication as a valid defense to assault. Accordingly, we reverse the trial court's conviction for assault because the lower court failed to instruct the jury on the lesser included offense of simple assault. Similarly, we reverse the trial court's conviction for assault with intent to kill because we find that jury instruction on intoxication hopelessly confusing. In order to guide the trial court on retrial, we will now decide whether voluntary intoxication is a defense to assault. California appellate courts are in conflict on whether the crimes of simple assault and assault with a deadly weapon are "specific intent" or "general intent" crimes. But there is no real difference; only a linguistic one between an act to do an act already performed and an intent to do an act in the future. Thus a distinction between the two must rest with other considerations. Simple assault and assault with a deadly weapon are general intent crimes even though they require a specific mental state. However, assault with intent to murder is a specific intent crime. If the intent to murder is negated by intoxication or mental illness, then a defendant is found guilty of only assault. Arson, for example, is a general intent crime, so it also cannot be negated by intoxication. Murder is a specific intent crime despite there being no further act required. Defendants lacking the specific intent required for murder are found guilty of manslaughter. Accordingly, on retrial, the trial court *should not* instruct the jury to consider evidence of the defendant's intoxication.

Remanded; with instructions that trial court instruct jury to disallow intoxication as a defense.

Regina v. Kingston

Court of Appeal, Criminal Division, 4 All E.R. 373 (1993)

FACTS

Penn, in an attempt to blackmail Defendant Kingston, lured a 15-year old boy to his apartment, drugged him, and invited Kingston to sexually abuse him, knowing of the defendant's sexual deviancies. In order to lower the defendant's inhibitions to commit the crime, Penn drugged Kingston's coffee and invited him to rape the boy, which he did. During the act, Penn photographed and audiotaped him. Consequently, Kingston was charged with sexual assault. At trial, Kingston presented the defense/excuse of involuntary intoxication. The trial judge instructed the jury that Kingston should be found guilty if he intended to assault the boy and should acquit the defendant only if it found that he did not intent to assault the boy. Kingston was convicted of sexual assault and appealed, arguing that he is entitled to acquittal even if he acted intentionally, if his intent arose out of circumstances which he bears no blame.

Is involuntary intoxication a defense to criminal prosecution?

Involuntary intoxication provides no defense to criminal prosecution, though it may mitigate the sentence.

COURT OF APPEAL: Involuntary intoxication is a defense to criminal prosecution if the intoxication was as the result of another's trick or fraud, and if the defendant would not have formed the required requisite criminal intent but for the intoxication. If drink or drug, surreptitiously administered, causes a person to lose his self-control and form an intent which he would not otherwise have formed, the law should exculpate him because the operative fault is not his. The law permits a finding that involuntary intoxication quashes *mens rea*, such that the intent formed was not criminal. In the case before us, the judge effectively withdrew this defense from jury's consideration, which was in error. Conviction reversed. The prosecution then appealed to the House of Lords.

HOUSE OF LORDS: We disagree with the conclusion reached by the Court of Appeal, and hold that involuntary intoxication is no defense to criminal prosecution, though it may allow a lesser sentence. Here, the defendant's sexual tendencies would ordinarily have been kept in check. The drug temporarily changed Kingston's disposition, lowering his ability to resist temptation so that his desires overrode his resistance. Thus, the drug enabled the desire. Here, Kingston contends he is without moral fault, but this is irrelevant to whether he had the *mens rea* necessary to constitute sexual assault. To recognize a new defense of this type, that is, adopt involuntary intoxication as a defense, would set a dangerous precedent, because 1) it would defend against all offenses except strict liability; 2) would provide a complete defense which would not allow prosecution for lesser charges; and 3) would be subjective in nature, since it would be judged only by whether the particular defendant's defendant's inhibitions were overcome by the drug. Unless the interests of justice require it, it should not be adopted unless necessary. Here, there is no such obligation, since the sentencing judge can apply a myriad of lesser sentences to mitigate the harm.

Court of Appeal reversed; the conviction is reaffirmed.

M'Naughten's Case
House of Lords, 8 Eng. Rep. 718 (1843)

FACTS

Defendant M'Naghten was under the mistaken delusion that the Tories [the conservative political party in the U.K.; Labor being the liberal political party] were in his city and followed and persecuted him wherever he went, entirely destroying his peace of mind and wishing to murder him. As a result, he came to London to kill the Prime Minister, Robert Peel. M'Naghten instead shot and killed Peel's secretary, Edward Drummond, who he believed was Peel. M'Naghten was arrested and was charged with attempted murder. At trial, evidence was presented that M'Naghten was acutely insane and delusional. At trial, the judge instructed the jury to acquit M'Naghten as insane if they found he was not sensible at the time he committed the murder and not "in a sound state of mind." The jury returned a verdict of "not guilty, on the ground of insanity." The verdict attracted great public attention and roused debate about the limits of the insanity defense. Consequently, the English Judiciary was invited to the House of Lords for the purpose of answering questions regarding the insanity defense. Among the questions asked of the Judges were: What is the proper jury instruction for an insanity defense? How should the issue of insanity be framed and conveyed to the jury? The famous *M'Naghten* Rule is found in the answers to these two questions.

What is the proper jury instruction for an insanity defense?

A jury pondering an insanity defense should be instructed to acquit as insane a defendant who, at the time of the act, had a defect of reason caused by a mental disease which made him unable to understand or appreciate the nature or quality of his wrongful acts.

A jury considering an insanity defense should be instructed to acquit as insane a defendant who, at the time of the act, had a defect of reason caused by a mental disease which made him unable to understand or appreciate the nature or quality of his wrongful acts. We submit that jurors ought to be told that every man is presumed sane, possessing sufficient reason to be responsible for his crimes, until the contrary be proved. To establish an insanity defense, it must be clearly proved that, at the time of the act, the accused was laboring under such a defect of reason, from disease of the mind, as not to know the nature and quality of the act, or that the act was wrong. If the accused was conscious of that the act he was doing was wrong and if the act was also unlawful at the time, he will be punished. The key, therefore, is whether he possessed sufficient reason to know what he was doing was wrong.

See Rule above.

The King v. Porter
55 L.R. 182 (1933)

FACTS

The presiding trial judge instructed the jury regarding the law of insanity; specifically, the *M'Naghten* Rule.

Can an abnormal person or one who is very peculiar in his disposition or temperament [stupid, obtuse, lacks self-control, impulsive or infirmed, for example] successfully raise the insanity defense when he nevertheless understood the wrongfulness of his act at the time of the crime?

The elements of the insanity defense are: 1) at the time of the act, his state of mind must have been one of disease, disorder or disturbance; and 2) his state of mind must have been of such a character as to prevent him from knowing that the physical nature of the act he was doing or of knowing that what he was doing was wrong.

An abnormal person or one who is very peculiar in his disposition or temperament *cannot* successfully raise the insanity defense when he understood the wrongfulness of his act at the time of the crime. The purpose of the law in punishing people is to deter others from committing similar offenses. Conversely, it is useless for the law to attempt to deter people from committing crimes by punishing them if their mental condition prevents them from understanding that what they are doing is unlawful and wrong. While many people who come into a Criminal Court are abnormal and very peculiar in their dispositions and temperament; some can still appreciate what they are doing and quite able to appreciate the threatened punishment of the law and the wrongness of their acts. These people will be held criminal liable for their wrongful acts. Their differences alone do not justify a finding of not guilty, with more. In order to determine if one has a mental disorder sufficient to justify a finding of not guilty on the ground of insanity, one must first consider the condition of the mind at the time the act complained of was done. Second, the state of mind must have been one of disease, disorder or disturbance. Mere excitability of a normal man, passion, even stupidity, obtuseness, lack of self-control, and impulsiveness, are quite different from a state of disease or disorder or mental disturbance arising from some infirmity – temporary or long-standing. If that existed it must then have been of such a character as to prevent him from knowing the physical nature of the act he was doing or of knowing that what he was doing was wrong.

See Rule above.

Blake v. United States

United States Court of Appeals, 407 F.2d 908 (5th Cir. 1969)

FACTS

Defendant Blake robbed a bank and was charged and convicted of bank robbery after unsuccessfully raising the defense of insanity at his trial. He thereafter appealed, arguing that the definition of insanity given to the jury for determining whether he was not guiltily by reason of insanity was outmoded and prejudicial. Blake was discharged from the Navy after he suffered an epileptic seizure. Thereafter, he received electro-shock treatment, and was hospitalized for two to three months a year later. He subsequently married, had children, and became a heavy drinker and began using drugs. He was subsequently hospitalized again, spent time in psychiatric institutions and received further electro-shock treatments. Eventually he adjudged incompetent and institutionalized. After discharge, he continued psychiatric treatment, divorced, remarried and was arrested for shooting his second wife. He was thereafter placed in a mental hospital for several months, and then was released on probation. He was sentenced to prison after violating probation. He married his third wife, divorced her and married his fourth wife. Blake robbed the bank in question because he claimed it mishandled his trust over a number of years. At trial, conflicting psychiatric testimony was proffered that indicated Blake was suffering from schizophrenia, marked with psychotic episodes, one of which happened during the robbery; but also that he was simply sociopathic and not suffering from any mental sickness.

Can the accused successfully raise the defense of insanity when the defendant "substantially" lacks the mental capacity to appreciate the wrongfulness of the crime [or to conform to the law] or must there be a complete lack of mental capacity?

Under the Model Penal Code, the defendant may be found not guilty by reason of insanity if he lacks "substantial" capacity to appreciate the wrongfulness of the conduct or to conform to the law.

We do not think that there need be a complete lack of mental capacity in order for one to be found not guilty by reason of insanity as rarely, if ever, is one completely lacking in mental capacity. Blake argues that we should adopt the Model Penal Code's standard of lack of "substantial" capacity to appreciate the wrongfulness of the conduct or to conform to the law should be used. We agree. And while the government argues the standard set forth in *Davis v. United States* should be applied; that there must be a "complete" lack of mental capacity in order for insanity to be a defense, the facts of this case do not show that Blake suffered from a severe mental disease which the jury might have found impaired his control over the conduct in question. Hence, under the *Davis* standard, he could not prevail. The same cannot be said applying the MPC standard. Taking into account the current knowledge regarding mental illness, we think that the "substantiality" type standard under the Model Penal Code's should control. A person, as Blake here, may be a schizophrenic or may merely have a sociopathic personality. He may or may not have

Blake v. United States
United States Court of Appeals, 407 F.2d 908 (5th Cir. 1969)

been in a psychotic episode at the time of the robbery. Nevertheless, he was not unconscious or incapable of distinguishing right and wrong nor was his will completely destroyed in terms of the *Davis* definition. We therefore adopt the Model Penal Code standard, but substitute the term "wrongfulness" in the first paragraph of the MPC for "criminality." This substituted term is a broader term which includes cases where the accused appreciated that his conduct was criminal but, because he was delusional, believed it to be morally justified.

 See Rule above.

United States v. Lyons

U.S. Court Of Appeals, 739 F.2d 994 (1984)

FACTS

Defendant Robert Lyons was indicted for knowingly and intentionally securing controlled narcotics. At trial, Lyons offered an insanity defense, arguing that he had become addicted to painkillers taken to treat painful ailments, and offered evidence in the form of expert witnesses who testified that his addiction caused physiological and psychological changes effectively leaving him substantially incapable of conforming his conduct to the law. The trial court excluded this evidence, holding evidence of mere narcotics addiction, standing alone without other psychological or physiological involvement, cannot support an insanity defense. Lyons was convicted and appealed, arguing just the opposite: that the proffered evidence does support a showing of a "mental disease or defect" as caused by his drug use.

Is evidence of mere drug addiction, without more, admissible to sustain the defense of insanity?

A person is not responsible for his criminal conduct on the grounds of insanity *only* if at the time of that conduct, as a result of mental disease or defect, he is unable to appreciate the wrongfulness of that conduct – thus, evidence of drug addiction is admissible to prove a defendant suffered from a mental disease or defect which made him unable to appreciate his action's wrongfulness, but inadmissible to prove he acted under an irresistible impulse which made him unable to conform to the law.

We adopted the *Model Penal Code's* definition of insanity in *Blake v. United States* because then-current knowledge of behavioral science supported such a result. It now appears our conclusion was premature. Consequently, we now overrule the *Blake* standard because the volitional prong insanity defense — a lack of capacity to conform one's conduct to legal requirements — is not in harmony with contemporary scientific knowledge. Today, most psychiatrists believe they lack sufficient scientific basis to measure a person's capacity for self-control. Moreover, such testimony tens to confuse jurors and requires that such proof be made by the federal prosecutor "beyond a reasonable doubt;" an all but impossible task. As such, we now hold that a person is deemed not guilty by reason of insanity only if, at the time of his conduct, he was unable to appreciate the wrongfulness of that conduct as a result of mental disease or defect. In the instant case, the defendant's proposed evidence suggests he suffered from a mental disease or defect, which might have rendered him unable to understand his actions' wrongfulness. Thus, justice demands that he be allowed to present that evidence to support his insanity defense.

Conviction reversed and remanded.

State v. Crenshaw
Washington Supreme Court, 659 P.2d 488 (1983)

FACTS

While on honeymoon with his new wife in Canada, Defendant-petitioner Crenshaw became involved in a brawl and deported back to the State of Washington. When his wife rejoined him two days later, Crenshaw "sensed" she had been unfaithful to him while still in Canada. To that end, he beat her unconscious in a motel room, went to a nearby store, stole a knife and returned only to fatally stab her 24 times. As if this were not enough, Crenshaw then drove to the farm where he worked, borrowed an ax, and returned to decapitate his wife. Crenshaw then tried to conceal his crime by cleaning the hotel room of blood and fingerprints and hiding the body and severed head. Thereafter, he picked up two hitchhikers and attempted to enlist their help in dumping his wife's car in a river. The hitchhikers contacted the police, who was apprehended and confessed voluntarily. Crenshaw was tried for first degree murder and pleaded the insanity defense. Crenshaw testified he followed the Muscovite religious faith, which requires husbands to kill adulterous wives and proffered evidence of his history of mental problems. The court instructed the jury that, under the *M'Naghten* rule as codified in the State of Washington, it may acquit the defendant by reason of insanity if it found that as a result of mental disease or defect, the defendant's mind was affected to such an extent that the defendant was unable to perceive the nature and quality of the acts or was unable to tell right from wrong." The terms "right and wrong" according to the jury instruction "refers to [the] knowledge of a person at the time of [the commission of] an act that he was acting contrary to the law." The jury found Crenshaw guilty of first degree murder. He subsequently appealed, arguing that the jury instruction erroneously misstated and defined "right and wrong" as a legal wrong rather than in the moral sense.

Can a defendant successfully raise an insanity defense under the *M'Naghten* test if he knew his act was illegal but he [subjective standard] did not it to be morally wrong?

Under the *M'Naghten* test, a defendant will be held criminally liable if he understands that his act was wrong from society's viewpoint [objective standard] and also knew his acts were illegal - the exception being where a party performs a criminal act knowing it is morally and legally wrong, but because of mental defect believed that the act is ordained by God.

Under the *M'Naghten* test, a defendant will be held criminally liable if he understands that his act was wrong from society's viewpoint [objective standard] and also knew his acts were illegal; the exception being where a party performs a criminal act knowing it is morally and legally wrong, but because of mental defect believed that the act is ordained by God. Under the *State v. White* holding, we held that "when *M'Naghten* is used, all who might possibly be deterred from the commission of criminal acts are included within the sanctions of the criminal law." Given this prospective, the trial court could assume that one who knew

State v. Crenshaw
Washington Supreme Court, 659 P.2d 488 (1983)

the illegality of his act was not beyond reach of criminal law. Consequently, the trial court's jury instruction here was correct. Alternately, the jury instruction below is correct because, at least in this case, a legal wrong is synonymous with moral wrong. Under *M'Naghten*, "moral wrong" must be judged by society's morals, not the individual's, because holding otherwise would allow criminals to escape punishment solely because they believed their acts were not morally wrong. In the case before us, there was expert testimony which showed that Crenshaw knew his actions were wrong by society's standards. Hence, we conclude Crenshaw understood his acts were both illegal and considered morally wrong by society. The narrow exception to the societal standard of moral wrong [where a party performs a criminal act, knowing it is morally and legally wrong, but believing, because of mental defect, that the act was ordained by God] is not applicable here because the defendant argued only that Muscovites believe it is their duty to kill their unfaithful wives, and not that God commanded it to be so. As such, we follow the *People v. Schmidt* holding that where a religious group's rituals encourage illegal acts, a member is still criminally liable for performing those acts, the aforementioned exception notwithstanding.

C See Rule above.

State v. Guido
New Jersey Supreme Court, 191 A.2d 45 (1993)

FACTS

Defendant Adele Guido wanted a divorce from her husband, the deceased, while the decedent insisted on holding on to her despite his inability or unwillingness to end his extra marital affair and assume the role of responsible husband and parent. Consequently and as a result, she shot and killed her husband. According to her testimony, she claimed to have taken a pistol from her suitcase and gone to her room intending to kill herself, but then reconsidered. Seeing her husband sleeping, she raised the weapon and fired into him until it was empty. She was charged with 2nd degree murder and claimed temporary insanity at trial. Expert testimony was proffered by two court-appointed psychiatrists and opinioned that she suffered from "anxiety neurosis" but was nevertheless legally sane at the time of the shooting. Their opinion was changed to "legal" insanity only after the two had discussions with defense counsel, though their underlying medical findings were unchanged. At trial, the prosecutor accused the doctors of collaborating with defendant's attorney to defraud the court. The psychiatrists explained they changed their conclusions because the doctors concluded, after their pretrial debate with the defendant's attorney, that their view of *M'Naghten* was too narrow and that "anxiety neurosis" did indeed qualify as a "disease" under *M'Naghten*. Nevertheless, Guido was convicted of 2nd degree murder and sentenced to 24 years' imprisonment. On appeal, Guido argued that the psychiatrists should be allowed to change their conclusions without prejudice.

May expert witnesses change their conclusions of sanity or insanity without prejudice with respect to an insanity defense raised at a criminal trial?

Expert witnesses may change their conclusions of sanity or insanity without prejudice if done in good faith, with or without altering their medical findings.

Expert witnesses may change their conclusions of sanity or insanity without prejudice if done in good faith, with or without altering their medical findings. During the trial, defense counsel and psychiatrists were subject to unwarranted humiliation, even though it appeared, as the charge continued against them, that their change in the report was honest, if mistaken. The doctors explained they originally understood that the "disease of the mind" required by the *M'Naghten* rule means a psychosis and not the same lesser illness or functional abnormality. The psychiatrists explained they changed their conclusions because the doctors concluded, after their pretrial debate with the defendant's attorney, that their view of *M'Naghten* was too narrow and that "anxiety neurosis" did indeed qualify as a "disease" under *M'Naghten*. *M'Naghten's* rule does not identify the exact diseases excused, but specifies the requisite effect the disease must create [that at the time of the act, the accused must have labored under a defect of reason such that he did not

State v. Guido

New Jersey Supreme Court, 191 A.2d 45 (1993)

---

know the nature and quality of the act he was doing, or did not know the act was wrong]. And while the emphasis is on the state of mind, it is nonetheless required that that state be due to "disease," not something else. We do resolve the problem here; rather simply reveal the unfairness of charging the defense with fraud for changing their report based on a good faith change in their understanding of the legal meaning of "disease."

 Judgment reversed.

United States v. Brawner
U.S. Court of Appeals, 471 F.2d 969 (D.C. Cir. 1972)

FACTS

It would appear from the text that a mentally ill defendant was charged with first degree murder. The defendant could not successfully raise the defense of legal insanity entitling him to full exoneration from the crime because he was able to understand the quality and nature of his [unlawful] act and was able to control it. However, the defendant argued that his impaired mental condition prevented him from forming a specific deliberate intent to kill, a required element of the crime for which he was charged [first degree murder]. He thus argued that he was entitled to and qualified for the lesser offense of voluntary manslaughter. In support of his position, he introduced expert testimony. The trial judge refused to allow this testimony and the defendant was convicted as charged. Thereafter, the defendant appealed.

Can defendants who are *not* legally insane still introduce evidence of mental illness to show that they lacked the requisite criminal intent necessary for the commission of a crime?

Expert testimony about a defendant's abnormal mental condition is relevant and admissible if it negates or establishes the specific mental condition that is an element of the crime, even if the defendant is not legally insane.

Expert testimony about a defendant's abnormal mental condition is relevant and admissible if it negates or establishes the specific mental condition that is an element of the crime, even if the defendant is not legally insane. Earlier cases call this doctrine "diminished responsibility," however we find this term confusing and misleading. Procedurally, the issue of abnormal mental condition which negates intent may arise in different ways. For example, the defendant may offer evidence of a mental condition which does not qualify as a "disease," or he may tender evidence that qualifies as a mental disease, yet the jury may find that he was still aware that his act was wrongful and was able to control it. A conviction for first degree murder [a/k/a deliberate and premeditated murder] requires a finding of a subjective specific intent to kill; the mere act itself does not prove premeditation. Thus, if the defendant's mental condition prevented him from forming the specific intent necessary to commit the crime, the defendant may present expert testimony to that effect, and may qualify for a lesser charge. The judge will then determine whether such testimony has the requisite scientific support and probative value to warrant its admission into evidence.

See Rule above.

Clark v. Arizona

Supreme Court of the United States, 126 S. Ct. 2709 (2006)

FACTS

Petitioner Clark was charged with first-degree murder under an Arizona statute prohibiting intentionally or knowingly killing a police officer in the line of duty. At his bench trial, Clark did not contest that he shot the officer or that the officer died, but relied on his own undisputed paranoid schizophrenia at the time of the incident to deny that he had the specific intent to shoot an officer or knowledge that he was doing so. Accordingly, the prosecutor offered circumstantial evidence that Clark knew the victim was a police officer and testimony indicating that Clark had previously stated he wanted to shoot police and had lured the victim to the scene to kill him. In presenting the defense case, Clark claimed mental illness, which he sought to introduce for two purposes. First, he raised the affirmative defense of insanity, putting the burden on himself to prove by clear and convincing evidence that, in the words of another state statute, "at the time of the [crime, he] was afflicted with a mental disease or defect of such severity that [he] did not know the criminal act was wrong." Second, he aimed to rebut the prosecution's evidence of the requisite *mens rea,* that he had acted intentionally or knowingly to kill an officer. Ruling that Clark could not rely on evidence bearing on insanity to dispute the *mens rea,* the trial court cited the Arizona Supreme Court's decision in *State* v. *Mott* which refused to allow psychiatric testimony to negate specific intent and held that Arizona does not allow evidence of a mental disorder short of insanity to negate the *mens rea* element of a crime. The judge issued a first-degree murder verdict, finding that in light of that the facts of the crime, the expert evaluations, Clark's actions and behavior both before and after the shooting, and the observations of those who knew him, Clark had not established that his schizophrenia distorted his perception of reality so severely that he did not know his actions were wrong. Clark moved to vacate the judgment and life sentence, arguing, among other things, that Arizona's insanity test and its *Mott* rule each violate due process. He claimed that the Arizona Legislature had impermissibly narrowed its insanity standard in 1993 when it eliminated the first of the two parts of the traditional *M'Naghten* insanity test. The trial court denied the motion. Affirming, the Arizona Court of Appeals held, among other things, that the State's insanity scheme was consistent with due process. The court read *Mott* as barring the trial court's consideration of evidence of Clark's mental illness and capacity directly on the element of *mens rea.*

(1) Does due process prohibit Arizona's use of an insanity test stated solely in terms of capacity to tell whether an act charged as a crime was right or wrong? (2) Does Arizona violate due process in restriction consideration of defense evidence of mental illness and incapacity to its bearing on a claim of insanity thus eliminating its significance directly on the issue of the mental element of the crime charged?

(1) Due process does not prohibit Arizona's use of an insanity test stated solely in terms of the capacity to tell whether an act charged as a crime was right or wrong (2) the Arizona Supreme Court's *Mott* rule does not violate due process.

Clark v. Arizona
Supreme Court of the United States, 126 S. Ct. 2709 (2006)

 Due process does not prohibit Arizona's use of an insanity test stated solely in terms of the capacity to tell whether an act charged as a crime was right or wrong. The first part of the landmark English rule in *M'Naghten's Case* asks about cognitive capacity: whether a mental defect leaves a defendant unable to understand what he was doing. The second part presents an ostensibly alternative basis for recognizing a defense of insanity understood as a lack of moral capacity: whether a mental disease or defect leaves a defendant unable to understand that his action was wrong. Although the Arizona Legislature at first adopted the full *M'Naghten* statement, it later dropped the cognitive incapacity part. Under current Arizona law, a defendant will not be adjudged insane unless he demonstrates that at the time of the crime, he was afflicted with a mental disease or defect of such severity that he did not know the criminal act was wrong.

The Arizona Supreme Court's *Mott* rule does not violate due process. *Mott* held that testimony of a professional psychologist or psychiatrist about a defendant's mental incapacity owing to mental disease or defect was admissible, and could be considered, only for its bearing on an insanity defense, but could not be considered on the element of *mens rea*. Of the three categories of evidence that potentially bear on *mens rea* - (1) everyday "observation evidence" either by lay or expert witnesses of what Clark did or said, which may support the professional diagnoses of disease and in any event is the kind of evidence that can be relevant to show what was on Clark's mind when he fired his gun; (2) "mental-disease evidence," typically from professional psychologists or psychiatrists based on factual reports, professional observations, and tests about Clark's mental disease, with features described by the witness; and (3) "capacity evidence," typically by the same experts, about Clark's capacity for cognition and moral judgment (and ultimately also his capacity to form *mens rea*) - *Mott* imposed no restriction on considering evidence of the first sort, but applies to the latter two. Although the trial court seems to have applied the *Mott* restriction to all three categories of evidence Clark offered for the purpose of showing what he called his inability to form the required *mens rea*, his objection to *Mott*'s application does not turn on the distinction between lay and expert witnesses or the kinds of testimony they were competent to present. Rather, the issue here is Clark's claim that the *Mott* rule violates due process.

The reasons supporting the Arizona rule satisfy due process. The first such reason is Arizona's authority to define its presumption of sanity (or capacity or responsibility) by choosing an insanity definition and placing the burden of persuasion on criminal defendants claiming incapacity as an excuse. Consistent with due process, a State can require defendants to bear that burden, see *Leland* and Clark does not object to Arizona's decision to require persuasion to a clear and convincing degree before the presumption of sanity and normal responsibility is overcome. If a State is to have this authority in practice as well as in theory, it must be able to deny a defendant the opportunity to displace the sanity presumption more easily when addressing a different

Clark v. Arizona

Supreme Court of the United States, 126 S. Ct. 2709 (2006)

---

issue during the criminal trial. Yet just such an opportunity would be available if expert testimony of mental disease and incapacity could be considered for whatever a factfinder might think it was worth on the *mens rea* issue. The sanity presumption would then be only as strong as the evidence a factfinder would accept as enough to raise a reasonable doubt about *mens rea*; once reasonable doubt was found, acquittal would be required, and the standards established for the insanity defense would go by the boards. What counts for due process is simply that a State wishing to avoid a second avenue for exploring capacity, less stringent for a defendant, has a good reason for confining the consideration of mental disease and incapacity evidence to the insanity defense. For these reasons, there is also no cause to claim that channeling evidence on metal disease and capacity offends any " 'principle of justice so rooted in the traditions and conscience of our people as to be ranked as fundamental,' " *Patterson*.

Affirmed.

Robinson v. California
Supreme Court of the United States, 370 U.S. 660 (1962)

FACTS

A California statute makes it a criminal offense for a person to "be addicted to the use of narcotics." Defendant-appellant Robinson was convicted after a jury trial in the Municipal Court of Los Angeles in violation of the statute. The evidence against him was given by two Los Angeles police officers. Officer Brown testified that he had observed "scar tissue and discoloration on the inside" of the appellant's right arm, and "what appeared to be numerous needle marks and a scab which was approximately three inches below the crook of the elbow" on the appellant's left arm. The officer also testified that the appellant under questioning had admitted to the occasional use of narcotics. Officer Lindquist testified that he had examined the appellant the following morning in a Los Angeles jail, and based upon his than ten years of experience as a member of the Narcotic Division of the Los Angeles Police Department, stated that "these marks and the discoloration were the result of the injection of hypodermic needles into the tissue into the vein that was not sterile." He further testified that the scabs were several days old at the time of his examination, and that the appellant was neither under the influence of narcotics nor suffering withdrawal symptoms at the time he saw him. This witness also testified that the appellant had admitted using narcotics in the past. The appellant testified in his own behalf, denying the alleged conversations with the police officers and denying that he had ever used narcotics or been addicted to their use. He explained the marks on his arms as resulting from an allergic condition contracted during his military service. His testimony was corroborated by two witnesses. The trial judge instructed the jury that the statute made it a misdemeanor for a person "either to use narcotics, or to be addicted to the use of narcotics . . . . The existence of such a chronic condition may be ascertained from a single examination, if the characteristic reactions of that condition be found present." The judge further instructed the jury that the appellant could be convicted under a general verdict if the jury agreed either that he was of the "status" or had committed the "act" denounced by the statute. "All that the People must show is either that the defendant did use a narcotic in Los Angeles County, or that while in the City of Los Angeles he was addicted to the use of narcotics . . . ." Under these instructions the jury returned a verdict finding the appellant "guilty of the offense charged." An appeal was made to the Appellate Department of the Los Angeles County Superior Court which affirmed the judgment of conviction. The case comes before the U.S. Supreme Court.

Does the punishment and imprisonment a person solely because of their narcotic addiction constitute cruel and unusual punishment under the 8th and 14th Amendments?

To the extent that a state law which requires imprisonment for the use of, or addiction to, narcotics is interpreted to allow imprisonment for addiction alone, such law inflicts cruel and unusual punishment in violation of the 14th Amendment.

Robinson v. California

Supreme Court of the United States, 370 U.S. 660 (1962)

As so construed and applied, the statute inflicts a cruel and unusual punishment in violation of the Eighth and Fourteenth Amendments. The broad power of a State to regulate the narcotic drugs traffic within its borders is not at issue here. More than forty years ago, in *Whipple v. Martinson*, we explicitly recognized the validity of the State's exercise of its police power to regulate the administration, sale, prescription and use of dangerous and habit-forming drugs . . ." In the interest of discouraging the violation of such laws, or in the interest of the general health or welfare of its inhabitants, a State might establish a program of compulsory treatment for those addicted to narcotics. Such a program of treatment might require sanctions, penal or otherwise or the administration of public health education, for example. In short, it is not for us to decide. Upon that premise we turn to the California law in issue here. It would be possible to construe the statute under which the appellant was convicted as one which is operative only upon proof of the actual use of narcotics within the State's jurisdiction. But the California courts have not so construed this law. The appellant could be convicted, they were told, if they found simply that the appellant's "status" or "chronic condition" was that of being "addicted to the use of narcotics." This statute, therefore, is not one which punishes a person for the use of narcotics, for their purchase, sale or possession, or for antisocial or disorderly behavior resulting from their administration. It is not a law which even purports to provide or require medical treatment. Rather, we deal with a statute which makes the "status" of narcotic addiction a criminal offense, for which the offender may be prosecuted "at any time before he reforms." California has said that a person can be continuously guilty of this offense, whether or not he has ever used or possessed any narcotics within the State, and whether or not he has been guilty of any antisocial behavior there. Thus, we hold that a state law which imprisons a person thus afflicted as a criminal, even though he has never touched any narcotic drug within the State or been guilty of any irregular behavior there, inflicts a cruel and unusual punishment in violation of the Fourteenth Amendment. To be sure, imprisonment for ninety days is not, in the abstract, a punishment which is either cruel or unusual. But the question cannot be considered in the abstract. Even one day in prison would be a cruel and unusual punishment for the "crime" of having a common cold. We are not unmindful that the vicious evils of the narcotics traffic have occasioned the grave concern of government. There are, as we have said, countless fronts on which those evils may be legitimately attacked. We deal in this case only with an individual provision of a particularized local law as it has so far been interpreted by the California courts.

The conviction is reversed.

Powell v. Texas
Supreme Court of the United States, 392 U.S. 514 (1968)

FACTS

In late December 1966, Defendant-appellant Leroy Powell (Powell) was arrested and charged with being found in a state of intoxication in a public place, in violation of Texas Penal Code, Art. 477 (1952), which reads as follows: "Whoever shall get drunk or be found in a state of intoxication in any public place, or at any private house except his own, shall be fined not exceeding one hundred dollars." A psychiatrist (Dr. Wade), after examining Powell, testified that Powell is a "chronic alcoholic," who by the time he is intoxicated is not able to control his behavior, and who has reached this point because he has an uncontrollable compulsion to drink. When asked, on cross-examination, whether Powell's act in taking the first drink when he was sober was a "voluntary exercise of his will," Dr. Wade answered yes. He qualified his answer, however, by stating that "these individuals have a compulsion, and this compulsion, while not completely overpowering, is a very strong influence, an exceedingly strong influence, and this compulsion coupled with the firm belief in their mind that they are going to be able to handle it from now on causes their judgment to be somewhat clouded." He admitted that when Powell is sober he knows the difference between right and wrong. Powell testified regarding the history of his drinking problem, his many arrests for drunkenness, that he was unable to stop drinking, that when he was intoxicated he could not control his behavior, and that he did not remember his arrest on the occasion for which he was being tried. He admitted, on cross-examination, that he had one drink on the morning of the trial and had been able to discontinue drinking. Appellant was subsequently found guilty and fined $20. He appealed to the County Court at Law No. 1 of Travis County, Texas, where a trial *de novo* was held. His counsel urged that appellant was "afflicted with the disease of chronic alcoholism," that "his appearance in public [while drunk was] . . . not of his own volition," and therefore that to punish him criminally for that conduct would be cruel and unusual, in violation of the Eighth and Fourteenth Amendments to the United States Constitution. The trial judge in the county court, sitting without a jury, made certain findings of fact, infra, at 521, but ruled as a matter of law that chronic alcoholism was not a defense to the charge. He found appellant guilty, and fined him $50. There being no further right to appeal within the Texas judicial system, appellant appealed to this Court; we noted probable jurisdiction.

Can a state court find as a matter of law that chronic alcoholism is not a defense to the crime of public intoxication when interpreting a state law?

The 8th Amendment prohibition against cruel and unusual punishment is not violated when a state imposes sanctions for public behavior (public intoxication) which violates its law.

The lower court's "findings of fact" were not such in any recognizable, traditional sense, but were merely premises of a syllogism designed to

Powell v. Texas
Supreme Court of the United States, 392 U.S. 514 (1968)

bring this case within the scope of *Robinson v. California*. The record here is utterly inadequate to permit the informed adjudication needed to support an important and wide-ranging new constitutional principle. There is no agreement among medical experts as to what it means to say that "alcoholism" is a "disease," or upon the "manifestations of alcoholism," or on the nature of a "compulsion." Faced with the reality that there is no known generally effective method of treatment or adequate facilities or manpower for a full-scale attack on the enormous problem of alcoholics, it cannot be asserted that the use of the criminal process to deal with the public aspects of problem drinking can never be defended as rational. Appellant's conviction on the record in this case does not violate the Cruel and Unusual Punishment Clause of the Eighth Amendment. Appellant was convicted, not for being a chronic alcoholic, but for being in public while drunk on a particular occasion, and thus, as distinguished from *Robinson v. California*, was not being punished for a mere status. It cannot be concluded, on this record and the current state of medical knowledge, that appellant suffers from such an irresistible compulsion to drink and to get drunk in public that he cannot control his performance of these acts and thus cannot be deterred from public intoxication. In any event, this Court has never articulated a general constitutional doctrine of mens rea, as the development of the doctrine and its adjustment to changing conditions has been thought to be the province of the States.

 The conviction is affirmed.

United States v. Moore
United States Court of Appeals, 486 F.2d 1139 (D.C. Cir. 1973)

FACTS

Defendant-appellant Moore, a heroin addict, was charged with heroin possession and drug trafficking. Moore admitted at trial that he was an addict and possessed heroin for personal use, but contested any allegation that he was a seller. Moore argued that as an addict, he had an overpowering need for the drug which compelled him to possess it. Therefore, he argued, he should not be held responsible for being in the possession of the drug. The trail judge disagreed and excluded expert testimony concerning the nature of Moore's heroin addiction and declined to instruct the jury that a non-trafficking addict could not be convicted of possession. Moore was convicted and subsequently appealed.

Is proffered evidence of the appellant's long and intensive drug addiction a defense to a charge of drug possession?

Drug addiction provides no defense to a charge of and subsequent prosecution for drug possession.

Drug addiction provides no defense to a charge of and subsequent prosecution for drug possession. We believe it is clear from the evidence that Moore was not merely an addict, but engaged in the drug trade. However, even if he were merely a personal user and not a trafficking addict, his conviction must be sustained. Moore argues that common law requires that he is entitled to dismissal of the indictment or a jury trial on this issue because the "common law has long held that capacity to control one's behavior is a prerequisite for criminal responsibility." We disagree. Drug addition comes in many varieties and varying degrees, some of which do not result in a loss of control. To hold otherwise, and allow the defense to be raised in all cases of addition, would run contrary to public policy, since it would tend to exonerate any crime carried out by a hard-core addict while under the influence of drugs. Our holding is consistent with *Robinson*, which prohibits criminalizing addiction, but does not prohibit criminalizing addiction-compelled acts. *Powell* also does not prohibit such a holding.

Conviction affirmed.

Commonwealth v. Tluchak

Superior Court of Pennsylvania, 70 A.2d 657 (1950)

FACTS

Defendant-appellants Tluchak and his wife entered into a written contract to sell their farm to the prosecutor and his wife. The agreement did not include any personal property but it did cover "All buildings, plumbing, heating, lighting fixtures, screens, storm sash, shades, blinds, awnings, shrubbery and plants." When the purchasers took possession of the farm, they discovered that certain articles which had been on the premises at the time the agreement of sale was executed were missing. Thereafter, the defendants were charged with larceny and separately convicted and found guilty of the crime. Defendants requested new trials; but the lower court overruled their motions. Mr. Tluchak was sentenced to pay a fine of $50 and to make restitution; sentence was suspended in his wife's case. Defendants separately appealed their respective convictions.

Can the defendants be found guilty of larceny if they sold but refused or failed to deliver the goods to the purchasers?

When one is in the lawful possession of the goods or money of another, he cannot commit larceny by feloniously converting them to his own use because he already has a vested right of possession and larceny is a crime against the possession of another's goods, not mere custody.

The defendants cannot be found guilty of larceny if they sold but refused or failed to deliver the goods to the purchasers. Tluchak and his wife had possession of the goods, not mere custody of them. The evidence indicates that they were allowed to retain possession without trick or artifice and without fraudulent intent to convert them. Presumably title passed upon payment of the purchase price; nevertheless Tluchak and his wife retained lawful possession afterward. Thus, "One who is in lawful possession of the goods or money of another cannot commit larceny by feloniously converting them to his own use, for the reason that larceny, being a criminal trespass on the right of possession, cannot be committed by one who, being invested with that right, is consequently incapable of trespassing on it."

Judgments and sentences reversed and appellants discharged without delay.

Topolewski v. State

Supreme Court of Wisconsin, 109 N.W. 1037 (1906)

FACTS

Defendant-appellant Topolewski, an employee of the Plankinton Packing Company, wanted to collect on a debt owed to him by Mat Dolan, a former employee of the same company. Since Dolan was unable to repay the debt, Topolewski conjured up a scheme which would allow Dolan to satisfy what was owed by helping Topolewski steal some meat from the company. Topolewski discussed the details of the plan with Dolan, who then secretly let the company in on the scheme. Dolan and the company then agreed to set up Topolewski. Dolan and Topolewski hatched a plan whereby Dolan would order some barrels of meat to be placed on one of the company's loading platforms normally used to deliver meat to customers. Topolewski would then arrive, pretending to be a customer, and pick up the meat. Dolan would make this arrangement through Mr. Layer, the person in charge of the wholesale department. Mr. Layer was informed about the scheme and the plan to trap Topolewski. Layer ordered four barrels of meat to be packed and placed on the loading platform for Topolewski to pick up. Layer next notified Ernst Klotz, the platform boss, that a customer was coming to pick up the barrels. When Topolewski arrived to pick up the meat, Klotz allowed him to load the barrels onto his wagon, but did not actually physically help him. Topolewski take the fourth barrel but told Klotz that he wanted it marked and sent to him with a bill and told Klotz that he had ordered the barrels the prior night through Dolan. Topolewski then rode away with three barrels of meat, worth $55.20. Topolewski was caught and found guilty of having stolen three barrels of meat from the packing company. Topolewski subsequently appealed.

Is a person guilty of larceny where the owner of the property aids in the commission of the offense?

The larceny element of a trespassory taking does not take place where the taking is facilitated by the owner or at the owner's request.

In *Reg v. Lawrence*, the court held that larceny does not take place where property is delivered by a servant to a defendant under the direction of the master, regardless of the defendant's purposes. Here, the company placed the barrels on the loading platform with the knowledge that Topolewski would arrive to pick it up. The platform was the usual place for delivering such goods to customers. While Klotz did not assist Topolewski in taking the barrels, he stood by and allowed Topolewski to pick up the barrels, assisted him in arranging the wagon, and made arrangements for the delivery of the fourth barrel. Klotz was instructed that someone was to come and pick up the meat; thus, he had every reason to believe that Topolewski had a right to take the property. His conduct, for all intents and purposes, amounted to a delivery of the three barrels to Topolewski. In *Rex v. Egginton*, a servant

Topolewski v. State

Supreme Court of Wisconsin, 109 N.W. 1037 (1906)

informed his master that he had been approached to assist in the robbing of the master's house. The master instructed the servant allow the thieves to steal certain items. The master intended to have the thieves arrested after they accomplished their purpose. Nevertheless the court held that the crime of larceny was complete because the master did not direct the servant to deliver the property to the thieves or consent to its taking. In the instant case, the element of trespass is absent. The company intended to set a trap for Topolewski, but in setting the trap the company constructively aided in the commission of the crime and, in essence, consented to the taking. Thus, there was no trespass by Topolewski; and there can be no larceny without a trespass. In sum, "where the owner of property by himself or his agent, actually or constructively, aids in the commission of the offense, as intended by the wrongdoer, by performing or rendering unnecessary some act in the transaction essential to the offense, the would be criminal is not guilty of all the elements of the offense." If, however, Topolewski had merely disclosed to Dolan a scheme to steal meat from the loading dock should an opportunity present itself, and if that intent was then communicated to the company, then this case would have had a different result.

Conviction reversed.

Nolan v. State
Maryland Court of Appeals, 131 A.2d 851 (1957)

FACTS

Defendant Nolan, the office manager of the Federal Discount Corporation, was convicted of embezzlement. He and a co-worker/accomplice appropriated money from their employer, a finance company engaged in the business of making loans and collections. As payments were received from customers, they would be placed in the cash drawer. At the end of the day, the accomplice would prepare a report showing the daily cash receipts. Nolan would then appropriate some of the cash from the drawer, and his accomplice would recompute the adding tapes to equal the remaining cash.

Is an employee who unlawfully appropriates goods from his employer's possession [after delivery to him to employer] guilty of the crime of embezzlement?

Goods which have reached their destination are constructively in the owner's possession although he may not yet have touched them and, therefore, after such termination of transit, the servant who converts them is guilty of larceny, not of embezzlement.

If the goods were taken from the owner's possession, the crime is larceny, not embezzlement. Goods which have reached their destination are constructively in the owner's possession although he may not yet have touched them and, hence, after such termination of transit, the servant who converts them is guilty of larceny, not of embezzlement. Here, the money was not taken by Nolan until it had been placed in the cash drawer and balanced at the end of the day. At that point [when it was in the cash drawer] and also at the point when it was taken, the cash was in the [constructive] possession of the Federal Discount Corporation. Thus, the evidence is insufficient to find Nolan guilty of embezzlement. The case will be remanded for further proceedings in order that the State, if it deems proper, may try Nolan on an indictment for embezzlement and larceny, if such an indictment is returned against the defendant.

See Rule above.

Burns v. State

Supreme Court of Wisconsin, 128 N.W. 987 (1911)

FACTS

Defendant Burns, a constable, arrested an insane man named Adamsky, after a pursuit. Another of the pursuers gave to Burns a roll of money that had been thrown away by the insane man during his flight. Evidence was presented that Burns misappropriated the funds, and a jury convicted him of larceny by bailee under a Wisconsin statute.

Did the court err by instructing the jury that if Burns converted to his own use any of the insane man's money he did so as a bailee?

A person who has been given possession of the property of another or recovers that which has been lost or carelessly thrown away is known as a bailee - if he who has possession gives the property to a 3rd party, that person [the 3rd party] assumes the duties of the original bailee and can be held criminally liable for "larceny by a bailee" if he misappropriates it.

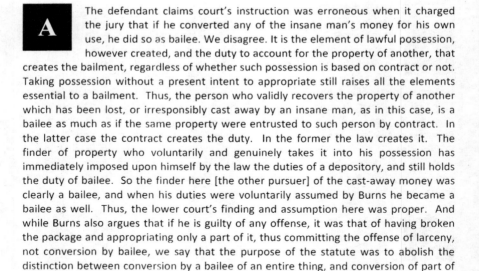

The defendant claims court's instruction was erroneous when it charged the jury that if he converted any of the insane man's money for his own use, he did so as bailee. We disagree. It is the element of lawful possession, however created, and the duty to account for the property of another, that creates the bailment, regardless of whether such possession is based on contract or not. Taking possession without a present intent to appropriate still raises all the elements essential to a bailment. Thus, the person who validly recovers the property of another which has been lost, or irresponsibly cast away by an insane man, as in this case, is a bailee as much as if the same property were entrusted to such person by contract. In the latter case the contract creates the duty. In the former the law creates it. The finder of property who voluntarily and genuinely takes it into his possession has immediately imposed upon himself by the law the duties of a depository, and still holds the duty of bailee. So the finder here [the other pursuer] of the cast-away money was clearly a bailee, and when his duties were voluntarily assumed by Burns he became a bailee as well. Thus, the lower court's finding and assumption here was proper. And while Burns also argues that if he is guilty of any offense, it was that of having broken the package and appropriating only a part of it, thus committing the offense of larceny, not conversion by bailee, we say that the purpose of the statute was to abolish the distinction between conversion by a bailee of an entire thing, and conversion of part of the contents.

Thus defendant's conviction is proper and is therefore affirmed.

State v. Riggins
Supreme Court of Illinois, 132 N.E.2d 519 (1956)

FACTS

Defendant Marven E. Riggins was the owner and operator of a collection agency in Rockford, Illinois. He maintained an office, full and part-time employees, and a clientele of about 500 clients for whom he collected delinquent accounts. In February, 1953, he approached Dorothy Tarrant, the complaining witness in this case and the operator of Cooper's Music and Jewelry, and asked her if he could collect her company's delinquent accounts. Tarrant agreed and as part of their oral agreement, Riggins was to receive ¹/₄ of the money recovered on those accounts that were "city" accounts and ½ of those accounts designated "out-of-city" accounts. It was further agreed that he need not account for the amounts collected until a bill was paid in full, at which time he was to remit by check what was rightfully owed to Tarrant. The parties operated under this agreement for almost two years. During that time, Tarrant exercised no control over Riggins as to the time or manner of collecting the accounts, and with her knowledge he commingled funds collected for all his clients in a single bank account. He also used this account as a personal account, from which he drew for business, family and personal expenses.

Can a collection agent be convicted of embezzlement?

A collection agent who "receives money in a fiduciary capacity" for a client falls within the reach of Ill. Rev. Stat, chap. 38, the Illinois embezzlement statute.

Illinois' embezzlement statute provides that embezzlement is a felony and includes anyone who fraudulently converts to his own use the property of another. Specifically, the statute provides "a clerk, agent, servant, or apprentice of any person . . . receiving any money . . . in his fiduciary capacity . . . shall be punished by the criminal statutes of this state for . . . larceny . . . irrespective of whether any such officer, agent, clerk, servant . . . has or claims to have any commission or interest in such money." Clearly, Riggins acted as agent for Tarrant in collecting her delinquent accounts. That is, he transacted business and/or managed her affairs, which was authorized to do by her as part of the authority she expressly delegated to him. Under the terms of the agreement, he was required to render a full account of all matters entrusted to him. Specifically, he was required to account for the amounts he collected when the bill was paid in full. He did not fulfill this duty. Thus, we conclude that Riggins, as an "agent" of Tarrant, having received money in a "fiduciary capacity," and thereafter misappropriating those funds, falls within the embezzlement statute.

See Rule above.

Hufstetler v. State

Alabama Court of Appeals, 63 So. 2d 730 (1953)

FACTS

Defendant Hufstetler drove to a gasoline service station in Forney, Alabama in a car with two or three other passengers inside. When they arrived, a man in the back seat got out, went into the service station's store and asked if there was a telephone. Peter Whorton, the owner and operator of the store and service station, told him there was no telephone and the man said he wanted some gasoline. He then went back and got in the car. Whorton asked the man how much gas he wanted, and he was told to "fill it up." Whorton put 6½ gallons of gasoline in the car and the man in the back seat then told him to get a quart of oil. When Whorton went for the oil, Hufstetler drove off with all of his passengers in the car without paying. The gasoline was valued at $1.94. The accused was convicted by the court without a jury on a charge of petit larceny; the defendant did not testify nor offer any evidence.

Can the accused be held criminally liable for petit larceny when he drove his car away without paying for gas?

When one obtains the property of another by fraud or trick, even with the consent of the owner, he may be prosecuted for the crime of larceny.

The accused can be held criminally liable for petit larceny when he drove his car away without paying for gas. We arrive that this conclusion after answering the only question of critical concern before us: whether, on the basis of the evidence presented, the judgment of conviction can be sustained. Hufstetler's attorney urges that Whorton voluntarily parted with the possession and ownership of the gasoline. However in this case, the circumstances clearly show that by the application of the well known doctrine of aid and abet, Hufstetler secured the possession of the gasoline by trick or fraud. The obtaining of the property by the consent of the owner under such conditions will not necessarily prevent the taking from being larceny. In other words, an actual trespass is not always required to be proven. This is because the trick or fraud invalidates the transaction, and it will be deemed that the owner still retained the constructive possession. Also, it is logical to conclude that Whorton had no indention of parting with the ownership of the gasoline until he was paid. Thus, the element of intent can be inferred from the factual background.

Affirmed.

Graham v. United States

U.S. Court of Appeals, 187 F.2d 87 (D.C. Cir. 1950)

FACTS

Defendant-appellant Graham, an attorney, was indicted for two counts of grand larceny for having stolen money from one Francisco Gal in the amounts of $100 and $1,900. Gal, an immigrant employed as a cook, had been arrested and charged with disorderly conduct. During this time, Gal was seeking American citizenship and was afraid that his arrest would impede or bar his application for citizenship. To that end, he hired Graham as an attorney. Unfortunately, Gal's command of the English language was less that perfect, as evidenced by his testimony whereby he stated that Graham told him he would have to "talk to the policeman" because "money was talk." He further testified that Graham told him he would charge him $200 for a fee; that he would have to pay an additional $2,000 for the police; and that Graham told him "don't mention the money for nobody and the police either." All in all, Gal testified that he paid Graham $2,200. The police officer who originally arrested Gal testified that after he came to Graham's office, and after talking with him, told Gal that he wasn't in any trouble. The officer testified that Graham did not at any time offer to or actually give him [the officer] money. Graham testified that the entire payment was intended as a fee for legal services; that he had never mentioned money for the police; and that no part of the money was in fact paid to the police or anyone else, but was kept by him [Graham] for professional services rendered. Graham argues two principal arguments: 1) the evidence supports a directed verdict in his favor; and 2) trial court erred in not sufficiently distinguishing between the situation where one obtains complete title to another's property by fraud or trick and the case where possession only is obtained

 Did the trial court err in not sufficiently distinguishing between the situation where one obtains complete title to another's property by fraud or trick and the case where possession only is obtained?

 One who obtains money from another upon the representation that he will perform certain service for the latter, intending at the time to convert the money, and actually converting it, to his own use, is guilty of larceny.

 The trial court did not err by not distinguishing between the situation where one obtains complete title to another's property by fraud or trick and the case where possession only is obtained. Graham's principal arguments are, first, that the evidence supports the proposition that Gal voluntarily gave Graham complete title to the money and therefore Graham is entitled to a directed verdict. We disagree. If the jury believed Gal's testimony and did not believe Graham, we think it possible for the jury to conclude beyond a reasonable doubt that Graham fraudulently induced Gal to give him the $2,000 to be used to bribe the police, that Graham did not intent so to use the money, and converted it to his own use. This would be larceny by trick. Graham's second contention is that the trial court's charge to the jury was erroneous in not sufficiently distinguishing between the situation where one obtains complete title to another's property by fraud or trick and the case

Graham v. United States

U.S. Court of Appeals, 187 F.2d 87 (D.C. Cir. 1950)

---

where possession only is obtained. Title 2201 of Title 22 of the D.C. Code provides: "Whoever shall feloniously take and carry away anything of value of the amount or value of $50 or upward . . . shall suffer imprisonment of not less than one nor more than ten years." Interpreting this statute, this court has held that one who obtains money from another upon the representation that he will perform certain service therewith for the latter, intending at the time to convert the money, and actually converting it, to his own use, is guilty of larceny. In classic terminology, "the distinction drawn by the common law is between the case of one who gives up possession of a chattel for a special purpose to another who by converting it to his own use is held to have committed a trespass, and the case of one who, although induced by fraud or trick, nevertheless actually intends that title to the chattel shall pass to the wrongdoer." What this means is that under the circumstances in this case, Graham can be found guilty of larceny, because title to the money remained in Gal [the complainant] until the accomplishment of the purpose for which he gave Graham [the defendant] the money – that is, until final delivery of the money to the officers whom Gal was led to believe were to be bribed.

 The judgment of the District Court is affirmed.

People v. Ashley

Supreme Court of California, 267 P.2d 271 (1954)

FACTS

Defendant Ashley, the business manager of a corporation chartered for the purpose of "introducing people" was charged with feloniously taking money from two women and convicted of grand theft under the California Penal Code. Ashley obtained loan of $7,200 from Mrs. Russ, a 70 year-old woman and promised her that the loan would be secured by a first mortgage on certain improved property of the corporation, and that the money would be used to build a theater on other property owned by the corporation. In fact, the corporation leased but did not own the improved property, and no theater was ever built, the having been used instead to meet the corporation's operating expenses. After Ashley received the money, Mrs. Russ frequently quarreled with him over his failure to deliver the promised first mortgage. She finally received a note of the corporation secured by a second trust deed on some unimproved property owned by the corporation. She testified that she accepted this security because Ashley told her to "take that or nothing." She subsequently received four postdated checks in payment of the loan. After it became apparent that these checks would not be paid, Ashley requested an extension. Mrs. Russ granted the extension after Ashley threatened to kill himself if she refused, so that she might be paid from the proceeds of his life insurance policies. Defendant Ashley also obtained $13,590 from a Mrs. Neal, representing that the corporation intended to use the money to buy the El Patio Theater. Neal was initially told that the loan would be secured by a trust deed on the theater building and that she would have good security for her loan because the corporation was worth $500,000. However, after obtaining the money, Ashley issued Mrs. Neal a note of the corporation for $13,500. Subsequently, Neal loaned the corporation an additional $4,470, receiving a note for $17,500 in exchange for the previous note. Mrs. Neal testified that when she hesitated in making the additional loan, Ashley placed a gun on his desk and made threats. The corporation never bought the theater, Mrs. Neal never received the trust deed, and the money was deposited to the corporation's account. The case went to the jury with instructions relating to larceny by trick and device and obtaining property by false pretenses.

 Did the defendant knowingly and with intent to deceive make false promises to obtain property in violation of California statute?

 To support a conviction of theft for obtaining property by false pretenses, it must be shown that the defendant made a false pretense or representation with intent to defraud the owner of his property, and that the owner was in fact defrauded.

 Initially, we point out that Ashley's defense was that there was no unlawful taking of any sort; it was not based on distinctions between title and possession. We note the differences: Larceny by trick is the appropriation of the property of another [possession only], the possession of which was fraudulently acquired. Obtaining property by false pretenses is the fraudulent or

People v. Ashley

Supreme Court of California, 267 P.2d 271 (1954)

---

deceitful acquisition of both title and possession. To support a conviction of theft for obtaining property by false pretenses, it must be shown that Ashley made a false pretense or representation with intent to defraud the owners of their property, and that the owners were in the fact defrauded. It is unnecessary to prove that Ashley benefited personally from the fraudulent acquisition. The false pretense or representation must have materially influenced the owners to part with their property. In our State, false promises can provide the foundation of a civil action for deceit, however, something more than nonperformance is required to prove the defendant's intent not to perform his promise. Moreover, in cases of obtaining property by false pretenses, it must be proved that any misrepresentations of fact alleged by the prosecutor were made knowingly and with intent to deceive. If such misrepresentations are made innocently or inadvertently, they can not form the basis for a prosecution for that crime. If false promises were not false pretenses, the legally sophisticated, without fear of punishment, could perpetrate on the unwary fraudulent schemes like that revealed by the record before us.

 The judgment and order denying the motion for a new trial are affirmed.

Nelson v. United States
U.S. Court of Appeals, 227 F.2d 21 (D.C. Cir. 1955)

FACTS

Defendant-appellant Nelson appealed from a conviction for obtaining goods by false pretenses. Defendant had purchased merchandise for resale over a period of months from Potomac Distributors of Washington, D.C. Inc. By September 18, 1952, his account was in arrears more than thirty days on which date Potomac sought immediate possession of two television sets and a washing machine. Consequently, Schneider, the secretary-treasurer for Potomac, told Nelson that no further credit could be extended to him. Nelson offered to give security for the desired items as well as for the delinquent account by representing himself as the owner of a Packard automobile for which he paid $4,260.50. He failed, however, to disclose to Potomac that $3028.08 was owed and secured by a chattel mortgage in favor of City Bank. Instead, he represented that he owed only one payment of $55, not yet due. Relying on such representations, Potomac delivered two televisions worth $136 each to Nelson, taking in return a demand note for the entire indebtedness, past and present, secured by the chattel mortgage on the Packard and the television sets. When Nelson's promised payment was not forthcoming, Schneider attempted to locate him but learned he had left town. The Packard about that time was in a collision, incurring damage of about $1,000, and was thereupon repossessed on behalf of the bank which held the prior lien for Nelson's car purchase indebtedness.

Did defendant's misrepresentations constitute a material fraud?

The intent to injure or defraud is presumed when the unlawful act, which results in loss or injury, is proved to have been knowingly committed.

Nelson argues that Potomac could not have been defrauded because the car had an equity value of over $900 when he offered it as security - roughly five times the value of the two TV sets. This fact is immaterial. Nelson sold two TV sets and apparently had taken payment even though he had nothing to deliver to his customers. He could not get the sets from Potomac without offering security for his past due account is well as for his present purchase. In order to get them, he lied. He now complains because his victim believed him when he lied. He argues that the misrepresentations were not material although the victim, Potomac testified, and the jury could properly find, that it would not have parted with its goods except in reliance upon his statements. He argues that there was no proof of an intent to defraud. We take a contrary position. Wrongful acts knowingly or intentionally committed can neither be justified nor excused on the ground of innocent intent. The intent to injure or defraud is presumed when the unlawful act, which results in loss or

Nelson v. United States

U.S. Court of Appeals, 227 F.2d 21 (D.C. Cir. 1955)

injury, is proved to have been knowingly committed – the intent is presumed from the result of the action.

 Affirmed.

State v. Harrington
Supreme Court of Vermont, 260 A.2d 692 (1969)

FACTS

Defendant-respondent John B. Harrington was an attorney retained by Norma Morin to obtain a divorce from her husband, Armand Morin. As Mrs. Morin was without funds, Harrington agreed to work on a contingent fee basis. The couple owned assets worth approximately $50,000, including a motel where the two had previously lived. In order to secure the divorce and a favorable settlement, Harrington and Mrs. Morin arranged to obtain evidence of Mr. Morin's infidelity by hiring a woman, armed with a tape recorder, to entice him into having sex with her in one of his motel rooms. At the appropriate moment, Harrington and his associates entered the room and took pictures of Mr. Morin and the woman naked in bed. Several days later, Harrington, in the presence of Mrs. Morin, dictated a letter to Mr. Morin proposing a settlement of the divorce action in which she would receive her divorce, give up her interest in the marital assets, waive alimony, and receive a lump sum of $175,000. The letter stressed Mrs. Morin's present state of insolvency and also provided that Mr. Morin would also receive all recordings and photos taken in the hotel room after he accepted the offer. Finally, the letter stated that if Mr. Morin did not accept the offer, divorce proceedings would be brought alleging adultery, disclosing the infidelity as well as revealing other improprieties Mr. Morin was involved in. A photograph from the hotel room was included in the letter.

Did the letter constitute a threat in violation of Vermont's extortion statute?

A demand for settlement of a civil action, accompanied by a malicious threat to expose the wrongdoer's criminal conduct, if made with intent to extort payment and against the wrongdoer's will, constitutes the crime of blackmail within the meaning of Vermont's extortion statute.

The letter constituted a threat in violation of the Vermont's extortion statute. 13 V.S.A. 1701, the relevant statute at issue, provides that "[a] person who maliciously threatens to accuse another of a crime or offense, or with an injury to his person or property, with intent to extort money or other pecuniary advantage, or with intent to compel the person so threatened to do an act against his will, shall be imprisoned in the state prison not more than two years or fined not more than $500." Harrington maintains that his letter does not constitute a threat to accuse Mr. Morin of the crime of adultery. Instead, he argues that implicit threats in the letter were not to accuse Mr. Marin of adultery, but merely to bring to light an embarrassing, reputation-ruining divorce proceeding unless a stipulation could be negotiated. The statute is aimed at blackmailing, and a threat of any public accusation is as much within the purview of the statute as a threat of formal complaint, and is much easier made, and may be quite as likely to accomplish its purpose. There is nothing in the statute that requires such a restricted meaning of the word "accuse," and

State v. Harrington

Supreme Court of Vermont, 260 A.2d 692 (1969)

to restrict it thus would destroy the efficacy of the act. In further support of a motion for acquittal, Harrington also urges that the totality of the evidence does not exclude the inference that he acted merely as an attorney, attempting to secure a divorce for his client on the most favorable terms possible. We disagree. Quite clearly, the veiled threats in Harrington's letter exceeded the limits of his representation of Mrs. Morin in the divorce action. A demand for settlement of a civil action, accompanied by a malicious threat to expose the wrongdoer's criminal conduct, if made with intent to extort payment, against his will, constitutes the crime alleged in the indictment.

 Judgment affirmed.

FACTS

Defendant Fichtner is the manager of the Hill Supermarket in Freeport and Co-defendant McGuinness is the assistant manager. Fichtner was charged with two counts of extortion due to the fact that he and McGuinness, aiding and abetting one other, obtained $25 from one Smith, with his consent, which was induced by a wrongful use of fear. On January 18, 1951, Smith purchased several items in the store amounting to $12, but left without paying for a 53¢ jar of coffee, which he had concealed in his pocket. Fichtner asked Smith to return to the store, and then threatened to call the police to have Smith arrested for petit larceny, with resulting publicity in the newspapers and over the radio, unless he paid $75 and signed a paper admitting that during the course of several months he had unlawfully taken merchandise from the store in that amount. Smith insisted that the only merchandise he had ever stolen was the jar of coffee that evening and a 65¢ roll of bologna one week prior. Nevertheless, he finally signed the paper admitting that he had taken $50 worth of merchandise from the store during a period of four months. That evening Smith paid $25 in cash and promised to pay the balance in weekly installments of $5. Smith testified that he was induced to sign the paper and make the payment because Fichtner threatened to accuse him of petit larceny and to expose him to the disgrace of the criminal charge and the resulting publicity. It is undisputed that the $25 was "rung up" on the store register, went into the company funds, and Fichtner received no part of the money. During the following week, Smith reported the incident to the police and Fichtner was arrested. Fichtner testified that over the course of several weeks he saw Smith steal merchandise in the amount of $5.61, and he honestly believed that during the several months Smith had been shopping there that he had stolen merchandise in the amount of $75.

Was the proffered evidence adequate to sustain the defendant's conviction for extortion?

The extortion statutes were intended to prevent the collection of money by the use of fear induced by means of threats to accuse a debtor of a crime.

The proffered evidence was adequate to sustain the defendant's conviction for extortion. Fichtner requested the court to instruct the jury that if it found that Fichtner honestly believed that the amount which Smith paid or agreed to pay represented the amount of the merchandise he had previously stolen then Fichtner must be acquitted. The court refused this request "except as already charged." We believe that the portion of the main charge which states that extortion is committed only when one obtains property from another by inducing fear in that other by threatening to accuse him of crime unless he pays an amount over and above what was rightfully due, was more deferential to Fichtner than

People v. Fichtner
New York Supreme Ct., Appellate Div., Second Dept., 118 N.Y.S.2d 392 (1952)

---

that which he was entitled to receive by the law. We arrive at this conclusion because, in our opinion, the extortion statutes were intended to prevent the collection of money by the use of fear induced by means of threats to accuse a debtor of a crime. It thus makes no difference whether the debtor stole any goods or even how much he stole. Under this rational, Fichtner may properly be convicted even though he believed Smith was guilty of the theft of the supermarket's goods in an amount either equal to or less, or greater than any sum of money obtained from Smith. Moreover Fichtner's good faith in thus enforcing payment of the money alleged to be due to the supermarket provides no defense to the crime he is charged with.

Conviction affirmed.

State v. Miller
Supreme Court of Oregon, 233 P.2d 786 (1951)

FACTS

Defendant Miller induced the Hub Lumber Company to agree to guarantee his indebtedness to the Howard Cooper Corporation on the false representation that he owned a tractor free of encumbrances and on his executing a chattel mortgage thereto as security. In reality, Miller was purchasing the tractor under a conditional sales contract. Thereafter, he was convicted of obtaining property from the Hub Lumber Company by false pretenses.

Does obtaining an agreement to agree to guarantee one's indebtedness to another, induced by false pretenses, a crime under Oregon law?

Under Oregon law, in order to be convicted of obtaining property by false pretenses, the "property" must be something capable of being possessed, such as worldly goods or possessions, tangible things and things to which title can be transferred.

Obtaining an agreement to agree to guarantee one's indebtedness to another, induced by false pretenses, is not a crime under Oregon law. Specifically, statute §23-537 O.C.L.A. reads: "If any person shall, by any false pretenses or by any privity or false taken, and with intent to defraud, obtain or attempt to obtain, from any other person any money or property whatsoever, or shall obtain or attempt to obtain with the like intent the signature of any person to any writing, the false making whereof would be punishable as forgery, such person, upon conviction thereof, shall be punished by imprisonment." Reduced to its simplest terms, this indictment means that by false pretenses Miller induced the Hub Lumber Company to agree to pay his indebtedness to the Howard Cooper Corporation if he should fail to pay it. The question is whether this amounts to an allegation that, in the sense of the statute, Miller obtained "any property" from the Hub Lumber Company. If not, then the indictment does not charge a crime. We recognize that "property" under the statute must be something capable of being possessed and the title to which can be transferred. Here, the *benefit* of the guaranty which the Hub Lumber Company gave to the Howard Cooper Corporation for Miller's advantage could not be possessed, nor could there be any such thing as holding title to it. Had the indictment alleged that Miller obtained the *signature* of the Hub Lumber Company or its agent to a guaranty of Miller's indebtedness, we would have had an entirely different situation. This failure to so allege was not due to mistake or oversight, rather because no written guaranty was ever executed — it was simply an oral agreement.

The indictment, in our opinion, does not allege a crime, and the judgment must therefore be reversed and the action dismissed.

United States v. Girard

U.S. Court of Appeals, 601 F.2d 69 (2nd Cir. 1969)

FACTS

Defendant-appellant Girard, a former DEA agent, began discussions with one James Bond regarding a proposed illegal venture that involved smuggling a planeload of marijuana from Mexico into the United States. Girard told Bond that for $500 per name he could, through an inside source, secure reports from the DEA files that would show whether any participant in the proposed operation was a government informant. Unfortunately for Girard, Bond himself became an informant and disclosed his conversations with Girard to the DEA. Thereafter, the dealings between the two were conducted under the surveillance of the DEA. Bond asked Girard to secure reports on four men whose names were furnished to him by DEA agents. DEA records are kept in computerized files, and the DEA hoped to identify the inside source by monitoring access to the four names in the computer bank. In this manner, the DEA learned that Girard's informant was Lambert, a DEA agent who obtained the reports through a computer terminal located in his [Lambert's] office. Defendant-appellants, including Girard, were convicted of the unauthorized sale of government property under §18 U.S.C. 641 and for conspiring to accomplish the sale under §18 U.S.C. 371. The defendants appealed.

 Does government information constitute "property" as embraced by §18 U.S.C. 641, the statute forbidding the unauthorized sale of government property?

 The Government has a property interest in its private records and although the contents of a writing is an intangible, it is nonetheless a thing of value which it may be protected by statute.

 Government information constitutes "property" within the meaning of §18 U.S.C. 641, the statute forbidding the unauthorized sale of government property. Section 641, so far as is relevant here, provides that whoever without authority sells any "record . . . or thing of value" of the United States or who "receives . . . the same with intent to convert it to his use or gain, knowing it to have been embezzled, stolen, purloined or converted," shall be guilty of a crime. Girard contends that the statute covers only tangible property such that the sale of information, which has an *intangible* quality, does not violate the statue. We disagree. Like the District Judge, we are impressed by Congress' repeated use of the phrase "thing of value" in §641 and its predecessors. The word "thing" notwithstanding, the phrase is generally construed to cover tangibles as well as intangibles. Although the content of a writing is an intangible, it is nonetheless a thing of value and the existence of protections for writings was judicially recognized for many years, predating the birth of copyright law. Thus, we are satisfied that the Government has a property interest in certain of its private records which it may protect by statute as a thing of value. The District Judge also rejected Girard's constitutional challenge to section 641 based upon alleged vagueness and overbreadth. We again agree with his ruling. Where, as here, we are not dealing with Girard's exercise of a First Amendment freedom, we should not search for statutory vagueness that did not exist for the defendants themselves. Neither should we find a constitutional violation simply because the statute might conceivably trespass upon the First Amendment rights of others. In view of the statute's plainly legitimate sweep in regulating conduct, it is not so substantially overbroad that any overbreadth that may exist cannot be cured on a case by case basis.

The judgments are affirmed.

Regina v. Stewart

Supreme Court of Canada, 41 C.C.C.3d 481 (1988)

FACTS

A union attempting to organize the approximately 600 employees of the Constellation hotel in Toronto, Canada, was unable to obtain the names, addresses and telephone numbers of the employees because of a hotel policy that such information he treated as confidential. Defendant Stewart, a self-employed consultant, was hired by someone he assumed to be acting for the union to obtain the names and addresses of the employees. Stewart offered a security guard at the hotel named Hart a fee to obtain this information. Instead of providing the name, Hart reported this request to his security chief and to the police. Consequently, a telephone conversation between Hart and Stewart was recorded, and Stewart was indicted for, among other crimes, counseling the offense of theft. Stewart was acquitted by a single judge court, but on appeal, the Ontario Court of Appeal reversed and entered the verdict of conviction. Stewart then appealed to the Supreme Court of Canada.

 Is confidential information, an intangible, considered "property" within the meaning of the law of theft?

 Confidential information is not "property" for the purposes of the law of theft.

 In this case, we are not dealing with the theft of a list or any other tangible object containing confidential information, but with the theft of confidential information *per se*, a pure intangible. The assumption that no tangible object would have been taken was part of the agreed statement of facts, and the case was argued throughout on that basis. The word "anything" is not in itself a bar to anything, including any intangible, whatever its nature. Thus its meaning must be determined with the context of the Code. It is clear that to be the object of theft, "anything" must be property in the sense that to be stolen, it has to belong in some way to someone. It is possible that, with time, confidential information will come to be considered as property in the civil law or by civil statutory enactment. But even if it were, it would not mean that it would automatically qualify as property for the purposes of criminal law. Whether or not confidential information is property under the Criminal Code should be decided in a comprehensive way, taking into account the competing interests of the free flow of information, of one's right to confidentiality or one's economic interests in certain kinds of information. These are choices to be made, in my view, by the legislature and not of the judiciary.

 Appeal allowed; acquittal restored.

United States v. Siegel

U.S. Court of Appeals, 717 F.2d 9 (2nd Cir. 1983)

FACTS

Defendants Abrams and Siegel were both officers and directors of Mego International, a publicly held manufacturer and distributor of toys and games. They were charged with and convicted of violating the wire fraud statute by engaging in a scheme to defraud Mego and its stockholders by violating their fiduciary duties to act honestly and faithfully in the best interest of the corporation and to account for the sale of all Mego property entrusted to them. The fraudulent scheme involved the creation of a hidden cash fund derived from cash sales of merchandise that had been closed out, marked down for clearance, or returned as damaged. These "off the books" sales all together generated sales of $100,000 in cash. The indictment charged that Abrams and Siegel used the cash for pay-offs to union officials and to other persons dealing with the corporation.

Was evidence of self-enrichment sufficient to prove violations of the wire fraud statute?

The *wire* fraud statue, §18 U.S.C. 1343, provides that anyone who devised or intended to devise any scheme to defraud or obtain money by means of false pretenses, representations, or promises, transmits or causes to be transmitted by means of wire, radio or television communication in interstate or foreign commerce . . . any writings, pictures, signs, signals . . . shall be fined not more than $1000 or imprisoned not more than 5 years in, or both.

The *mail* fraud statute, §18 U.S.C. 1341, is violated when a fiduciary fails to disclose material information which he is under a duty to disclose to another under circumstances where the non-disclosure could or does result in harm the other.

Whether there was evidence of self-enrichment was an issue on appeal, which generally dealt with the sufficiency of the evidence to prove violation of the *wire* fraud statute. The *wire* fraud statue, §18 U.S.C. 1343, provides that anyone who devised or intended to devise any scheme to defraud or obtain money by means of false pretenses, representations, or promises, transmits or causes to be transmitted by means of wire, radio or television communication in interstate or foreign commerce . . . any writings, pictures, signs, signals . . . shall be fined not more than $1000 or imprisoned not more than 5 years in, or both. The *mail* fraud statute, §18 U.S.C. 1341, is violated when a fiduciary fails to disclose material information which he is under a duty to disclose to another under circumstances where the non-disclosure could or does result in harm the other. While we have described the mail fraud and wire fraud statutes as seemingly limitless in *United States v. Von Barta*, we have also recognized in *United States v. Bronston,* that a mere breach of fiduciary duty, standing alone, may not necessarily constitute a mail fraud. However, to be clear,

United States v. Siegel

U.S. Court of Appeals, 717 F.2d 9 (2nd Cir. 1983)

we have held that the statute is violated when a fiduciary fails to disclose material information which he is under a duty to disclose to another under circumstances where the non-disclosure could or does result in harm the other. In the case before us, there was testimony which showed that Abrams and Siegel personally received the proceeds from the cash sales and either pocketed them or placed them in the corporate safe deposit box; that the cash sales generated in excess of $100,000 and that approximately $31,000 was accounted for. Given this evidence, we conclude that the jury could have inferred that Abrams and Siegel used some or all of the remainder of the proceeds for their own benefit, and could have fairly concluded beyond a reasonable doubt that they were involved in a scheme to misappropriate the proceeds from the sale of Mego assets for their own self-enrichment.

 Affirmed.

People v. Brown
Supreme Court of California, 38 P. 518 (1894)

FACTS

Defendant-appellant Brown, a seventeen-year-old boy, had been in an argument with another boy named Yount. Yount had thrown oranges at Defendant-appellant Brown, and Brown wanted to get back at him so Brown entered Yount's house and tried to take his bicycle, but instead took Frank's bicycle. Brown claimed to have taken the bicycle to get back at Yount, but intended to return the bike the next day. Brown drove the bicycle into a grove, and hid himself and the bicycle under some brush so that no one could find him until he planned to return it that evening. However, Frank found him (and his bicycle) hiding under the brush first. The jury was instructed that larceny may occur even though the party taking the property intended only to temporarily deprive the owner of the goods. The trial judge provided an example as well. The jury found Brown guilty and he appealed.

Can the crime of larceny be committed by one who only temporarily intends to deprive the owner of his property?

Larceny requires that the taking be with the intent to permanently deprive the owner of his possession.

The judge incorrectly charged the jury. The court instructed the jury that larceny may take place if the accused only intended to temporarily deprive the owner of the property. We disagree. We believe that judicial authorities are consistent in holding that the felonious intent must be the intent to permanently deprive the owner of the property. The judge's illustration regarding the man taking the horse is too broad in its terms to accurately state the law. Under the judge's example, the accused may or may not be guilty of larceny - it would be a pure question of fact for the jury to decide. Felonious intent requires the accused to have intended to *permanently* deprive the owner of his property - not just to convert the property to his own use.

Judgment reversed.

Regina v. Feely
Court of Appeal, 2 W.L.R. 201 (1973)

FACTS

Defendant Feely, a branch manager for a firm of bookmakers, was sent a circular [as were all branch managers] by the head office that the practice of borrowing money from tills was to cease. Nevertheless, Feely took about £30 from a branch safe the following month. Four days later, Feely was transferred to another branch. His successor discovered a cash shortage of £40, for which Feely gave him an IOU. Though his successor did not report the deficiency, a member of the firm's security staff did. Feely was asked to give an explanation. In so doing, he accounted for about £10 for some bets he had paid out, but as to the remaining £20, he said that he had taken it because he was "stuck for cash." Feely stated he borrowed the £30 intending to pay it back and that his employers owed him about £70 from which he wanted them to deduct the money. Trial testimony showed that the firm did owe him that amount. Nevertheless, Feely was convicted of the theft of the £30.

Can the promise and honest and reasonable belief by the accused to repay money taken serve as a valid defense to a charge of theft?

The issue of whether the defendant acted dishonestly or not is a matter for the jury to decide, not the judge, in a criminal trial for theft.

The jury should have been allowed to decide, not the judge, whether the defendant's alleged taking of the money was dishonest. The jurors were not permitted to do so, and with such a result, a guilty verdict was returned by them without haven given thought to what was probably the most import issue of the case. The trial judge directed the jury that if Feely had taken the money from either the safe or the till, it was no defense for him to say that he had intended to repay it or that his employers owed him more than enough to cover what he had taken. At no point during the trial did the judge allow the jury to decide whether the prosecution had proved it case: that Feely had taken the money dishonestly. Instead, the judge took it upon himself and decided as a matter of law what was "dishonest" and he expressed his view to the jurors. We do not believe that judges should define what "dishonestly" means. Jurors, when deciding whether a taking was dishonest can be reasonably expected to apply the current standards of ordinary decent people, as they should. That is their function. That is what they do. Here, the jury should have been left to decide whether Feely's alleged taking of the money had been dishonest. Because they were not permitted to do so, we allow the appeal.

Appeal allowed.

People v. Reid

New York Court of Appeals, 508 N.E.2d 661 (1987)

FACTS

[Two cases consolidated on appeal to the New York Court of Appeals, the State's highest court] Defendant-appellants Reid and Riddles were convicted of armed robbery, despite evidence that they were only trying to recover money owed to them. In one case, the trial court, conducting a trial without a jury, stated that it credited the testimony of Reid that he had taken the money to satisfy a debt, but the court denied him the defense of claim of right because he used force.

 May the defendants validly assert claim of right defenses? Specifically, does a good-faith claim of right by a defendant(s) negate the intent to commit robbery by he who uses force to recover cash allegedly owed him?

 A good-faith claim of right does not undo the intent to commit robbery by a defendant who uses force to recover cash allegedly owed him.

 The issue presented here is whether a good-faith claim of right, which negates larcenous intent in certain thefts, negate the intent to commit robbery by a defendant who uses force to recover cash allegedly owed him. We hold that it does not. Accordingly, we affirm the order of the Appellate Division in each case. The Appellate Divisions have uniformly ruled that claim of right is not a defense to robbery; their determinations have been based upon the interpretation of the applicable statutes and a policy decision to discourage self-help, and they are consistent with what appears to be the emerging trend of similar appellate court decisions from other jurisdictions. For similar reasons, we conclude that the claim of right defense is not available in this case and we need not decide whether an individual who uses force to recover a specific chattel which he owns may be convicted of robbery. However, it should be noted, that because taking property "from another owner thereof" is an element of robbery, a person who recovers property which is his own may not be guilty of robbery. Consequently, we find the lower courts in both cases correctly denied defendants' requests to assert claim of right defenses; Reid's request to assert claim of right defense was properly denied.

 Defendants' requests were properly denied.

Linda R. S. v. Richard D.

Supreme Court of the United States, 410 U.S. 614 (1973)

FACTS

Appellant, the mother of an illegitimate child, brought a class action to enjoin the "discriminatory application" of Art. 602 of the Texas Penal Code providing that any "parent" who fails to support his "children" is subject to prosecution, but which by state judicial construction applies only to married parents. Appellant sought to enjoin the local district attorney from refraining to prosecute the father of her child. The three-judge District Court dismissed appellant's action for want of standing: Held:

Does a mother of an illegitimate child have standing to attack the constitutionality of Art. 602 of the Texas Penal Code when the law applies only married parents?

Although appellant has an interest in her child's support, application of Art. 602 would not result in support but only in the father's incarceration, and a private citizen lacks a judicially cognizable interest in the prosecution or non-prosecution of another.

Appellant, the mother of an illegitimate child, brought this action in United States District Court on behalf of herself, her child, and others similarly situated to enjoin the "discriminatory application" of Art. 602 of the Texas Penal Code. A three-judge court was convened pursuant to 28 U.S.C. 2281, but that court dismissed the action for want of standing. We postponed consideration of jurisdiction until argument on the merits and now affirm the judgment below. Article 602, in relevant part, provides: "any parent who shall willfully desert, neglect or refuse to provide for the support and maintenance of his or her child or children under eighteen years of age, shall be guilty of a misdemeanor, and upon conviction, shall be punished by confinement in the County Jail for not more than two years." The Texas courts have consistently construed this statute to apply solely to the parents of legitimate children and to impose no duty of support on the parents of illegitimate children. In her complaint, appellant alleges that one Richard D. is the father of her child, that Richard D. has refused to provide support for the child and that although appellant made application to the local district attorney for enforcement of Art. 602 against Richard D., the district attorney refused to take action for the express reason that, in his view, the fathers of illegitimate children were not within the scope of Art. 602.

Recent decisions by this Court have greatly expanded the types of "personal stake[s]" which are capable of conferring standing on a potential plaintiff. Although the law of standing has been greatly changed in the last 10 years, we have steadfastly adhered to the requirement that, at least in the absence of a statute expressly conferring standing, federal plaintiffs must allege some threatened or actual injury resulting from the putatively illegal action before a federal court may assume jurisdiction. Applying this test to the facts of this case, we hold that, in the unique context of a challenge to a

Linda R. S. v. Richard D.
Supreme Court of the United States, 410 U.S. 614 (1973)

criminal statute, appellant has failed to allege a sufficient nexus between her injury and the government action which she attacks to justify judicial intervention. To be sure, appellant no doubt suffered an injury stemming from the failure of her child's father to contribute support payments. But the bare existence of an abstract injury meets only the first half of the standing requirement. As this Court made plain in Flast v. Cohen, supra, a plaintiff must show "a logical nexus between the status asserted and the claim sought to be adjudicated. . . . Such inquiries into the nexus between the status asserted by the litigant and the claim he presents are essential to assure that he is a proper and appropriate party to invoke federal judicial power." Here, appellant has made no showing that her failure to secure support payments results from the non-enforcement, as to her child's father, of Art. 602. Although the Texas statute appears to create a continuing duty, it does not follow the civil contempt model whereby the defendant "keeps the keys to the jail in his own pocket" and may be released whenever he complies with his legal obligations. On the contrary, the statute creates a completed offense with a fixed penalty as soon as a parent fails to support his child. Thus, if appellant were granted the requested relief, it would result only in the jailing of the child's father. The prospect that prosecution will, at least in the future, result in payment of support can, at best, be termed only speculative. Certainly the "direct" relationship between the alleged injury and the claim sought to be adjudicated, which previous decisions of this Court suggest is a prerequisite of standing, is absent in this case.

Affirmed.

Inmates of Attica Correctional Facility v. Rockefeller

United States Court of Appeals, 477 F.2d 375 (2nd 1973)

FACTS

Plaintiffs are certain present and former inmates of New York State's Attica Correctional facility including the mother of an inmate that was killed when Attica was retaken following an inmate uprising in September 1971. The complaint alleges that before, during and after the prisoner revolt which resulted in the killing of 32 inmates and the wounding of many others, the defendants, including the Governor of New York and other State officials committed, conspired to commit or aided and abetted in the commission of various crimes against the complaining inmates. It is charged that state officers intentionally killed some of the inmate victims without provocation during the recovery of Attica, that state officers assaulted and beat prisoners after the prison had been successfully retaken and that medical assistance was maliciously denied to over 400 inmates wounded during the recovery of the prison. Plaintiffs request relief in the nature of mandamus (1) against state officials, requiring the State of New York to submit a plan for the independent and impartial investigation and prosecute the offenses charged; and (2) against the U.S. Attorney, requiring him to investigate, arrest and prosecute the same officers for having committed the federal offenses. The motions of the federal and state defendants to dismiss the complaint were granted by the district court.

Is there any mandatory duty upon the state officials to bring such prosecutions?

There is no mandatory duty upon the state officials to bring such prosecutions - New York law reposes in its prosecutors discretion to decide whether or not to prosecute in a given case, which is not subject to review in the state courts.

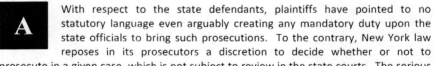

With respect to the state defendants, plaintiffs have pointed to no statutory language even arguably creating any mandatory duty upon the state officials to bring such prosecutions. To the contrary, New York law reposes in its prosecutors a discretion to decide whether or not to prosecute in a given case, which is not subject to review in the state courts. The serious charge that the state's investigation is proceeding against inmates but not against state officers, if shown to be accurate, might lead the Governor to supplement or replace those presently in charge of the investigation. But the gravity of the allegation does not reduce the inherent judicial capacity to supervise.

The order of the district court is affirmed.

United States v. Armstrong

Supreme Court of the United States, 517 U.S. 456 (1996)

FACTS

In response to their indictment on "crack" cocaine and other federal charges, respondents filed a motion for discovery or for dismissal, alleging that they were selected for prosecution because they are black. The District Court granted the motion over the Government's argument, among others, that there was no evidence or allegation that it had failed to prosecute nonblack defendants. When the Government indicated it would not comply with the discovery order, the court dismissed the case. The *en banc* Ninth Circuit affirmed, holding that the proof requirements for a selective-prosecution claim do not compel a defendant to demonstrate that the Government has failed to prosecute others who are similarly situated.

Is a defendant entitled to discovery on a claim that he was singled out for prosecution on the basis of his race with more?

For a defendant to be entitled to discovery on a claim that he was singled out for prosecution on the basis of his race, he must make a threshold showing that the Government declined to prosecute similarly situated suspects of other races.

Under the equal protection component of the Fifth Amendment's Due Process Clause, the decision whether to prosecute may not be based on an arbitrary classification such as race or religion. *Oyler* v. *Boles*. In order to prove a selective-prosecution claim, the claimant must demonstrate that the prosecutorial policy had a discriminatory effect and was motivated by a discriminatory purpose. To establish a discriminatory effect in a race case, the claimant must show that similarly situated individuals of a different race were not prosecuted. *Ah Sin* v. *Wittman*, 198 U.S. 500. *Batson* v. *Kentucky*, 476 U.S. 79, and *Hunter* v. *Underwood*, 471 U.S. 222, distinguished. Although *Ah Sin* involved federal review of a state conviction, a similar rule applies where the power of a federal court is invoked to challenge an exercise of one of the core powers of the Executive Branch of the Federal Government, the power to prose cute. Discovery imposes many of the costs present when the Government must respond to a prima facie case of selective prosecution. Assuming that discovery is available on an appropriate showing in aid of a selective-prosecution claim, see *Wade* v. *United States*, 504 U.S. 181, the justifications for a rigorous standard of proof for the elements of such a case thus require a correspondingly rigorous standard for discovery in aid of it. Thus, in order to establish entitlement to such discovery, a defendant must produce credible evidence that similarly situated defendants of other races could have been prosecuted, but were not. In this case, respondents have not met this required threshold.

See above.

Brady v. United States

Supreme Court of the United States, 397 U.S. 742 (1970)

FACTS

In 1959, petitioner was charged with kidnapping in violation of 18 U.S. C. 1201(a). Since the indictment charged that the victim of the kidnapping was not liberated unharmed, petitioner faced a maximum penalty of death if the verdict of the jury should so recommend. Petitioner, represented by competent counsel throughout, first elected to plead not guilty. Apparently because the trial judge was unwilling to try the case without a jury, petitioner made no serious attempt to reduce the possibility of a death penalty by waiving a jury trial. Upon learning that his codefendant, who had confessed to the authorities, would plead guilty and be available to testify against him, petitioner changed his plea to guilty. His plea was accepted after the trial judge twice questioned him as to the voluntariness of his plea. Petitioner was sentenced to 50 years' imprisonment, later reduced to 30. In 1967, petitioner sought relief under 28 U.S.C. 2255, claiming that his plea of guilty was not voluntarily given because 1201(a) operated to coerce his plea, because his counsel exerted impermissible pressure upon him, and because his plea was induced by representations with respect to reduction of sentence and clemency. It was also alleged that the trial judge had not fully complied with Rule 11 of the Federal Rules of Criminal Procedure. After a hearing, the District Court for the District of New Mexico denied relief. The court held that 1201(a) was constitutional and found that petitioner decided to plead guilty when he learned that his codefendant was going to plead guilty: petitioner pleaded guilty 'by reason of other matters and not by reason of the statute' or because of any acts of the trial judge. The court concluded that 'the plea was voluntarily and knowingly made.' The Court of Appeals for the Tenth Circuit affirmed, determining that the District Court's findings were supported by substantial evidence and specifically approving the finding that petitioner's plea of guilty was voluntary.

Does the rule that a plea must be intelligently made to be valid require that a plea be vulnerable to later attack if the defendant did not correctly assess every relevant factor entering into his decision?

The rule that a plea must be intelligently made to be valid does not require that a plea be vulnerable to later attack if the defendant did not correctly assess every relevant factor entering into his decision.

The record before us also supports the conclusion that Brady's plea was intelligently made. He was advised by competent counsel, he was made aware of the nature of the charge against him, and there was nothing to indicate that he was incompetent or otherwise not in control of his mental faculties; once his confederate had pleaded guilty and became available to testify, he chose to plead guilty, perhaps to ensure that he would face no more than life imprisonment or a term of years. Brady was aware of precisely what he was doing when he admitted that he had kidnapped the victim and had not released her unharmed.

Brady v. United States

Supreme Court of the United States, 397 U.S. 742 (1970)

It is true that Brady's counsel advised him that 1201(a) empowered the jury to impose the death penalty and that nine years later in *United States v. Jackson*, the Court held that the jury had no such power as long as the judge could impose only a lesser penalty if trial was to the court or there was a plea of guilty. But these facts do not require us to set aside Brady's conviction. Often the decision to plead guilty is heavily influenced by the defendant's appraisal of the prosecution's case against him and by the apparent likelihood of securing leniency should a guilty plea be offered and accepted. Considerations like these frequently present imponderable questions for which there are no certain answers; judgments may be made that in the light of later events seem improvident, although they were perfectly sensible at the time.

The rule that a plea must be intelligently made to be valid does not require that a plea be vulnerable to later attack if the defendant did not correctly assess every relevant factor entering into his decision. A defendant is not entitled to withdraw his plea merely because he discovers long after the plea has been accepted that his calculus misapprehended the quality of the State's case or the likely penalties attached to alternative courses of action. More particularly, absent misrepresentation or other impermissible conduct by state agents, a voluntary plea of guilty intelligently made in the light of the then applicable law does not become vulnerable because later judicial decisions indicate that the plea rested on a faulty premise. The fact that Brady did not anticipate *United States v. Jackson*, does not impugn the truth or reliability of his plea. We find no requirement in the Constitution that a defendant must be permitted to disown his solemn admissions in open court that he committed the act with which he is charged simply because it later develops that the State would have had a weaker case than the defendant had thought or that the maximum penalty then assumed applicable has been held inapplicable in subsequent judicial decisions. This is not to say that guilty plea convictions hold no hazards for the innocent or that the methods of taking guilty pleas presently employed in this country are necessarily valid in all respects. This mode of conviction is no more foolproof than full trials to the court or to the jury. In the case before us, nothing in the record impeaches Brady's plea or suggests that his admissions in open court were anything but the truth. Although Brady's plea of guilty may well have been motivated in part by a desire to avoid a possible death penalty, we are convinced that his plea was voluntarily and intelligently made and we have no reason to doubt that his solemn admission of guilt was truthful.

 Affirmed.

Bordenkircher v. Hayes

Supreme Court of the United States, 434 U.S. 357 (1978)

FACTS

The respondent, Paul Lewis Hayes, was indicted by a Fayette County, Ky., grand jury on a charge of uttering a forged instrument in the amount of $88.30, an offense then punishable by a term of 2 to 10 years in prison. After arraignment, Hayes, his retained counsel, and the Commonwealth's Attorney met in the presence of the Clerk of the Court to discuss a possible plea agreement. During these conferences the prosecutor offered to recommend a sentence of five years in prison if Hayes would plead guilty to the indictment. He also said that if Hayes did not plead guilty and "save the court the inconvenience and necessity of a trial," he would return to the grand jury to seek an indictment under the Kentucky Habitual Criminal Act, which would subject Hayes to a mandatory sentence of life imprisonment by reason of his two prior felony convictions. Hayes chose not to plead guilty, and the prosecutor did obtain an indictment charging him under the Habitual Criminal Act. A jury found Hayes guilty on the principal charge of uttering a forged instrument and, in a separate proceeding, further found that he had twice before been convicted of felonies. As required by the habitual offender statute, he was sentenced to a life term in the penitentiary. The Court of Appeals drew a distinction between "concessions relating to prosecution under an existing indictment," and threats to bring more severe charges not contained in the original indictment - a line it thought necessary in order to establish a prophylactic rule to guard against the evil of prosecutorial vindictiveness. Quite apart from this chronological distinction, however, the Court of Appeals found that the prosecutor had acted vindictively in the present case since he had conceded that the indictment was influenced by his desire to induce a guilty plea. The ultimate conclusion of the Court of Appeals thus seems to have been that a prosecutor acts vindictively and in violation of due process of law whenever his charging decision is influenced by what he hopes to gain in the course of plea bargaining negotiations.

Is the Due Process Clause of the Fourteenth Amendment violated when a state prosecutor carries out a threat made during plea negotiations to re-indict the accused on more serious charges if he does not plead guilty to the offense with which he was originally charged?

In this case, the Due Process Clause of the Fourteenth Amendment is not violated when the state prosecutor carried out a threat made during plea negotiations to re-indict the accused on more serious charges if he did not plead guilty to the offense with which he was originally charged.

It is not disputed here that Hayes was properly chargeable under the recidivist statute, since he had in fact been convicted of two previous felonies. In our system, so long as the prosecutor has probable cause to believe that the accused committed an offense defined by statute, the decision whether or not to prosecute, and what charge to file or bring before a grand jury, generally rests entirely in his discretion. Within the limits set by the legislature's constitutionally valid definition of chargeable offenses, "the conscious exercise of some selectivity in enforcement is not in itself a federal constitutional violation" so long as "the selection was [not] deliberately based upon an unjustifiable standard such as race, religion, or other arbitrary classification." To hold that the prosecutor's desire to induce a guilty plea is an "unjustifiable standard," which, like race or religion, may play no part in his charging decision, would contradict the very premises that underlie the concept of plea bargaining itself. Moreover, a rigid constitutional rule that would prohibit a prosecutor from acting forthrightly in his dealings with the defense could only invite unhealthy subterfuge that would drive the practice of plea bargaining back into the shadows from which it has so recently emerged. There is no doubt that the breadth of discretion that our country's legal system vests in prosecuting attorneys carries with it the potential for both individual and institutional abuse. And broad though that discretion may be, there are undoubtedly constitutional limits upon its exercise. We hold only that the course of conduct engaged in by the prosecutor in this case, which no more than openly presented the defendant with the unpleasant alternatives of forgoing trial or facing charges on which he was plainly subject to prosecution, did not violate the Due Process Clause of the Fourteenth Amendment.

Judgment of the Court of Appeals is reversed.

Williams v. New York

Supreme Court of the United States, 337 U.S. 2412 (1942)

FACTS

A jury in a New York state court found appellant guilty of murder in the first degree. The jury recommended life imprisonment, but the trial judge imposed sentence of death. In giving his reasons for imposing the death sentence the judge discussed in open court the evidence upon which the jury had convicted stating that this evidence had been considered in the light of additional information obtained through the court's 'Probation Department, and through other sources.' Consideration of this additional information was pursuant to 482 of New York Criminal Code which provides: ... Before rendering judgment or pronouncing sentence the court shall cause the defendant's previous criminal record to be submitted to it, including any reports that may have been made as a result of a mental, psychiatric (sic) or physical examination of such person, and may seek any information that will aid the court in determining the proper treatment of such defendant. The Court of Appeals of New York affirmed the conviction and sentence over the contention that as construed and applied the controlling penal statutes are in violation of the due process clause of the Fourteenth Amendment of the Constitution of the United States in that the sentence of death was based upon information supplied by witnesses with whom the accused had not been confronted and as to whom he had no opportunity for cross-examination or rebuttal.

Are the controlling New York penal statues as construed violative of the due process clause of the Fourteen Amendment?

The controlling penal statutes are not in violation of the due process clause of the Fourteenth Amendment of the Constitution of the United States even though the sentence of death was based upon information supplied by witnesses with whom the accused had not been confronted and as to whom he had no opportunity for cross-examination or rebuttal.

The considerations we have set out admonish us against treating the due-process clause as a uniform command that courts throughout the Nation abandon their age-old practice of seeking information from out-of-court sources to guide their judgment toward a more enlightened and just sentence. New York criminal statutes set wide limits for maximum and minimum sentences. Under New York statutes a state judge cannot escape his grave responsibility of fixing sentence. In determining whether a defendant shall receive a one- year minimum or a twenty-year maximum sentence, we do not think the Federal Constitution restricts the view of the sentencing judge to the information received in open court. The due-process clause should not be treated as a device for freezing the evidential procedure of sentencing in the mold of trial procedure. It is urged, however, that we should draw a constitutional distinction as to the procedure for obtaining information where the death sentence is imposed. We cannot accept the contention. Leaving a sentencing judge free to avail himself of out-of-court information in making such a fateful choice of sentences does secure to him a broad discretionary power, one susceptible of abuse. But in considering whether a rigid constitutional barrier should be created, it must be remembered that there is possibility of abuse wherever a judge must choose between life imprisonment and death. And it is conceded that no federal constitutional objection would have been possible if the judge here had sentenced appellant to death because appellant's trial manner impressed the judge that appellant was a bad risk for society, or if the judge had sentenced him to death giving no reason at all. We cannot say that the due-process clause renders a sentence void merely because a judge gets additional out-of-court information to assist him in the exercise of this awesome power of imposing the death sentence. Appellant was found guilty after a fairly conducted trial. His sentence followed a hearing conducted by the judge. Upon the judge's inquiry as to why sentence should not be imposed, the defendant made statements. His counsel made extended arguments. The case went to the highest court in the state, and that court had power to reverse for abuse of discretion or legal error in the imposition of the sentence. That court affirmed. We hold that appellant was not denied due process of law.

Affirmed.

United States v. Thompson

U.S. District Court, District of Massachusetts, 190 F. Supp. 2d 138 (2002)

FACTS

Mr. Thompson plead guilty to distribution of cocaine base (crack). The charges grew out of a joint federal-state investigation of crack cocaine trafficking at the Bromley Health Housing Development. Mr. Thompson was sentenced to a term of imprisonment of 60 months, representing a downward departure of 17 months based on his extraordinary family circumstances. The First Circuit vacated the defendant's sentence and remanded for re-sentencing. On re-sentencing, he again argued for extraordinary family circumstances and argued for a departure based upon his extraordinary post-sentencing rehabilitation.

 Under the facts of the instance case, does First Circuit case law allow a downward departure on resentencing because of "extraordinary circumstances" and/or "extraordinary circumstances reflecting rehabilitation after an earlier [now vacated] sentence for the same crime?"

 As it applies here, First Circuit case law has allowed a downward departure on resentencing because of "extraordinary circumstances reflecting rehabilitation after an earlier [now vacated] sentence for the same crime" but not simply for "extraordinary circumstances" under the facts of this case.

 Mr. Thompson has spent a number of years in prison under his original sentence. His children have suffered, but the family ids coping. Whatever the costs of their adjustment, and whatever their continuing pain, which I do not mean to minimize, they cannot be characterized as extraordinary under the applicable First Circuit law. Which respect to defendant's second alleged ground for departure, First Circuit case law has allowed a downward departure on resentencing because of "extraordinary circumstances reflecting rehabilitation after an earlier [now vacated] sentence for the same crime." Although the ground is no longer available to defendants in future cases, it is available to Mr. Thompson because of the timing of his plea and sentencing. His record warrants departure on this ground. Accordingly, I depart downward to level 25 and sentence Mr. Thompson to 60 months.

 Defendant's record warrants departure. It is so ordered.

Blakely v. Washington
Supreme Court of the United States, 542 U.S. 296 (2004)

FACTS

Petitioner pleaded guilty to kidnapping his estranged wife. The facts admitted in his plea, standing alone, supported a maximum sentence of 53 months, but the judge imposed a 90-month sentence after finding that petitioner had acted with deliberate cruelty, a statutorily enumerated ground for departing from the standard range. The Washington Court of Appeals affirmed, rejecting petitioner's argument that the sentencing procedure deprived him of his federal constitutional right to have a jury determine beyond a reasonable doubt all facts legally essential to his sentence.

Did the sentencing procedure deprive the accused of his federal constitutional right to have a jury determine, beyond a reasonable doubt, all facts legally essential to his sentence?

Because the facts supporting petitioner's exceptional sentence were neither admitted by petitioner nor found by a jury, the sentence violated his Sixth Amendment right to trial by jury.

This case requires the Court to apply the rule of *Apprendi* v. *New Jersey,* that, "[o]ther than the fact of a prior conviction, any fact that increases the penalty for a crime beyond the prescribed statutory maximum must be submitted to a jury, and proved beyond a reasonable doubt." The relevant statutory maximum for *Apprendi* purposes is the maximum a judge may impose based solely on the facts reflected in the jury verdict or admitted by the defendant. Here, the judge could not have imposed the 90-month sentence based solely on the facts admitted in the guilty plea, because Washington law requires an exceptional sentence to be based on factors other than those used in computing the standard-range sentence. Petitioner's sentence is not analogous to those upheld in *McMillan* v. *Pennsylvania* and *Williams* v. *New York* which were not greater than what state law authorized based on the verdict alone. Regardless of whether the judge's authority to impose the enhanced sentence depends on a judge's finding a specified fact, one of several specified facts, or *any* aggravating fact, it remains the case that the jury's verdict alone does not authorize the sentence. This Court's commitment to *Apprendi* in this context reflects not just respect for longstanding precedent, but the need to give intelligible content to the fundamental constitutional right of jury trial. This case is not about the constitutionality of determinate sentencing, but only about how it can be implemented in a way that respects the Sixth Amendment. The Framers' paradigm for criminal justice is the common-law ideal of limited state power accomplished by strict division of authority between judge and jury. That can be preserved without abandoning determinate sentencing and at no sacrifice of fairness to the defendant.

Reversed and remanded.

Mclaren Legal Publishers LLC

For a full catalog please visit our website:

mclarenpublishing.com